Sport in the global society
General Editors: J.A. Mangan and Boria Majumdar

# Japan, Sport and Society

# Sport in the global society
General Editors: J.A. Mangan and Boria Majumdar

The interest in sports studies around the world is growing and will continue to do so. This unique series combines aspects of the expanding study of *sport in the global society*, providing comprehensiveness and comparison under one editorial umbrella. It is particularly timely, with studies in the aesthetic elements of sport proliferating in institutions of higher education.

Eric Hobsbawm once called sport one of the most significant practices of the late nineteenth century. Its significance was even more marked in the late twentieth century and will continue to grow in importance into the new millennium as the world develops into a 'global village' sharing the English language, technology and sport.

Other titles in the series

# Japan, Sport and Society

Evolving for centuries in relative isolation, sport in Japan developed a unique character reflective of Japanese culture and society. In recent decades, Japan's drive towards cultural and economic modernization has consciously incorporated a modernization of its sports cultures. *Japan, Sport and Society* provides insights into this process, revealing the tensions between continuity and change, tradition and modernity, the local and the global in a culture facing the new economic and political realities of our modern world. The book explores three broad areas of interest:

- sport and modern society in Japan
- current issues in social reconstruction and reproduction through sport
- modernization, globalization and sport in Japan

Providing unprecedented access to new work from Japanese scholars, and raising key questions of globalization and cultural identity, this text represents a fascinating resource for students and researchers of sport and society.

**Joseph Maguire** is Professor of Sociology of Sport in the School of Sport and Exercise Sciences at Loughborough University, UK.

**Masayoshi Nakayama** is Professor of Sport Sociology in the Faculty of Education at Shimane University, Japan.

# Japan, Sport and Society

Tradition and change in a globalizing world

Edited by Joseph Maguire and Masayoshi Nakayama

Routledge
Taylor & Francis Group

LONDON AND NEW YORK

First published 2006 by Routledge, an imprint of Taylor & Francis
2 Park Square, Milton Park, Abingdon, Oxon OX14 4RN

Simultaneously published in the USA and Canada
by Routledge
270 Madison Ave, New York, NY 10016

*Routledge is an imprint of the Taylor & Francis Group*

Typeset in Goudy by
GreenGate Publishing Services, Tonbridge, Kent
Printed and bound in Great Britain by
The Cromwell Press, Trowbridge, Wiltshire

*British Library Cataloguing in Publication Data*
A catalogue record for this book is available from the British Library

*Library of Congress Cataloging in Publication Data*
Japan, sport, and society : tradition and change in a globalizing world /
edited by Joseph Maguire and Masayoshi Nakayama.
      p. cm. – (Sport in the global society)
   Includes bibliographical references and index.
   1. Sports–Social aspects–Japan. 2. Globalization–Japan. I. Maguire,
Joseph A., 1956– II. Nakayama, Masayoshi, 1949– III. Title. IV. Series.
GV706.5.J37 2005
306. 4'82'0952–dc22

2005017957

ISBN 10:  0-7146-5358-6 (hbk)
ISBN 10:  0-7146-8293-4 (pbk)

ISBN 13:  978-0-7146-5358-7 (hbk)
ISBN 13:  978-0-7146-8293-8 (pbk)

# Contents

# Illustrations

## Figures

## Tables

# Series editors' foreword

In the early 1980s, the distinguished historian Natalie Davis pondered on the professional consequences for her, of the New History: '... the impact of anthropology on my own historical reflection has been to reinforce my sense not of the changeless past, but of the varieties of human experience'.[1] Replace the term 'anthropology' with the term 'sociology' and the essential virtue of *Japan, Sport and Society* is revealed. It is a sociological inquiry into the varied response to sport in contemporary Japan with, inevitably, implicit historical undertones and overtones, which if read in conjunction with recent historical studies of Japanese sport in the series Sport in the Global Society including *The Missing Olympics: The 1940 Tokyo Games* by Sandra Collins,[2] ensures an academic repast of 'haute cuisine' rather than merely 'nouvelle cuisine', and allows a desirable scholastic ambition to be realised: 'It is essential to comprehend the relationship between changes in the structural features of a society and changes in the beliefs, values and ideologies held by members of that society'.[3]

*Japan, Sport and Society* has other virtues. It explores significant issues involving sport in contemporary Japan that have wider relevance for 'the modern global village': the extent to which sport forges bonds of friendship between cultures, the degree to which it can assist the creation of shared cosmopolitan values among nations, the range of its capacity for provoking insular responses to intrusive cultural imports. Metaphorically speaking, it courageously ventures into Plato's murky Caves of Shadows of shifting realities and surreal shapes.

In short, it confronts the complex question of just how far modern sport is an agent of synthesis and syncretism.

As Asia increasingly infiltrates the consciousness of the American and the European with the burgeoning of the economies of India and China, not to mention the looming talismanic Beijing 2008,[4] this volume, when read conjointly with its companion historical inquiries in Sport in the Global Society, is a timely reminder not only of the variety of the human experience of sport, but of the fact that Japan was a front runner in the Asian 'race' to absorb, adapt and utilise modern sport which is now embedded in its politics, culture and society.

J.A. Mangan
Boria Majumdar
July 2005

## Notes

1  Natalie Z. Davis, 'The possibilities of the past' in Theodore K. Rabb and Robert I. Rotberg (eds), *The New History: The 1980s and Beyond*, Princeton: Princeton University Press, 1982, p. 275.

2  See Sandra Collins, *The Missing Olympics: The 1940 Tokyo Games*, London: Routledge, 2005. Also in the series Sport in the Global Society, see J.A. Mangan and Ikuo Abe, 'Sportsmanship – English inspiration and Japanese response: F.W. Strange and Chiyosaburo Takeda' in J.A. Mangan and Fan Hong (eds.) *Sport and Asian Society: Past and Present*, London: Frank Cass, 2003, pp. 99–128 and J.A. Mangan and Takeshi Komagome, 'Militarism, sacrifice and emperor worship: the expendable male body in fascist Japanese martial culture' in J.A. Mangan (ed.), *Superman Supreme: Fascist Body as Political Icon: Global Fascism*, London: Frank Cass, 2000, pp. 181–204. In addition, see A. Guttmann and L. Thompson, 'Educators, imitators and modernizers: The arrival and spread of modern sport in Japan' in J.A. Mangan (ed.) *Europe, Sport, World: Shaping Global Societies* (European Sports History Review, No. 3), London: Frank Cass, 2001, pp. 23–48.
The International Journal of the History of Sport has also published articles of relevance, see, for example, Shinsuke Tanada, 'Diffusion into the Orient: The introduction of modern sports in Kobe, Japan', *IJHS*, Vol. 5, No. 3, December, 1998, 372–376; Ikuo Abe, Yasuharu Kiyohara and Ken Nayajima, 'Fascism, sport and society in Japan', *IJHS*, Vol. 9. No. 1, 1992, 1–28, and with reference to Japanese imperialism and sport, see Nam Gil Ha and J.A. Mangan, 'A curious conjunction: Sport, religion and nationalism and the nodern history of Korea', *IJHS*, Vol. 11, No. 3, December 1994. Finally, two monographs deserve special mention: Donald T. Roden, *School Days in Imperial Japan: A Study in the Culture of a Student Elite*, Berkeley: UCP, 1980, and A. Guttmann and L. Thompson, *Japanese Sports: A History*, Hawaii: HUP, 1991.

3  Gerald Bernbaum, 'Sociological techniques and historical study' in *History, Society and Education* published by the History of Education Society, London: Methuen, 1971.

4  For succinct considerations of the talismanic role anticipated for Beijing 2008, see Fan Hong, Ping Wu and Huan Xiong, 'Beijing ambitions: An analysis of the Chinese elite sports system and its Olympic strategy for the 2008 Olympic Games', pp. 510–529 and Dong Jinxia, 'Women, nationalism and the Beijing Olympics: Preparing for glory' (pp. 530–545) in Boria Majumdar and Fan Hong (eds.) *Modern Sport: The Global Obsession/Essays in Honour of J.A. Mangan*, London: Routledge, 2005.

# Introduction

*Joseph Maguire and Masayoshi Nakayama*

The aim of this collection is to bring the work of Japanese scholars in the area of sport, culture and Japanese society to the attention of a wider audience. Work of this kind is, in fact, not new. In 1967, in the second volume of the *International Review of Sport Sociology*, the official publication of the recently formed International Committee for Sport Sociology (ICSS), Kyuzo Takenoshita published both a paper on 'The Social Structure of the Sport Population in Japan' and a separate overview of 'The Sociological Research Work of Sport in Japan'. In the latter paper, Takenoshita concluded: 'sociology of sport in Japan is but at its start, and how to get it developed will be a matter of the future' (1967: 180). That development has certainly occurred, so much so that the Japanese Society for Sport Sociology, formed in 1991, has its own journal, *The Japan Journal of Sport Sociology*, and arguably the largest national sociology of sport membership.

The role that Japanese scholars have played in the development of the sociology of sport has also involved their participation in the International Sociological Association (ISA) congresses, North American Society for the Sociology of Sport (NASSS) conferences and the International Sociology of Sport Association's (ISSA) World Congresses. Japanese members have also served on the ICSS/ISSA Executive Boards. We have, then, a rich tradition of research available to draw on. Yet, despite such progress, few scholars in the West have accessed such research. In the last two decades there has been a significant growth in books written by Westerners concerning Japan (Hendry, 1995, 1998). Such work has also focused on the notion of Japanese 'uniqueness' and 'strangeness' (Dale, 1986; Joseph, 1993). More recently, Japanese popular culture has been the focus of increased attention (Hammond, 1997; Ivy, 1995; Martinez, 1998; McCreery, 2000). Other work has examined issues that are raised in this collection concerning modernization, globalization and national identity (Befu and Guichard-Anguis, 2001; Yoshino, 1992).

Some work has also highlighted issues of sport (Joseph, 1993, cf chapter 13; Kelly, 1998; Pempel, 1998; Watts, 1998), which complements work done by Westerners in the sociology of sport (Guttmann and Thompson, 1991a; Horne and Manzenreiter, 2002). Work on sport in Japan has been done by Westerners who reside in Japan (Thompson, 1998), while others have considered the spread of Japanese 'sports' to other cultures (Frühstück and Manzenreiter, 2001). Further, the broader topic of leisure in Japan has been considered in an edited collection by Linhart and Frühstück, 1998.

The purpose of this collection is to bring together a selection of Japanese researchers and topics. In designing this collection we wished to highlight several key issues regarding Japanese culture and society. These include questions of: continuity and change, tradition and modernity, the invention of tradition and habitus codes, and the local and the global. Tracing the diffusion of Western sports to Japan lies outside the scope of this book (Guttmann and Thompson, 2001b). It is clear that over the past two centuries sections of Japanese society resisted both modernization/Westernization and the sports that followed in the wake of these processes. In the interwar years, Western-style sports were discouraged and the state promoted a nationalist form of budo. 'Imported sports' were seen as undesirable and a break with tradition. That this tradition was itself invented was glossed over (Inoue, 1998).

Nevertheless, questions of body habitus also contoured the reception of Western sport culture and attempts were made to replace the 'western spirit in sports with the Japanese spirit of budo' (Shun, 1998: 172). Such observations also highlight the degree to which cultures can indigenize Western sports and whether it is possible to maintain the diversity of body cultures in a global figuration that also promotes sameness and homogeneity (Maguire, 2005). Considering the case of baseball, Suishu Tobita, who gained a reputation as the guru of the sport from the 1920s to his death in 1965, observed that baseball is 'more than a game. It has eternal value. Through it, one learns the beautiful and noble spirit of Japan' (cited in Joseph, 1993: 237).

Clearly, then, the study of 'sport' can tell us much about the societies within which they are located. Yet, the study of sport can also reveal something about relations between societies and civilizations (Maguire, 1999). In this regard several questions arise. Does sport assist in building friendship between people and nations? Does sport extend some degree of emotional identification between members of different societies and civilizations? Through the cultural interchange that sport provides, does an array of more cosmopolitan emotions develop within and between the peoples of different nations? Or, conversely, do people, from dominant and/or subordinate positions in different societies, react negatively to the encroachment of alien values, artifacts and cultural products, of which modern sport was a prime example in the twentieth century? Considered in this light, we have also to ask the question whether such global sport processes extend or contract emotional identification between members of different societies. The evidence from the study of Japanese sport is mixed: the chapters which follow seek to examine these processes in more detail.

The book is divided into three sections. In Part One, we consider the 'Making of sport and modern Japanese society'. Here, chapters by Yoshinobu Hamaguchi on innovation in martial arts, Yuko Kusaka on the emergence and development of Japanese school sport and Koichi Kiku on the development of the Japanese baseball spirit capture aspects of change in Japanese society over the past century. All are tied together by a sensitive probing of continuity and change in sport, culture and society over time.

In Part Two, we focus on the sociological processes of 'Social reconstruction, reproduction and sport'. In Chapter Four, Masayoshi Nakayama considers economic developments and the value aspect of sport. Given the challenges arising from the growth of Western sport, Kanji Kotani in Chapter Five focuses on questions of sustainable sport and environmental problems. Here, he gives us an example on how green sport can help both in the sport world and in the wider community. Chapter Six, by Hidesato Takahashi considers the role that voluntary associations play in the formation of sport spectatorship and what this reveals about wider aspects of Japanese society. Issues of gender are considered by Keiji Matsuda in Chapter Seven. In doing so, Matsuda weaves together several issues of sport, culture and Japanese society.

Part Three focuses on questions of 'Modernization, globalization and sport'. All three chapters conduct a critical examination of the processes involved and how they have impacted on Japanese sport and society. Chapter Eight, by Hitoshi Ebishima and Rieko Yamashita, considers the FIFA 2002 World Cup and places this football phenomenon in various Japanese cultural contexts. In Chapter Nine, Hideki Nishimura explores how the wisdom to be gained through physical cognition in sport is lost or 'buried' in the process of modernization that Japan has undergone since opening up to the West. The book concludes with the work of Takayuki Yamashita who, in Chapter Ten, examines how globalization processes are changing the 'field of Japanese sport'.

We hope that you find the book fruitful and interesting. In editing this collection, we have both learned more about how we understand sport, culture and society – about the societies from which we come, about the assumptions we make about other cultures – and what we can learn from each other. Our hope is that we have contributed to the progress that Kyuzo Takenoshita predicted would be made back in 1967.

## References

Befu, H. and Guichard-Anguis, S. (eds) (2001) *Globalizing Japan: Ethnography of the Japanese Presence in Asia, Europe, and America*. London: Routledge.

Dale, P. (1990). *The Myth of Japanese Uniqueness*. London: Routledge.

Frühstück, S. and Manzenreiter, W. (2001) Neverland lost: Judo cultures in Austria, Japan and elsewhere struggling for cultural hegemony at the Vienna Budokan. In H. Befu, and S. Guichard-Anguis, (eds) (2001) *Globalizing Japan. Ethnography of the Japanese Presence in Asia, Europe, and America*. London: Routledge, pp. 69–93.

Guttmann, A. and Thompson, L. (1991a) *Japanese Sports: A History*. Hawaii: University of Hawaii Press.

Guttmann, A. and Thompson, L. (1991b) Educators, imitators, modernizers: The arrival and spread of modern sport in Japan. *The European Sports History Review*, 3, pp. 23–48.

Hammond, P. (ed.) (1997) *Cultural Difference, Media Memories: Anglo-American Images of Japan*. London: Cassell.

Hendry, J. (1995) *Understanding Japanese Society*. London: Routledge.

Hendry, J. (ed.) (1998) *Interpreting Japanese Society* (2nd edn). London: Routledge.

Horne, J. and Manzenreiter, W. (2002) *Japan, Korea and the 2002 World Cup*. London: Routledge.

Inoue, S. (1998) Budo: Invented tradition in the martial arts. In Linhart, S and Frühstück, S. (eds) (1998) *The Culture of Japan as Seen Through its Leisure*. New York: SUNY Press, pp. 83–94.

Ivy, M. (1995) *Discourses of the Vanishing: Modernity, Phantasm, Japan*. Chicago: University of Chicago Press.

Joseph, J. (1993) *The Japanese: Strange but not Strangers*. London: Penguin.

Linhart, S. and Frühstück, S. (eds) (1998) *The Culture of Japan as Seen Through its Leisure*. New York: SUNY Press.

Kelly, W. W. (1998) Blood and guts in Japanese professional baseball. In S. Linhart and S. Frühstück (eds) (1998) *The Culture of Japan as Seen Through its Leisure*. New York: SUNY Press, pp. 95–112.

Maguire, J. (1999) *Global Sport: Identities, Societies, Civilizations*. Cambridge: Polity Press.

Maguire, J. (2005) *Power and Global Sport: Zones of Prestige, Emulation and Resistance*. London: Routledge.

Martinez, D. P. (ed.) (1998) *The Worlds of Japanese Popular Culture: Gender, Shifting Boundaries and Global Cultures*. Cambridge: Cambridge University Press.

McCreery, J. (2000) *Japanese Consumer Behaviour: From Worker Bees to Wary Shoppers*. London: Curzon Press.

Pempel, T. J. (1998) Contemporary Japanese athletics: window on the cultural roots of nationalism-internationalism. In S. Linhart and S. Frühstück (eds) (1998) *The Culture of Japan as Seen Through its Leisure*. New York: SUNY, pp. 95–112.

Takenoshita, K. (1967a) The social structure of the sport population in Japan. *International Review of Sport Sociology*, 2, pp. 5–18.

Takenoshita, K. (1967b) The sociological research work of sport in Japan. *International Review of Sport Sociology*, 2, pp. 179–186.

Thompson, L. (1998) The invention of the Yokozuna and the championship system, or Futahaguro's revenge. In S. Vlastos (ed.) *Mirror of Modernity: Invented Traditions of Modern Japan*. Berkeley: University of California Press, pp. 174–190.

Vlastos, S. (ed.) (1998) *Mirror of Modernity: Invented Traditions of Modern Japan*. Berkeley: University of California Press.

Watts, J. (1998) Soccer *shinhatsubai*: What are Japanese consumers making of the J-League? In D. P. Martinez (ed.) *The Worlds of Japanese Popular Culture: Gender, shifting boundaries and global cultures*. Cambridge: Cambridge University Press, pp. 181–202.

Yoshino, K. (1992) *Cultural Nationalism in Contemporary Japan*. London: Routledge.

# Part I

# Making of sport and modern Japanese society

# Chapter 1

# Innovation in martial arts

*Yoshinobu Hamaguchi*

## Introduction

*Bujutsu* (arts and techniques in battle) is the collective term for traditional Japanese martial arts and includes *kendo, judo, kyudo* and *sumo*. It was one of the core values of the warrior class which was the ruling class before modernization. The warriors' values, and the social system represented by the warrior philosophy (*bushido*), were the foundation of traditional Japanese culture. With the radical change in national policy to one that encouraged internationalization and modernization from the middle of the nineteenth century, the practical value of *bujutsu* techniques diminished. As a result its popularity waned. However, *Bujutsu* came to be considered as the central guide to traditional moral education and became more commonly known as *budo*. Judo was developed by Jigoro Kano as part of this transition from *bujutsu* to *budo*. With the internationalization of sports, judo continued evolving and became an Olympic 'sport'. Judo continues to change as a result of globalization processes.

In this chapter an aspect of the Japanese modernization process will be examined with reference to the evolutionary process from *bujutsu* to *budo*. In addition, the transition of judo into a sport form and its subsequent global diffusion will also be considered. As part of this analysis, three components of sport in the broader cultural context are highlighted. These are cultural views of sports, the codes of behaviour in sports, and sports materials (Saeki, 1984: 67–98). Discussion of games as a specific example of a sport activity, as well as the structure of the sports world, which is a layered structure that contains the sport system as the whole, will be undertaken (Sugawara, 1980: 2–5). The components of sport activities will also be examined. These include: facilities; duration of time; prelusory goals; lusory means; allowable equipment and materials; the evaluation system; and, prescribed penalties for rule violations (Fraleigh, 1984: 68).

## Japanese martial arts before modernization

The word *bujutsu*, the original term for Japanese martial arts, come from the Chinese character *bu-*, battle or martial, and *jutsu*, techniques or arts. Such arts were originally practised by *bushi*, or the warrior class in Japan. *Bujutsu* have a very long history. In Japan a unique system of *bujutsu* developed due to specific geographical and historical factors. In terms of geography Japan is isolated from the Asian Continent. Because of this, Japan had only rarely been exposed to cultural influences from neighbouring countries. Japan is composed of four rather large islands surrounded by smaller islands. Nearly eighty per cent of the country is mountainous and the rest is coastal plains. With these geographic characteristics the population shares limited living space and has developed life styles and social value systems different from those of continental Asia.

When the Yamato Court established and united the nation states between the fourth and fifth century, the chief of the tribe, who became an emperor, started ruling these states as one nation. He was assisted by the aristocrats who participated in politics. Although the emperor remained titular head of state until the nineteenth century, the warrior class actually ruled the nation from the twelfth to the middle of nineteenth century. Japanese martial arts developed within this historical context.

*Bushi* originated from landlords (*jinushi*) and families with the political power (*gozoku*) around the tenth century. Their work was to look after the land that was allocated to them by the government and they started to militarize in order to protect their lands (Todo, 2000: 35). These aristocrats soon formed groups and, aided by their warriors, started to gain greater power in society. In the twelfth century, a warrior group gained sufficient power to rule in places other than Kyoto where the emperor traditionally lived.

From the mid-fifteenth to mid-sixteenth century is known as the Warring States period. This struggle for power is best described by the term *gekokujo* (the overturning of those on top by those below). *Bujutsu* developed further in this period as practical defensive and offensive skills for survival and for gaining wealth and power. *Bujutsu* encompassed a range of skills including horse riding, archery, sword-fighting, and unarmed combat, involving grappling with and throwing an opponent down (Nakabayashi, 1987: 10). Although matchlock muskets were introduced as early as 1543, during this period battles usually involved hand-to-hand fighting, mainly with swords.

As the Warring States period ended, Japan started to gain political and military stability. The various skills that warriors were required collectively to master, as *bujutsu*, began to develop independent cultural identities. The sword-hunt decree of 1588 disarmed all the farmers and only warriors were granted the privilege of carrying swords. Thus, swords became a symbol of the warrior class and *kenjutsu* (swordsmanship) assumed an important role in *bujutsu* (Sakai, 2003: 29).

The Edo period, between 1603 and 1867, was a relatively stable age under the rule of a warrior family (the Tokugawas). The Tokugawa regime established a social hierachy and people were divided into four classes called *shi-no-ko-sho*, that is: warrior, farmer, artisan, merchant. In 1639, the Tokugawa regime also adopted a policy of national seclusion, the exception being highly restricted trade with the Dutch and Chinese. Because of this seclusion, Japan developed its own prac-tices such as *kabuki, ukiyo-e, sado* and *ikebana*.

Martial arts in this period became less valued in terms of their practical use. Japan had political stability and members of the warrior class could no longer change their social status by using their combat skills. Instead, martial arts devel-oped to be part of the warrior class's education. In the same way as in other cultural activities, martial arts split into hundreds, or even thousands, of schools according to the different weapons used and the masters' ideas. Each martial art was developed independently.

The main method of practice was *kata* (set form practice) with real swords, and after the middle of the eighteenth century, a practice method that used bam-boo and wooden swords, with armour, became popular. Martial arts were less violent, and became more sport-like. Martial arts were becoming civilized. The late Edo period was socially stable and *bujutsu* thus took on an educational role. It had a philosophical dimension and a refined code of conduct (*bushido*) for war-riors, as well as maintaining the skills formerly used in battle. This paved the way for it to develop and change to *budo* in the next period.

## Japanese modernization and *budo*

After the arrival of American Commodore Matthew Perry, in 1853, Japan faced pressure to open the country up to the United States and European countries other than Holland. When in the Meiji period, after the Tokugawa regime returned political rule to the emperor in 1867, Japan opened its doors to the world and experienced rapid modernization. The government established facto-ries and developed modern industry in order to build up military strength under its policy of 'A rich country and a strong country' and the slogan 'Increase pro-duction and promote industry'. The government also announced a Conscription Ordinance in 1873 and men had to do three years of military service. Moreover, the government introduced an Education Order, based on the European model, under the slogan 'Civilization and enlightenment' and combined this with the land tax reform of 1873. The warrior class was phased out with both the abolition of the status system and the prohibition of carrying swords. *Bujutsu*, therefore, declined. In 1889, the Constitution of the Empire of Japan was promulgated and, in 1890 the Diet (Parliament) was organized. Thus, Japan was developing as a modern country.

This rapid Westernization, however, ensured that the country was marked by internal friction and external conflict. These tensions led to a re-apprecia-tion of *budo* in society. For example, the practical effectiveness of *kenjutsu* in close combat was acclaimed in the Satsuma Rebellion of 1877. Japanese mar-tial arts were also advocated as an educational tool for the cultivation of morals and strength of character in the Sino-Japanese war of 1894-95 and Russo-Japanese war of 1904–05. More concretely, *kenjutsu* became part of the compulsory training for the police in 1879 after the Satsuma Rebellion, and jujutsu began to be introduced as an element in the education and training of the police and the army in the 1880s.

In the process of modernization, Japanese martial arts were no longer of practical value in fighting battles. Spiritual education through a warrior way of life learnt through such training was, however, highly prized. With this change of attiude to martial arts, *bujutsu* became *budo*. Inoue (1998: 231) expresses this as the invention of *budo*. This involved a change from *jutsu* (battle skills) to *do* (the way of life). In addition, martial arts, which used to be the exclusive preserve of the warrior class and used as an educational medium in the hierarchical class system, started to be learned and practised by the whole nation, regardless of social status. This occurred in the context of the training associated with military service.

In 1895, the Japanese Martial Arts Federation, called *Dai Nihon Butokukai*, developed as a reforming organization for all Japanese martial arts. *Dai Nihon Butokukai* built *Butokuden* in Kyoto as its own training hall and, at the same time, established branch offices in every part of the country. *Dai Nihon Butokukai* became a foundational organization in 1909 which secured its social status. Moreover, in 1905, the Martial Arts teacher training school was established, and changed its name as it evolved: in 1910, *Bujutsu Gakko* (Martial Arts School); in 1912, *Bujutsu Senmon Gakko* (Martial Arts Special School) and, in 1919, *Budo Senmon Gakko* (Martial Arts Special School). In 1919, *Dai Nihon Butokukai* changed the name of all martial arts from *bujutsu* to *budo*. In 1926, in the school physical education (PE) curriculum, the term *budo* started to be used, differentiating it from team sports.

*Dai Nihon Butokukai* united all martial art schools that were then practising independently. This organization standardized Japanese martial arts: its proponents established a new *kata* form and developed and awarded common proficiency titles *kyoshi* and *hanshi*. This was different from the grading systems found in each school.

*Dai Nihon Butokukai* tried to develop *budo* by placing an emphasis on the spiritual and moral aspects of *budo* called *zissenn teki shushin*. To prevent *budo* becoming a competitive sport, it did not organize competitions but set up exhibition matches, in which there were no winning and losing sides. All the changes that *Dai Nihon Butokukai* developed were part of the innovative process involved in the transition from *bujutsu* to *budo* and Sakaue (1998: 180), who tried the same sort of innovation in kendo, notes that it was done only to eliminate the competitive aspects of kendo. This innovative view on *budo* became a common understanding in Japan, as *budo* has been differentiated from other sports subjects in the school PE curriculum.

*Budo* was adopted as a compulsory subject in 1931 as Japan moved towards militarism. *Budo* was used as an educational tool to encourage nationalism. After defeat in World War II, *Dai Nihon Butoku-Kai* was ordered to break up and *budo* was forbidden for several years. Soon after *budo* was resumed, the All-Japan Championships and the world championships took place. However, *budo* is not now competitive in terms of winning and losing, but is practised for its character building effect.

Kendo in *budo* has been practised in many countries and thirty-four countries are members of the International Kendo Federation (as of 1997). Judo is also part of *budo* and, by 1977, 178 countries were members of the International Judo Federation. Judo, however, with its Olympic Games status is now considered to be an exception in *budo*. How did judo, a reflection of traditional Japanese culture, develop in the process of globalization?

## The foundation of judo

Attention must first focus on the cultural system of judo that Jigoro Kano developed. In this way, the process and content of change in judo, along with internationalization of the world after the establishment of International Judo Federation, can be examined. Judo formed and developed from *jujutsu*, meaning techniques for hand-to-hand fighting and self-defence. It has a long history as one of the Japanese martial arts. Previously, there were different types of *Jujutsu* schools as well as of other martial arts. The formation of the Takeuchi School in 1653 is regarded as the beginning of individual organizational schools (*ryuuha*) and there were about seven hundred of these by the middle of the 1800s. Participants in *jujutsu* were obliged to wear uniform and, in some schools even a full set of armour, and to fight without using any weapons against opponents who could have various types of weapons. The aim was to overwhelm the opponent by means of superior skill rather than power.

Judo was developed by Jigoro Kano at one of the hundreds of *jujutsu* schools in 1882. His school quickly gained great influence and took a central role in the development of *jujutsu*. It is this school which laid the foundation of modern judo that has been diffused globally. Kano was born in 1859 into a rich family of the merchant class. After studying politics, economics and philosophy at *Tokyo Teikoku Daigaku* (Tokyo Imperial University), which had been established to develop modernization, Kano worked for more than two decades as a headmaster at *Tokyo Koto Shihan Gakko*, a teacher-training institution. He was appointed as the first Asian member of the International Olympic Committee (IOC) in 1909 and subsequently established the Japan Olympic Committee (JOC). Kano also established the sport governing body in 1911 as well as a teacher-training course for physical education in 1915. He was also elected as a member of the House of Lords in 1922. It can be said that Kano's family class and educational background were typical of the people involved in the modernization of Japan and he also contributed greatly to the development of judo.

## The concepts of Kano judo

Kano studied at a number of schools of *jujutsu* and also compared them with other *jujutsu* schools. He analysed each technique and movement that was developed reflecting each school's original theories and then re-constructed a new theory (Kodokan, 1987b: 102). From the beginning Kano was positive about introducing judo to foreign countries, and this made an important contribution to the development of judo.

Kano defined the principle of judo as *seiryoku zenyo*, which is an abbreviation for *seiryoku saiyuukou katsudo*, meaning the most economical use of body and mind energy. Kano also uses other expressions: maximum-efficient-movement for achieving the purpose (Kodokan, 1988: 7) and economized energy (Kano, 1932: 37). These expressions explain his vision of judo as using one's energy in the most economical and rational way to achieve a goal. *Jujutsu* techniques thus involved the ability to fight without weapons. Kano explains this as training for victory or defeat (Kodokan, 1987b: 11). When he established his dojo, *Kodaokan*, he described judo as a way of training for more than victory or defeat, the word '*jutsu*' meaning 'techniques' and '*do*' means 'way'.

In essence, *Kodokan* judo emphasizes acquiring an attitude while acquiring techniques, rather than just acquiring skills. The main purpose of judo is the pursuit of an economical and rational way of life. Training for victory or defeat is just part of the process of reaching this main goal. This philosophical view of judo was much the same as that taken when it was given an educational role and the term *bujutsu* was changed to *budo*. Where Kano differed from the educationists, however, was the latter's *budo* placed an emphasis on the ideas of *bushido*, and he did not. His emphasis was on *chusei no michi* which aims to cultivate a well-balanced person in learning and training (Kodokan, 1987a: 369).

Ideas and concepts concerning judo were summarized in *The Theory of Victory or Defeat and Its Application* which went through several revisions. The text was organized into four sections: fighting techniques, physical education, moral cultivation and the application of these to social life (Kodokan, 1987a: 154–8). The book starts with a discussion of the training methods involved for attack and defence and then considers judo in terms of the pursuit of rationalization in all aspects of life (Kodokan, 1987b: 53–63). The ultimate goal of *seiryoku zenyo* is to complete one's character building. *Seiryoku zenyo* is defined as the principle of judo and is not applied in a particular area of *budo*, but it was viewed by Kano as an universal principle that can be applied to all sorts of activities. *Kodokan* was established as an educational institution based on this principle.

In later years, the idea of *jita kyoei* (mutual welfare and benefit), which aims for social contribution, was combined with the principle of *seiryoku zenyo* (Hasegawa, 1981: 114). This concept of judo is, of course, not taught as the final goal of judo, but rather is explained as a consistent concept in the whole development process. Related to this discussion, Kano pointed out the difference between judo and sports: judo is a 'universal way' and sports are activities in which competitors compete, winning or losing. A further disadvantage of sports is that people easily become too emotional. Yet, given that people generally have an interest in sports and sports are effective in term of physical education, he encouraged the playing of sports.

## The training style of judo

Kano's concept of judo can be applied to every aspect of life. For example, Kano explains that by careful quality selection, reading good books can be the most efficient everyday activity and be consistent with the principle of *seiryoku zenyo* in one's mind. The most remarkable feature of Kano's ideas about judo was to teach judo as *bujutsu*, that is training for attack and defence. *Jujutsu* schools had a *kata* practice training style. Kano divided education into three areas: intellectual education; moral education and physical education. He also had a deep understanding of physical education that consisted of gymnastics, sports, and dance. He developed judo from *jujutsu*, considering that the theory and practice of judo would be learnt most efficiently, while learning judo could contribute to achieving goals in all three areas of education. There were three re-structured judo activities (Kodokan, 1987c: 12–19): 'lecture, questions and answers', '*randori*' (free practice), and '*kata*'. Theoretical study consisted of lecture, questions and answers. Kano thought that *Randori*, match-style practice following the rules, to be especially important as it differed essentially from *jujutsu's* mainly *kata* practice. *Randori* was carefully created by *Kano* based on those characteristics of sports that engage enthusiasm and spontaneously generate creative ideas. *Kata*, which requires repeated practice of set forms and the internalization of the techniques, was also regarded as necessary training. *Kata* practice enabled practitioners to gain a theoretical understanding of techniques in movements and acquire techniques that were too dangerous to practise in *randori*. *Kata* practice also had an element of gymnastics which complements physical movements that practitioners could not develop sufficiently in *randori*. Moreover, *Kata* practice had an element of dance that expressed emotional and aesthetic senses.

The principle of judo style training which Kano developed was to practise these elements through *kata*. In judo training style, *randori* represents one of Kano's greatest original ideas about re-structured judo. Although judo as a sport is mostly undertaken as a match-style practice, *randori* in Kano's conception of judo is not meant to decide a winner or loser, but to enable the practitioner to learn *seiryoku zenyo*. The teachers judge the results of the matches following the 'Regulation for the Refereeing of Judo Matches', which was compiled as a guide for the judo teachers in 1900. The 'Regulation for the Refereeing of *Kodokan* Judo' is still effective today in the domestic matches, while the IJF uses 'The Regulations and Rules of Matches', which means that there are two official sets of regulations.

## Characteristics of *kodokan* judo

When Kano established *Kodokan*, there were initially only nine students. Later the number of students increased rapidly and the organization and system of *Kodokan* were established in Kano's mission to develop judo. The establishment of dojo, the introduction of regulations and *kata*, the inauguration of organizations such as *yudansha-kai* (group for *dan* grade holders), the publication of journals, holding lecture meetings and registering *Kodokan* as a foundation to maintain good finances, were all features of this process. These events are evidence of the development of the organization and Kano's determination to make students more fully aware of his ideas and intentions.

Kano successfully established a full-time system education and teacher education of which, in turn, led to the diffusion of *Kodokan* judo into every part of the country. The introduction of a grading system in 1922 is worthy of special mention. Kano divided degrees of progress in judo into *dan* grade and *kyu* grade, and encouraged practitioners to practise towards each grade instead of awarding 'a certificate of completion'. He also encouraged an open communication of information with prospective teachers which would eventually lead their students to a full understanding of the whole concept and intentions of Kano judo. He kept writing about the way of life which should encompass more than simply *budo* techniques. Moreover, while Kano spent his own funds to develop judo and *Kodokan*, he considered that *Kodokan* should be financially self-sustaining and thus it was registered as a foundation in 1909.

It is also important to observe that Kano tried to have effective public relations. He invited many people to *Kodokan*, whether they were members or not, from Japan or abroad, and he himself visited many foreign countries to introduce *Kodokan* judo. He visited the UK three times, sent teachers to the UK and tried to have *The Budokwai* school in London become a British branch of *Kodokan* judo. In addition, he formulated the idea of establishing the World Judo Federation.

The establishment of *Kodokan* Culture Club in 1922 directly symbolizes Kano's intention for the development of judo. This culture club was a group that aimed to promote rationality in every aspect of life. However, the *Kodokan* did not achieve as much as Kano expected. Kano also established the *Kodokan* women's Judo club in 1926 and organized the All Japan Judo Championships in 1930. These championships were divided into four categories; professionals (including judo teachers), amateurs, categories by age, and women.

The judo Kano formed and developed was directed to follow its own path which was different from any other types of *budo*. *Kodokan* judo, which was systematically and organizationally developed by Kano, was, on the whole, supported by excellent judo teachers and had privileged status given that they kept the grading system to themselves. *Kodokan* became the dominant judo schools, whether Kano wished this or not. Nishiyama (1982: 291–2) describes *Kodokan* as a similar system to a head-school oriented society (*iemoto ruiji shakai*), which caused major conflicts in the process of judo internationalization. The spread of judo was evident in other respects: it was actively promoted as part of the training for the police and military who started practising it in 1886; it spread through the world with the systematization of the *jujutsu* section at *Dai Nishon Budokukai*; and it was adopted into the national school PE curriculum in 1911.

## Summary of innovation of judo by Kano

Considering his family class and educational background, Kano was typical of those people who were involved in the modernization and rationalization of Japan. He also took the lead in promoting the modernization of Japan in education and sports. Judo was based on European ideas of modernization and rationalization. The establishment of judo by Kano was aimed at changing the martial arts emphasis of *bujutsu* to *budo* with its concept of character building through the training of techniques. Although *budo* originated from the ideas of *bushido* that was developed when *bujutsu* were practised as a tool in the education of warriors, it is the character building aspect of Kano's judo that is different from the ideas of *bushido*. Through this, Kano aimed to rationalize every aspect of life. He also made use of *bujutsu* and the latest educational theory and developed judo as an overall system including the development of content and establishment of its organization. Aspects of those Japanese values which were attached to judo also prevented Kano's ideas from developing further. His concept of judo had become too diffuse in its emphasis on a way of life and his judo placed too great an emphasis on the effectiveness of practical techniques. This, combined with the fact that the whole organization was based on the Japanese head-school system, hindered further global development.

## Internationalization and change in judo

*Budo* was prohibited after World War II because it was regarded as the central idea of spiritual or philosophical education in militarism. Given this context it is not surprising that judo was also prohibited. Yet, during this same period the European Judo Federation was established in 1948 and the International Judo Federation (IJF) was formed in 1951. Japan was also invited to join the IJF. The first World Judo Championships took place in 1956. Risei Kano, a grandson of Jigoro, was appointed as the first president of the IJF. The regulations and rules of Kodokan judo were used in the Championships. The Championships took place without dividing competitors into divisions according to their weights until 1963. This was a period when several changes took place and judo officially became an Olympic sport at the Tokyo Olympic Games in 1964. When Charles Palmer was appointed as the president of the IJF for the next fifteen years (1965–1979), the internationalization of judo began to accelerate. This new stage of judo started with the introduction of the first regulations and rules of judo by the IJF in 1965 (*Kodokan* judo rules had been used until then).

From this point judo changed in many significant ways, for example: the introduction of detailed regulations and rules such as the various weight divisions and how to decide who had won, and the penalties to be imposed on competitors who showed a negative or inappropriate attitude during fighting. There were also several cultural innovations. These included a switch in emphasis from education through experiencing winning and losing situations (the development of rational spirit) to a sport whose object was to compete and win. In addition, in 1973, with the introduction of new scoring points: *ippon* _ *ippon, wazaari, koka,* the standard rules for winning and losing were altered. This sport-like process was matched by the introduction of a standard classification for fouls: *shido, chui, keikoku.* The regulations and rules of judo have thus continued to evolve in various ways. With an emphasis on outcome, on winning and losing, the verdict must be decided objectively – no matter how a match is conducted. These patterns of cultural change require further careful analysis.

Changes in the character of a judo contest have been matched by wider institutional changes. In particular, there co-exist two global organizations governing judo. As specified in the regulations of the IJF, judo is *Kodokan* judo that was established by Kano. In this sense, judo practitioners are all students of *Kodokan* and *Kodokan* is the ultimate organization for decision-making on any matter relating to judo. However, the IJF exists as a worldwide decision-making institute and Japan is but one of over 170 member nations. For the IJF, *Kodokan* is no more than one of the local dojos or just a judo institution. Thus, there are two different ultimate organizations for decision-making in the world of judo. The problematic situation has emerged from the different cultural backgrounds between *Kodokan* as a status-based organization as head of the Japanese judo schools and the IJF as a function-based organization.

Another feature symptomatic of the change that has taken place more recently is in the colour of the judo uniform. This had traditionally been white but, from 1997, one of the competitors had to wear a blue uniform to make it easier for spectators to distinguish between them. This is symbolic of judo's adoption of sport-like characteristics. Judo was becoming commodified and an element of spectacle was introduced in order to satisfy the demands of spectators and television. These trends require further investigation.

## Innovation of judo in global terms

Innovation in judo after World War II was mainly achieved by the IJF. While Japan and *Kodokan* had the greatest influence on judo until the 1964 Tokyo Olympics, since then this has declined. Although *Kodokan* was originally critical of the changes that the IJF implemented after the Tokyo Olympics, these remain in effect. While Kano placed an emphasis on the match-style training called *randori* to maintain practitioners enjoyment and interest in the activity, and thus be encouraged to tackle training voluntarily and positively, he also emphasized the original characteristics of *budo. Budo* is based on the idea of fighting in life-or-death situations and aims to be character-building through these fighting style activities. It is clear in this sense that the judo developed by Kano is judo as *budo.* The changes made by the IJF after World War II resulted in a shift away from this conception towards that of a form of sport where two competitors compete against each other, and winning and losing are judged within the context of safety and fairness. The rule changes outlined above signalled judo's global sport aspirations (Cashmore, 2000: 158–61).

## Conclusion

Japanese martial arts as *bujutsu* began to develop on warrior class lines around the beginning of the the tenth century and it was central to the culture of the ruling class until the nineteenth century. Japanese martial arts, especially in the Warring States period, between the fifteenth and sixteenth centuries, focused on practical skills needed in battle. As Japanese society became more politically and militarily pacified, Japanese martial arts were split into various schools and distinct cultural versions emerged in each school. In the Edo period, when the government adopted a policy of National Seclusion and established a class system, martial arts no longer had practical social value. In this context, the 'warriors' education adopted a new form and role. Schools of martial arts were split into hundreds of schools according to the different weapons used and masters' theories. The main training in each school was *kata* and each school developed its own system. In the case of *kenjutsu*, match-style training in armourwith bamboo and wooden swords was introduced in the middle of the eighteenth century. This signalled the beginning of the change from *bujutsu* to *budo*.

In the rapid modernization period which started in the late nineteenth century, the warrior class was phased out and *bujutsu* declined. New types of *bujutsu* began, however, with the establishment of the *Dai Nihon Budokukai* that unified various schools of *bujutsu*. *Bujutsu*, practical skills for fighting in life-or-death situations, came to be practised in a safe match field, which led to the form of *budo* that emphasized its philosophical and moral educational aspects, and forbade the use of such training for competitive purposes. After World War II, however, *budo* adopted some characteristics of sport and aimed at character building through its training.

Compared to judo, kendo has experienced a more moderate change and has kept traditional Japanese cultural characteristics and styles. It has been standardized but has retained common principles shared by different schools. On the other hand, judo development was based on *Kodokan*, a new school that unified various old *jujutsu* schools and rationalized the cultural form. In *Kodokan* judo, *randori* was introduced as one of the training styles. It is this that has become the modern sport of judo. In this sense it is not surprising that judo alone has been widely internationalized. Judo has gone far beyond the ideals of *budo*, and this is a source of regret within the judo subculture in Japan.

## References

Cashmore, E. (2000) *Sports Culture*, London: Routledge.

Fraleigh, W. P. (1984) *Right Action in Sport – Ethics for Contestants*. Champaign, IL: Human Kinetics.

Hasegawa J. (1981) *Kanou Jigoro no Kyouiku to Siso* (Education and Thought in Jigoro Kano), Tokyo: Meiji Shoin.

Inoue, S. (1998) 'Kindai Nihon niokeru Supotsu to Budo' (Sports and the martial arts in the making of modern Japan), in Japan Society of Sport Sociology (ed.), *Henyo suru*

*Genndai Shakai to Supotu* (Sport and the Transformation of Contemporary Society), Kyoto: Sekai Shisosya.

Kano, J. (1932) 'The contribution of Judo to education', *The Journal of Health and Physical Education*, 3–9, 37–40, 58.

Kodokan (ed.) (1987a) *Kano Jigoro Taikei* (Jigoro Kano's Writings), vol. 1, Tokyo: Honnotomosha.

Kodokan (ed.) (1987b) *Kano Jigoro Taikei* (Jigoro Kano's Writings), vol. 2, Tokyo: Honnotomosha.

Kodokan (ed.) (1987c) *Kano Jigoro Taikei* (Jigoro Kano's Writings), vol. 3, Tokyo: Honnotomosha.

Kodokan (ed.) (1988) *Kano Jigoro Taikei* (Jigoro Kano's Writings), vol. 9, Tokyo: Honnotomosha.

Nakabayashi, S. (1987) *Budo no Susume* (Introduction to Budo), unpublished book, Tsukuba: Isakusyuu-Kannkoukai.

Nishiyama, M. (1982) *Iemotosei no Tenkai* (The Development of the Head-of-School Based System), vol. 2, Kyoto: Yoshikawa Koubunkan.

Saeki, T. (1984) 'Spotsu no Bunnka' (Cultural aspects of sport), in R. Sugawara (ed.), *Supotsu Shakaigaku no Kiso Riron* (Basic Theory of Sport Sociology), Tokyo: Humaido Shupan.

Sakai, T. (2003) 'Budo to Toukenkan' (Significance of the sword in budo), in K. Irie (ed.) *Budo Bunka no Tankyu* (Investigation into the Culture of Budo), Tokyo: Humaido Shupan.

Sakaue, Y. (1998) 'Kendo no Kindaika to Sono Teiryuu' (Modernization of Kendo and its background), in T. Nakamura (ed.) *Nihon Bunka no Dokujisei* (The Originality of Japanese Culture), Tokyo: Sobun Kikaku.

Sugawara, R. (1980) 'Supotsu no Sekai to wa Nanika' (What is the structure of the sport world?), *Taiikuka Kyouiku*, 28 (11).

Todo, Y. (2000) 'Budo to bushido' (Budo and bushido), in M. Tanaka, Y. Todo, K. Higashi and N. Murata (eds), *Budo wo Siru* (What is Budo?), Tokyo: Humaido Shupan.

# Chapter 2

# The emergence and development of Japanese school sport

*Yuko Kusaka*

## Introduction

Sport-like activities existed before the Meiji era (1868–1912) in Japan. There were, for example, *shukyu* (circle football) in court, *kenjutu* (kendo), *jujutu* (judo) and *kyujutu* (Japanese archery). In addition, there existed a range of other activities including falconry, the marathon of *bushi*, sumo, horse racing, rowing, mountain climbing, and, for common people, swimming. However, in this chapter, the concept of sport is restricted to 'modern' sport. Modern sport is a recreation and a competitive exercise of physical skill that originated in the Western world. In 1868, the Meiji government wished to establish Japan as a modern nation. This was to be achieved by reform of economic, political, military and educational institutions, and by throwing off the ties of feudalism and the closed society of *bushi*. All of these changes were implicit in the slogan 'the wealth and military strength of a nation'.

The modernization models followed were mainly those of the Western world (USA, UK, Germany and France). The framework of modernization combined the 'Japanese spirit', formed from Buddhism and Confucianism, and the Western understanding of a free, democratic and utilitarian culture. It was possible for the Japanese to function within this framework because the religious, political and economic foundation for a modern social system already existed (Bellah, 1962).

The image of their citizens which the Meiji government sought to create was of people who thought freely and rationally, were independent and possessed of scientific knowledge, who lived in a humanistic way, had strong bodies and wills and who could build a wealthy nation. The aim of education was the creation of individuals who were gifted with wisdom, morality and strong bodies (Kinoshita, 1971; Takenoshita and Kishino, 1959).

## The introduction of modern sport into Japanese schools

Modern sport was introduced into Japanese schools at the beginning of the Meiji era, see Table 1 (Imamura, 1951, 1970; Takenoshita, 1950). These sports were recreational activities originally enjoyed after school by Japanese students.

Schools focused on modern sports. Baseball and tennis were the most popular, both before and after the Second World War. Baseball, in particular, was representative of sport in schools along with sumo, judo and kendo. On the other hand, play and recreational games, outdoor exercise such as running, jumping and throwing, croquet, lawn tennis, judo and kendo were also components of the subject of physical education. The introduction of Western sports stemmed from the actions of the American G. E. Leland and the Englishman F. W. Strange who were key persons in the development of Japanese physical education. These sports were added to normal gymnastics and military gymnastics. In Taisho 2 (1913), track and field, basketball and football (rugby), and in Taisho 15 (1926) soccer, handball, volleyball and sumo, were added to the curriculum. The inclusion of these sports as regular subjects helped to widen sports. Players who graduated from the higher teachers' colleges and found employment at local educational facilities (especially local teachers' training schools), played a very important role in the diffusion of sport to the majority of elementary, secondary and business schools. Sport as a regular subject, however, rarely developed naturally as a social institution in Japan. Japanese sports developed into school sports as extra-curricular activities (Inoue, 1970). It is to this that attention now turns.

*Table 2.1* Introduction of modern sport into Japanese schools

| Sports | Era (years) | Schools | Instructors | etc. |
|---|---|---|---|---|
| Baseball | M.5 (1872) | Kaisei-Gakko (univ. level) | Wilson and Maget (American) | |
| Tennis | as M.6 (1873) | | | Japanese who returned from foreign countries |
| Boating | as M.6 (1873) | Kaisei-Gakko | | |
| Soccer | as M.7 (1874) | Kogaku-Ryo (univ. level) | Johns, R. (English) | |
| Softballl | M.7 (1874) | Kogaku-Ryo | | |
| Hockey | M.8 (1875) | Kogaku-Ryo | | |
| Athletic sports and boating | M.7 (1874) | Kaigun-Heigaku -Ryo | English officer | |
| Athletic sports and skating | M.11 (1878) | Sapporo -Nogakko | Clerk, W. S. (American) | |
| Tennis | M.11 (1878) | Taiso-Denshujo | Leland, G. A. (American) | |
| Athletic sports and track and field, boating and cricket | M.16 (1883) | Tokyo-Univ. -Yobimon | Strange, W. F. (English) | |

## The development of school sport

Six main stages in the organization of Japanese school sport can be identified. Each was characterized by more elaborate behaviour, more complexity, and more formal rules and organizations than its predecessor. A central feature of the overall process was the gradual emergence of modern sport out of group recreational games. More concretely, the stages in the development of school sport were from, circa:

1873 (The beginning of the Meiji era) Recreational groups, seeking only ephemeral (temporary) pleasure in games, began to appear

1882 Groups of sports enthusiasts with an informal membership started to emerge. (They were still informal in terms of group composition and forms of activities and they began to play matches against each other)

1887 Formal sports groups (*Undo-bu*) (extra-curricular physical activity) became organized as part of school fraternity activities. This signalled the beginning of 'localization'

1897 Associations for contests or tournaments were formed in each sport community. By this time, the number of sport groups began to increase. Baseball was popularized to some degree

1921 National level organizations for individual sports were formed to unite and govern their communities (worlds). This signalled the beginnings of 'globalization'

1935 The Japanese (Amateur) Association of Sport was organized. This national and unifying organization preceded the development of Japanese (amateur) sport as a corporate body. Sport became one of Japan's cultural and social institutions.

After the Meiji restoration in 1868, Japan began to emerge from its long cultural and economic isolation. Many foreign teachers and technicians were invited by the Meiji government to assist at Japanese higher educational establishments in order to catch up with Western civilization. The Meiji government saw an urgent need to modernize Japanese society and its slogans were the advancement of civilization and economic and military development on the basis of nationalism (Kamishima, 1961). A special kind of education policy was needed to train the nation.

Education for the general population differed from education for the elite. The former consisted of elementary school programmes to create obedient workers who made up almost the whole population of Japan. The latter consisted of education programmes for the elite to train as competent leaders of Japanese society. They were students from the upper class. Most of these students were descendents of the *Bushi* (*Samurai*) class (*Shizoku*) who had the traditional attitude of *Bushido* (*Samurai spirit*). This was characterized by an emphasis on the moral excellence of Confucianism, a fighting spirit which was influenced partly by Zen-Buddism, and a consciousness of shame (Kusaka, 1996).

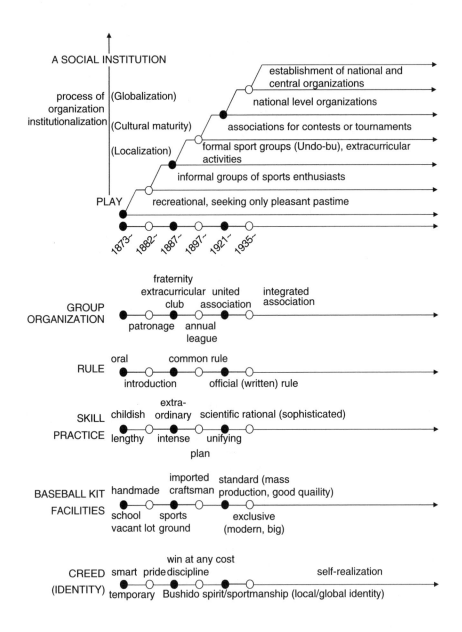

*Figure 2.1* The stages in the development of Japanese school sport (Kusaka, 1996)

## The appearance of recreation groups

Modern sport, introduced from a variety of foreign countries, began to be enjoyed as a recreation. For example, the origin of Japanese baseball was a by-product of the above-mentioned education policy. In 1873, H. Wilson, an American teacher of English, introduced baseball to the students of the *Kaisei-Gakko* (the predecessor of the Tokyo Empire University). Using his own bat and balls, he hit the balls and the students enjoyed catching them. The number of participants increased gradually; in the end, they played the game properly. E. H. Majet, also a teacher at this school, taught baseball, too. In 1876 they played baseball with Americans living in Yokohama and Tsukiji. In addition, students who returned to the school from the United States, taught the game to their friends and played together. The baseball cult grew gradually at this university. It spread to the neighbouring Tokyo Foreign Language School (the predecessor of the First National High School) whose students were eager to play baseball too. Peeping through the fence, they quickly imitated the game played by other students – even making their own ball and bat. Again, students returning from the U S A helped spread the baseball cult yet further.

In 1873, at the Tokyo *Kaitakushi-Kari-Gakko*, A. Bates and D. P. Penhallow taught baseball to the students after school. It was not easy to teach the game to young students who didn't understand English well. The game in those days was not necessarily played by eighteen persons, but was similar to the triangle baseball that is now played by children in Japan. The way the game was played depended entirely upon the players who were present at the time. There were only a few rough balls and bats, small vacant lots and simple oral rules. In these informal situations, unskilled players only enjoyed these spontaneous games occasionally. They had never experienced team sport before. This attraction was reinforced by the pride they took in playing American 'high collar' baseball.

## Informal groups of sport enthusiasts

At this stage students began to play sports seriously. From the 1880s, informal teams appeared in Tokyo. Table 2.2 provides the names of those teams.

Crude baseball skills were taught by Mr Hiraoka, using primitive equipment. They played without gloves, mitts and masks. Batters mostly tried to hit home runs. They were proud of playing a modern American game and competed with each other. Both victories and defeats contributed to the growth of the baseball cult. Thus, baseball had developed a heightened popularity by the 1890s. Codified baseball rules were introduced by several individuals including Mr Hiraoka in 1882, F. W. Strange's 'Outdoor Games' in 1883, Gendo Tsuboi's 'The method of Outdoor Games' in 1884 and by Morie Tanaka's 'How To Play Outdoor Games' in 1885. These rules made reference to *The Boys' Own Book* and Spalding's *The Baseball Guide* which were published in the USA at this period.

Table 2.2 Informal baseball teams appearing in the 1880s

| Year (Circa) | Teams |
| --- | --- |
| 1877 | The Tokyo College of Law (Tokyo-Daigaku-Hogakubu) |
| 1879 | The Shinbashi Club (The Athletic Club) |
| 1879 | The Hercules Club |
| 1882 | The Komaba Agricultural School |
| 1883 | The Tokyo College of Engineering (Kobu-Daigaku) |
| 1885 | Aoyama English School |
| 1885 | The Shirogane (platinum) Club of Hara Daigaku (predecessor to the University of Meiji Gakuen) |
| 1885 | The Saint Paul Club of Rikkyo-Daigaku (Christian school) |
| 1885 | Keio-Gijuku-Daigaku, which became The Mita Baseball Club in 1888 |
| 1885 | Daigaku-Yobimon |
| 1885 | The Tameike Club |
| | etc. |

These were not, however, the baseball rules of informal players. They played by different, oral rules, as called for by the occasion. It was only in 1895 that codified and uniform baseball rules were written down by the players of the First National High School.

In the rowing world, clubs appeared with names such as: The Members of Boat Club, The Sumida Rowing Club, The Row Club, The Oriental Rowing Club and The Pacific Rowing Club. These sports clubs were still based on acquaintanceships, private friendships among members, and retained the basic characteristics of recreational groups. Gradually, teams began to develop a spirit of competition. Spontaneously-formed, small sport-playing communities gradually began to take on the character of more formal groups. These informal groups of sport loving students evolved without official connection to their schools. To play the game and to win the game satisfied the players' pride. Belonging to a team gave the players status.

## The appearance of the sports club

After 1886, the spontaneous informal groups which appeared in the 1880s became a part of fraternity school extracurricular activities. They were given ideological and financial aid by the school organization, and today are known as the *Undo-bu*. These schools were higher educational facilities for elite students. Table 2.3 shows the names of those schools and fraternities, and the kinds of sport groups (*Undo-bu*).

*Table 2.3* Early fraternities and their clubs

| Year | Schools | Fraternities | Clubs |
|---|---|---|---|
| 1886 | Tokyo Imperial University | Undo-kai | Track and field, swimming. (In 1898, rowing, ball game, judo, kendo and kyudo/Japanese archery clubs were added.) |
| 1889 | Tokyo Higher Commercial School | Undo-kai | Rowing, judo and kyudo. |
| 1889 | Gakushuin | Hojin-kai Phys. Ed.-bu | Baseball, swimming, etc. |
| 1890 | 1st National High School | Koyu-kai | Rowing, kendo, kyudo, baseball, lawn tennis, track and field, long walk, etc. |
| 1890 | Tokyo Pref. High School | Koyu-kai | Undo, long walk, swimming, rowing, kendo, judo. |
| 1891 | 5th National High School | Ryunan-kai | Kendo, judo, outdoor games, etc. |
| 1892 | 3rd National High School | Jinshin-kai | Kendo and judo, kyudo, track and field, swimming and baseball. |
| 1892 | Keio-Gijuku | Phys.Ed.-kai | Kendo, judo, baseball, rowing, gymnastics, kyudo, gymnastic training and walking. |
| 1893 | 2nd National High School | Shoshi-kai | Martial arts. |
| 1896 | Tokyo Higher Teachers' College | Koyu-kai Undo-kai | Judo, kendo and bayonet, Japanese archery, heavy gymnastics and sumo, lawn tennis, football and baseball. (Every student had to belong to more than one club and to practise more than 30 minutes every day.) |
| 1897 | Tokyo Technical College (precursor of Waseda University) | Phys.Ed.-bu | Kendo, sumo, tennis, baseball, exercise outside school, heavy gymnastics, judo and kendo. |
| 1897 | Kyoto Imperial University | Dogaku-kai Undo-kai | Tennis, baseball, kyudo, kendo, judo, rowing and equestrianism. |
| 1898 | Tokyo Pref. Teachers' College | Shobu-kai | Kendo, judo, heavy gymnastics, baseball and tennis. (Every student had to belong to one club.) |
| 1898 | Tokyo Pref. Kansei High School | Koyu-kai | Rowing, kendo, long walk and swimming. |
| 1902 | Tokyo Higher Commercial School | Hitotsubashi-kai | Lawn tennis, rowing, etc. (Every student had to be a member of the rowing club.) |

In the development of these groups, the following features were evident: the appearance of recreational groups, the holding of intra-school meetings, the establishment of the *Undo-bu*, the increasing number of members and role differentiation, the institution of the *Senshu* (meaning a selected player), the establishment of regular team members, the achievement of winning and the creation of team traditions.

Each regular player wanted to win at any cost and fought for his own honour and pride, so defeat meant shame for him (private shame). He represented the school as well as the team, however, so he had to be a symbol of the school's customs, traditions and prestige. He was his school's selected fighter. School teachers, school mates and the old alumni placed responsibility for winning on the *Senshu*. Thus, defeat also meant public shame.

In the baseball world, The First National High School, *Gakushuin*, *Keio* and *Waseda* were the leading groups in Japan until the middle of the Meiji era. The games between the First National High School and Americans in Yokohama from 1896 to 1902, and the publication of the victories of the former in newspapers, was one of the stimuli for the baseball cult in Japan. This reflected the nationalistic trends of the time. Other, less manly activities were thought to be cowardly and un-*Bushido*-like. The number of baseball clubs gradually increased. Baseball spread to the middle schools (the equivalent of senior high schools today) in such big cities as Akita, Mito, Utsunomiya, Tokyo, Yokohama, and Kobe. Thus, from about 1900, baseball began to spread all over Japan. One of the reasons for the diffusion was the coaching of middle school teams in long vacations by the old alumni baseball players. Middle schools were also higher education establishments in the Meiji and the early Taisho eras (1912–1926).

In this period, and subsequently, there was a tendency for educational background to have a strong influence on future social and economic status. It was difficult to get into the middle and higher schools, both academically and economically. Thus, only a few young persons who grew up in affluent educational circumstances, that is, whose parents had higher social and economic status, could enter these higher schools. This occurred in spite of the official policy of equality of educational opportunities for all social strata of Japanese society. Figure 2.2 (Kusaka, 1987) shows the elite training system before the Second World War. It was almost exclusively these elite students who enjoyed sport at this stage.

Pupils had greater free time and use of the school grounds. Intense competition gave rise to some abuses, especially among the cheerleaders. Kinoshita, principal of the First National High School, admonished the students and reminded them not to forget the spirit of *Bushido*, not to be 'haughty in winning and not to be discouraged in losing'.

In baseball, from 1891 to 1904, the First National High School had the strongest team in Japan. Its baseball creed emphasized winning and cultivation of players with *Samurai*- and *Bushido*-like spirit. These were the roots of Japanese sport ideology before the Second World War. This is also one of the aspects of

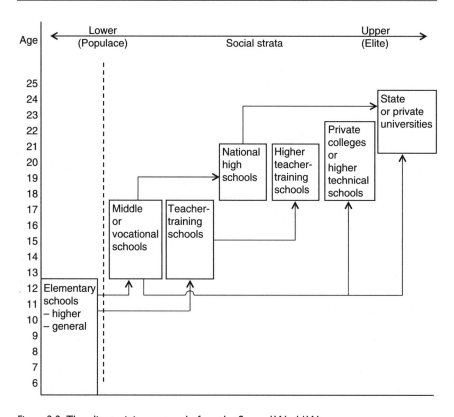

*Figure 2.2* The elite training system before the Second World War

the localization of modern sport in Japan. The teams of Waseda and Keio, the two oldest private universities, became stronger after 1902. The leading teams in other sports were the Tokyo Higher Teacher Training College and the Tokyo Higher Commercial College. Wasada and Keio led in tennis, and the Tokyo Empire University and the Kyoto Empire University in rowing.

## The appearance of associations for contests or tournaments

Sport teams which had begun to emerge after the 1890s began to arrange matches on an *ad hoc* basis. By 1902, groups which were of similar rank in terms of skill and status, began to arrange to play on a regular and more organized basis. This is when sport associations began to appear. Among a season's main fixtures were the First National vs. Commercial High School and the Waseda vs. Keio University in rowing, and the Tokyo Higher Teacher Training vs. Tokyo Higher Commercial School, the THTS vs. Waseda University, THTS vs. Keio and the

Tokyo Higher Commercial vs. Kobe Higher Commercial School in tennis. Especially popular, given the rivalry between the clubs, were the Waseda vs. Keio and the First vs. Third National High School matches.

In baseball, in 1905, the Waseda baseball team was led by university teacher Isoo Abe. He had made great efforts towards the development of the ideological aspects of Japanese baseball, arguing that the sport must contribute to the physical, spiritual and moral development or cultivation of players. The team had been to the USA for about two months to test their skills. The results were seven wins to nineteen losses against high school, college, university, adult and army teams. Owing to this experience, Japanese baseball developed rapidly in terms of skills and tactics, practice methods and the production of baseball equipment including bats, balls, gloves and spiked shoes. These developments corresponded with the technological developments in Japanese society. Japanese baseball was becoming more scientifically oriented.

In 1915 the Osaka Asahi Newspaper absorbed and organized both separate matches, and small district tournaments into the National Baseball Tournament of Middle Schools. In doing so the educational significance of the game for the young was stressed. Some seventy-two schools participated in the first tournament. In the second, third and fourth tournament years, respectively, 150, 229 and 410 teams participated. Thus these organizations stimulated the spread of baseball and inspired every school baseball club with the desire to win. Practice became more organized, coaches were recruited and the school organization helped them in their activities. School teachers and the old boys emphasized not only winning, but also the educational functions of baseball, insisting on fair play and the spirit of sportsmanship, sometimes referring to the *Bushido* spirit. By the 1920s, baseball had become the most popular sport.

The invention of the rubber ball led to the birth of the National Association of Boys' Softball, organized by the alumni in 1920. This also led to the birth of the National Association of Adults' Softball in 1927, called 'Sand-lot Baseball'. This is another aspect of the localization of modern sport in Japan. The former organization was dissolved by the Ministry of Education through the Baseball Restriction Act (the control of baseball matches) in 1932. There were worries about abuse of educational principles arising from too many competitions and tournaments being sponsored by local newspapers based on commercial values. The popularity of baseball is illustrated in Figure 2.3 (Kusaka, 1987).

Other sports also began to increase in number at this stage. Table 2.4 shows the increase in the number of schools. This was followed by a growth in the number of *Undo-bu*. In 1933, the rate of establishment of sports groups was 85 per cent in tennis (the calculation was 1,300 teams), 61 per cent in baseball (the calculation was about 1,000 teams), 30 per cent in basketball, and 20 per cent in both soccer and volleyball. Tournaments sponsored by newspapers and higher schools thus played important roles in the development of the organization and popularization of sport in Japan, especially in the formation of local branches of national associations.

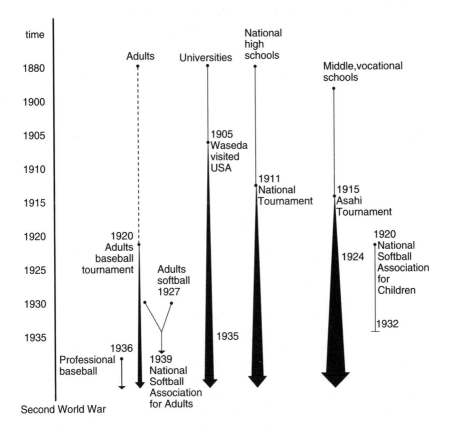

*Figure 2.3* The expansion of baseball communities in Japan

## National associations

National associations/federations began to form after 1920, within various sport communities. These associations were bureaucratic: they decided national and international levels of competition, made and acknowledged rules and conducted association-wide projects. Figure 2.4 shows the associations that were founded from 1920 to 1939.

The National Association of Sport/Physical Education was founded in 1911 by Jigoro Kano in order to enable Japan to participate in the Olympic Games. This association was an autocratic and outward-looking institution and did not include any substantial number of players. A central national association of amateur athletes was established by a substantial number of players in 1935. This National Association of (Amateur) Sport had articles that defined it as a co-operative foundation. Thus, in 1935, (school) sport became recognized in Japanese society as a cultural and social institution.

*Table 2.4* The increase in the number of schools before the Second World War

| Schools Year | Universities | National high schools | Higher technical schools | Teacher training schools | Middle schools | Vocational schools |
|---|---|---|---|---|---|---|
| 1887 | 1 | 6 | 61 | 45 | 48 | 27 |
| 1892 | 1 | 7 | 36 | 47 | 62 | 28 |
| 1897 | 2 | 6 | 45 | 47 | 157 | 99 |
| 1902 | 2 | 8 | 58 | 57 | 258 | 225 |
| 1907 | 3 | 7 | 66 | 69 | 287 | 368 |
| 1912 | 4 | 8 | 85 | 86 | 317 | 519 |
| 1916 | 4 | 8 | 90 | 92 | 325 | 571 |
| 1921 | 18 | 17 | 108 | 94 | 385 | 692 |
| 1926 | 37 | 31 | 139 | 102 | 518 | 853 |
| 1930 | 46 | 32 | 161 | 105 | 557 | 976 |
| 1935 | 45 | 32 | 177 | 102 | 557 | 1254 |

These developments were part of the processes of change in Japanese school sport organization from a time when only unorganized recreation groups existed. More formal sport groups appeared and grew mostly as a result of the increase in the number of schools which accompanied the development of Japanese capital-ism. Finally, the stage came when national level governing associations incorporated the smaller groupings. Other contributory factors involved in this were formalization processes, role differentiation and specialization of sport groups, the precise codification of sports rules and regulations, and provision of tournaments and associations. In addition, the advancement of patterned tech-niques, the improvements in sports equipment, which accompanied the technological development in Japanese society, and the formal acceptance of sport ideology, which mainly emphasized the moral and spiritual cultivation of players, all contributed to the institutionalization of Japanese (school) sport.

## The Japanization/localization of sport in Japan

The Japanese sporting creed had two main precepts. These were the winning principle and the cultivation principle. Players were honour-bound to strive to win. The teachers and the alumni who understood and aided students sport, for example, Isoo Abe (baseball), Shinzo Koizumi (tennis), Jigoro Kano (judo) and the many principals of middle schools and the National High Schools, also emphasized the notion of cultivation. In the period before the Second World War there were three principles that governed education: wisdom, morality and physicality. These had been emphasized by the nationalistic education policies of Arinori Mori and the morals of Confucianism in the 'Imperial Edict on

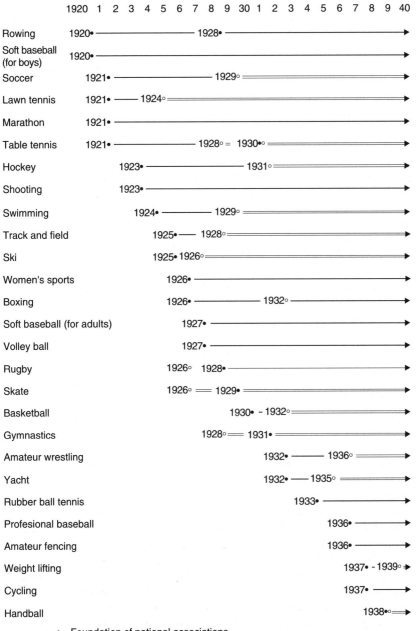

*Figure 2.4* Foundations of national associations (• –) and their affiliations to international federations (o =)

Education' since the Meiji era. Japanese sportsmen had to cultivate a range of virtues including: fairness; determination/endurance; self-control/discipline/obedience; co-operation/collaboration/team spirit; simplicity/cleanliness; and, doing one's best.

Manliness was concerned with the virtues of fairness and determination and student players had to play in a spirit of simplicity – which was almost a synonym for being an amateur. Sport was justified as the field which cultivated virtues such as physical training, judgment and calmness, while also promoting school and national prestige, and the vigour and physical fitness of the nation.

Japanese students had to play seriously. The notion of 'fun' could not justify their activities. In addition, sportsmanship and the spirit of fair play were replaced by the Japanese spirit or *Bushido* spirit. The Japanese highlighted Western ideals concerning these virtues, but insisted on drawing on the traditional ideas of Japanese culture, and thus sometimes replaced them with the spirit of Zen Buddism. However, no examination of the common and different factors involved in these beliefs was undertaken. The ideas of sportsmanship and fair play gradually permeated the Japanese players' attitudes towards their mind and body.

From this analysis, it is clear that in developing school sport in Japan, organizations, rules, skills and equipment (facilities) became gradually Westernized and internationalized. However, psychological aspects were given a local interpretation, or Japanized, especially before the Second World War. The framework was a Japanese spirit combined with Western knowledge – see Figure 2.5.

## The globalization of Japanese sport

It is possible to argue that the process involved in the globalization of Japanese culture and its people was reinforced by the playing of modern sports. However, as modern sports were introduced in the Meiji era, they also underwent a process of Japanization (localization). The individualistic (*Bushi/Bushido*) sports had already adopted a scientific approach in 1904 when Waseda University went to the USA. Nevertheless, substantial globalization of Japanese sport began upon affiliation with international sport federations – see Figure 2.4.

The military suppressed the playing of sport during the Second World War. After the war, however, young students soon began to play western games again. The emphasis of the physical education curriculum shifted from gymnastic exercise to recreation, sport as a leisure activity and for the promotion of sportsmanship. Track and field, swimming, skiing, gymnastics, judo, kendo, sumo, volleyball, basketball, handball, soccer, rugby, tennis, table tennis, badminton, softball, soft-baseball and dance were all included in the curriculum guidelines of the Ministry of Education in both 1949 and 1951.

The *Undo-bu* were seen as having an important role in the promotion of democratic physical education. Table 2.5 shows the increase in the number of

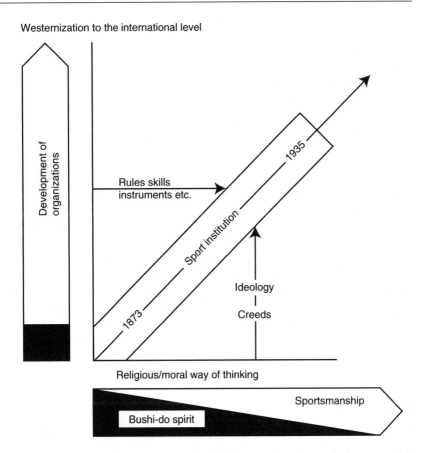

*Figure 2.5* Development of foreign sports through the combination of the Japanese spirit and Western knowledge

schools where all kinds of sports were being played. The theoretical justification for sport was moving towards notions of players' self-realization and self-identity formation.

## Conclusion

The idea of Japanese school sport germinated as student recreation and grew to have cultural meaning through students' values. School sport was then vested with educational values recognized by society and, by 1935, it was established as a cultural/social institution. The energy and passion of the people involved were a significant aspect of this cultural development. They were able to establish this cultural institution in society, as a function of something that has been described by Huizinga as 'fun' and by Csikszentmihalyi as 'flow'. This fact must illustrate a

*Table 2.5* Increase in numbers of schools after the Second World War

| Year | Elementary schools | Junior high schools | Senior high schools | Technical colleges | Junior colleges | Universities |
|------|------|------|------|------|------|------|
| 1948 | 25,273 | 16,285 | 3,575 | 0 | 0 | 12 |
| 1950 | 25,878 | 14,165 | 4,292 | 0 | 149 | 201 |
| 1962 | 26,615 | 12,674 | 4,637 | 19 | 305 | 260 |
| 1980 | 24,954 | 10,780 | 5,208 | 62 | 517 | 446 |
| 2003 | 23,808 | 11,159 | 5,472 | 64 | 541 | 686 |

universal truism applicable to players of all ages and countries. Without this motivation, no sport culture would be able to bloom – even in the UK or USA. As one baseball player wrote: 'I play baseball because it's fun, not because of the educational meanings'. It is a human desire to play and to seek to win.

Japanese sport creeds, such as the *Bushi* and *Bushido* principles, were also expressed by those involved. These creeds were the ideal types of Japanese school sport and focused on cultivation through sport, which was linked to and influenced by Zen Buddhism, Confucianism and Taoism. It is an example of the Japanization of modern sport. An older generation of Japanese sportsmen justified their activities by these ideals. Today, however, the justification for sport is changing to the self-realization and character-building of individual players and reflects the globalization of school sport in Japan.

## References

Bellah, R. N. (1962) *Tokugawa Religion* (Nipponn Kindaika to Shukyo Rinri), Tokyo: Miraisha.

Imamura, Yoshio (1951) *Nippon Taiikushi* (The History of Japanese Physical Education), Tokyo: Kaneko Shobo.

Imamura, Yoshio (1970) *Nippon Taiikushi* (The History of Japanese Physical Education), Tokyo: Humaido Shuppan.

Inoue, Kazuo (1970) *Gakkoutaiiku Seidoshi* (The History of School Physical Education), Tokyo: Taishukan Shoten.

Kamishima, Jiro (1961) *Kindainippon no Seishinkouzou* (The Spiritual Structure of Modern Japan), Tokyo: Iwanami Shoten.

Kinoshita, Hideaki (1971) *Nipponntaiikushi kenkyu Josetu* (The Introduction to Study of Physical Education in Japan), Humaido Shuppan.

Kusaka, Yuko (1987) 'The development of baseball organizations in Japan', *International Review for the Sociology of Sport*, 22–4: 263–279.

Kusaka, Yuko (1996) *Nipponn Supotubunka no Genryu* (The Headwaters of Sport Culture in Japan), Tokyo: Humaido Shuppan.

Takenoshita, Kyuzo (1950) *Taiiku 50nen* (The 50 Years of Physical Education), Tokyo: Jijitushinsya.

Takenoshita, Kyuzo and Kishino, Yuzo (1959) *Kindainippon Gakkoutaiikushi* (The History of Physical Education in Modern Japan), Tokyo: Toyokan Shuppansha.

# Chapter 3

# The Japanese baseball spirit and professional ideology[1]

*Koichi Kiku*

## Introduction

The purpose of this chapter is to discuss how the ideology of professional sport is developed from the basic 'spirit' of sport that plays an initial role in spiritual and physical education. Sport and economics have been deemed to be systematically related to each other, as a result of the autonomous development of principles and ideologies within sports institutions. The subject of this analysis is baseball, one of the most popular sports in Japan. The internal development of the ideology in professional baseball will be traced from the early Meiji era (late nineteenth century), when baseball was first introduced into Japan, to the early Showa era (early twentieth century), when a professional league was established. Based on the concept of historical sociology, the long chain of autonomic development of the ideology will be examined.

## Historical types of baseball spirit

The close relationship between history and sociology has been discussed from various points of view. Mills argued that social science itself should be a historical study and sociology, that deserves its name, should be all 'historical sociology' (Mills, trans. Suzuki 1965: 192). In fact, the theory of social science has been increasingly applied to historical researches (Miyashita, 1985: 100). Skocpol (1984) divided the theories that have been applied to historical studies into three strategies: 1) applying a general model to history, 2) using a concept for interpreting history, 3) analysing causal regularity in history. The latter was regarded as the most efficient, as it eliminated both particularization and generalization. It also abrogated the precedence of models and could determine the most suitable hypothesis for analysing factual historical instances. Hence, a general theory can be established without overstating particularities of individual cases, while the scope of applications is limited by using discourses based on historical facts (Skocpol, 1984: 362–386). This third strategy of causality analysis will be used in this study. The development of professionalism within the baseball institution in Japan, the most suitable hypothesis for this historical instance, will be analysed in the following sections (Kiku, 1988: 73–75).

## Ideology, creed and belief as spirit

Definitions of several concepts of institutional or professional sports have already been discussed (Kiku, 1984: 3–5). In this chapter, however, I would like briefly to define the concepts related to ideology, creed and belief, as a sphere of the sports spirit, based on the interpretation of symbol sphere[2] suggested by Gerth and Mills (1954: 22–23). Though definitions of ideology vary, here it is understood as a total generalization of a person's or group's belief in the significance of the world and a person's status within it (Barion: trans. Tokunaga, 1974: 152). It is a widespread idea that the value of sports justifies the existence of sport and clarifies its significance for people and society (Imamura, 1976: 766).

Sport ideology is envisaged as the form and system of a theoretically organized concept. In other words, it is the spirit of those who support and value the institution as well as its material significance and value. For the purpose of this analysis is, the ideological character of the spirit for a specific individual may be defined as belief, while that of a specific group as creed. If a creed reaches the point where the whole sports world appears to share it, it finally becomes ideology. In order to discuss the depth of ideology, however, it is necessary to have insight into belief and creed. While these three phases need to be distinguished, they should be understood as a whole concept (Kiku, 1993: 33).

## Historical types of baseball spirit in the formation of professional ideology

Considering that relations between sports and economics are institutionalized, the formation of a professional sports institution can be decreed by commercial interests. This phenomenon was observed when the professional baseball institution was established in Japan before the Second World War. The professional baseball league was officially formed when the foundation assembly was held at the Japan industry club in Marunouchi, Tokyo on February 5, 1936 (The Japan Professional Baseball League, 1936). The sponsoring companies for these professional teams were four newspaper publishers and three railroad firms, all then leading companies in the then Japanese economy.

This can be seen as a commercial ramification[3] of the baseball institution. Companies, or private enterprises, are businesses which conduct productive activities with the purpose of making profits (Imamura 1976: 785). Baseball developed autonomously and naturally in Japan until the professional league was established. The formation of the league provided a means for making profits in two ways: the consumerization of baseball spectators and the commercialization of baseball players.

Though professional baseball was a top-down economic institution, it also embraced the spirit of those who had been involved in the autonomous development of baseball or those responsible for the natural bottom-up development. This analysis also focuses on the latter aspect. To be more specific, two co-ordinate axes

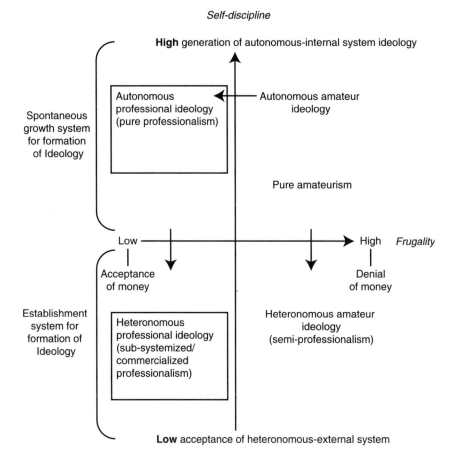

*Figure 3.1* Historical types of baseball ideology: frame of analysis

are used for analysing baseball ideology: the one representing the level of autonomy in the institution; the other representing positive/negative attitudes towards money (admission charging, purchase of equipment etc.). As shown in Figure 3.1, the four frames represent basic baseball ideologies. Needless to say, the latter axis, positive or negative attitudes towards money, is the most obvious concept dividing professionalism from amateurism. In this chapter, however, another autonomic/heteronomic axis is added and the ideology is segmented, as emphasis on objectivity is critical for the autonomous development of both professional and amateur institutions.

In addition to applying the framework to the connotation of baseball ideology, the historical aspect is also considered. Two principles of *Bushido*-spirit, self-discipline and stoical frugality, will be applied to the development of baseball ideology. Both principles were codes of the *samurai* warriors, but, as time went on, because victory was gradually stressed when they fought each other, self-discipline became more important than frugality. The formation of professional ideology in baseball has parallels in *Bushido*. The ideology could indicate that the ideal *Bushido*-style baseball based on self-discipline was reinforced by the affirmation of money. Based on this hypothesis, the way in which the baseball spirit was transformed in developing the professional league, will be discussed later.

Two types of ideologies, however, are concerned in this case: the ideology of autonomous development and the ideology of institutional development. The former ideology is based on self-discipline, where the benefits and ethos within baseball are autonomously maintained and developed over time. The latter ideology, on the other hand, does not have or has only a little self-discipline, so the existing benefits or ethos of an institution cannot be preserved, while the outward ideology, in this case an ideology based on economics, is prioritized. Based on the above understanding of the professional ideology, transitions of creed and ideology between the early Meiji era and the early Showa era will be elucidated in the following section. In order to do so, I would like to focus on the initiators, or those who played a role in developing the baseball ideology in Japan.

## Transitions in baseball spirit

Baseball was introduced into Japan in the early Meiji era, which was around 1872 to 1881. The game was played mainly by academic students and the sons of wealthy families. In those days, not long after the country had opened to foreign relations, it was modern and fashionable to be engaged in Western culture. At the beginning, baseball was one of these novelties, most of which were temporal pastimes for them. Students had never participated in outdoor sporting activities (Strange, 1883: 2). This was why they became enthusiastic about playing baseball. Gendo Tsuboi, who was the pioneer of outdoor sports in Japan, described, baseball as 'the most suitable outdoor sport for health and pleasure. It also inspires a sense of competitiveness' (Tsuboi and Tanaka, 1895: 66). He was the first person who admitted the merits of baseball as an outdoor sport, i.e. health, pleasure and competitiveness. Takeshi Hiraoka played a leading role in popularizing baseball among adults. He founded the Shinbashi Club (also known as Athletics) baseball team in 1878 and built the baseball field known as Recreation Park in Shinagawa Yatsuyama Garage in 1882 (Nakazawa, 1957: 3).

In order to maintain the facility and purchase necessary baseball equipment, it was decided that everyone should pay one Yen as a monthly fee.[4] The field should be levelled with a roller every Saturday. Made-in-the-USA balls, bats and other equipment should be used (The Daiichi High School Alumni Association 1895: 2). Hiraoka arranged for medals to be given to winners of games (Syono 1931: 8). Players were filled with pride when medals were awarded. Baseball players were wealthy enough to pay their own expenses for taking part. They were also 'proud' people who enjoyed high social status. For them, playing baseball was a sort of honour, as baseball was thought to be the greatest pastime of the day (Shimbun/Nippon 1896: July 20).

The situation changed around 1882 to 1887, when groups of informal baseball fans started to play the game and compete against each other. Until then, players enjoyed baseball as a casual pastime. But these games gradually became serious, as a sense of rivalry was created and competition was emphasized. The teams were competitive and full of fighting spirit (Tahara, 1929: 30). Each team asked its members to pay a membership fee in order to secure financial resources. In the case of the Tameike Club in Tokyo, for example, it was decided to charge daily membership fees for purchasing equipment. But the members brought their own equipment with them when they played ... the collected fees were left unused and kept in a large jingling wallet while the game was played (Tahara, 1929: 52). However, usually, a large portion of the fees teams paid was spent on purchasing baseball equipment. Most players were university graduates. Considering the fact that the percentage of those who studied at universities at that time was only 0.07 per cent (Ministry of Education in Japan, 1972: 211–247), it is clear that they belonged to the elite and wealthy class. Hence, organizing games between well-to-do club teams did not present any financial difficulties. They started to compete for a championship in the 1890s. Among many teams, Daiichi High School (also known as Ichiko) came into the spotlight.

## The generation of baseball ideology through *Bushido* spirit

The baseball club of Daiichi High School (hereafter called Ichiko) was established in 1886. F. W. Strange, a foreign teacher of English at the school, made a great effort to establish the club (The Dormitory of Daiichi High School 1930: 750–783). Generally speaking, from 1890s onwards, school sports clubs set out to win games against other schools and the students were devoted to hard training. Suishu Tobita, the father of school baseball, described training in Ichiko's baseball club as 'seriously hard' (Tobita, 1928: 61). The hard training in this club became legendary. What sustained such devotion to training was the Ichiko spirit – the spirit of indomitability and determination that aimed for victory at all costs (Nakano, 1922: 31–32). Baseball players had a creed which enabled them to survive hard training. Winning games became a matter of pride and honour for the players, as well as for the school. The success of the club enhanced the school's reputation. The club's extraordinary record of success between 1895 and 1902, fifty-six wins and only ten losses, was the result of their victory supremacist creed (Kusaka, 1985: 26).

According to 'The History of The Baseball Club' (The Daiichi High School Alumni Association 1972: 230–232), which was edited and published by the school alumni association in 1903, Ichiko's baseball club was a place for training members' minds. For outsiders, the achievement of Ichiko's baseball club represented school tradition. Baseball improved the insiders, or club members, and impressed outsiders, or the public. The whole contributed to enhance Ichiko's reputation. It also described baseball as becoming a 'tool for training the mind and building the character'. Baseball, then, generated the victory supremacist spirit in Ichiko's baseball players and was interpreted as a tool for improving the mind and morality.

Through this new interpretation, ideas of playing basketball for relaxation or as a pastime disappeared. Instead, victory through devotion to hard training was emphasized and the baseball pitch became a place for discipline and provided an opportunity for creating and enhancing the school's reputation. Furthermore, the nationalistic aspect of sports grew when Ichiko beat the foreigners' team based in Yokohama on May 23, 1896. Ichiko received countless congratulatory telegrams from schools all over Japan. Hirotsugu Kinoshita, the then school headmaster of Ichiko, said in his speech, 'According to the *Bushido* code, no matter how tough and cruel the battle is, one should not lose respect for the enemy. One should never be arrogant in winning or disappointed in losing. We have applied this *Bushido* approach to our baseball for years' (The Dormitory of Daiichi High School, 1930: 804). The school creed, bound up with the pre-modern *Bushido* spirit, turned out to be a logical and steadfast ideology. It would seem that Ichiko held two types of creed. One was the victory supremacist creed, like the old creed of *bushi* or warriors who felt ashamed when they were defeated. The other was the self-discipline creed, also based on the *Bushido*, in which players used the sport as an opportunity for their own physical and psychological training. Both of these creeds worked well together, without contradicting each other.

Baseball clubs at schools, which were usually organized by the alumni association, were financed by membership fees and individual donations. Because most equipment was imported and extremely expensive in those days, many clubs had financial problems. They were dependent on donations of money from parents or those of equipment from foreigners, and tried hard to save money (The Daiichi High School Alumni Association, 1894: 59). However, they never contemplated charging spectators, even when around 10,000 people gathered to watch Ichiko's game against the warship Detroit team on June 27th, 1896 (The Dormitory of Daiichi High School, 1930: 806). Baseball was the game of the *Bushido* spirit, which emphasized stoicism and frugality.

In general, in Japan, sports and *Bushido* were united from about 1897 (Furukawa, 1957: 86). This trend was described in 'The History of The Baseball Club' of Ichiko as follows (The Daiichi High School Alumni Association 1894: 232–234). It is worthy of quoting at some length:

Foreigners point out the following virtues of playing baseball:

- It develops the ability of judgment and agility
- It enhances cleverness

- It strengthens the body
- It fosters mutual co-operation.

They may be absolutely right, but our club would like to suggest additional virtues:

- The spirit of baseball is to pursue frugality
- The spirit of baseball is to play with bravery and fortitude
- The spirit of baseball is to devote oneself without hesitation.

Our baseball club is highly responsible for representing our school, whose tradition corresponds to the above virtues. The dormitory, on the other hand, is a place for practising self-discipline, the spirit of our baseball club. Both the club and the dormitory should collaborate to train the player's mind to achieve self-discipline as an objective ... The baseball players should behave with dignity without worring about their appearance. They should train hard and do their best to play baseball, even if they are covered with mud. It is not a matter of skills, but the spirit ... The spirit of bushi is required in every aspect of training.

The baseball creed at the time can be summarized as: (a) frugality (the spirit of baseball is to be frugal); (b) self-discipline based on *Bushido* (to achieve self-discipline as an objective); (c) victory supremacist (the spirit of *bushi* implies losing is shameful). Additionally, two typical aspects of *Bushido* philosophy were combined in the *Ichik* creed. The first is the *Roujyo* principle. *Roujyo* was a war tactic practised by *bushi*, of completely segregating themselves from the outside world and barricading themselves in their castle, until their enemy gave up. Like secluded *bushi* of the time, Ichiko students confined their lives to the club and the dormitory, cutting communication with the outside world for the sake of training and studying to become elites. *Shinken-shoubu* is another principle of *bushi*. It is a combined ideology of frugality and hard work according to *Bushido* (Kimura, 1960: 69). As these principles were all existent in *Bushido* from the medieval era in Japan, they integrated well into the baseball creed. Finally, it was extended to a general ideology for the whole baseball institution in Japan which created its own baseball playing ethos.

## The decline of frugality and the introduction of admission charges

From 1904 onwards, Waseda and Keio Universities, which are among the oldest privately run universities in Japan, stood out as more competitive in terms of baseball than Ichiko. The Bushido spirit, however, was still apparent in baseball. Because of the excessive rivalry, especially between the cheering clubs of these two universities, they regarded each other like enemies in wartime and even had to give up playing games (Hirose, 1940; Oota, 1930). *Bushido* baseball also spread to local areas, as seen in *Yakyu Ben-yo* (*Handbook of Baseball*, 1905), which was published by the alumni association of Daiichi Secondary School in Aichi prefecture (Tajima, 1905: 20–23). Then, from August to September 1911, a discussion took place about whether baseball was harmful for young students. This discussion was sparked off by an article in the *Asahi Shinbun*, one of the leading national newspapers in Japan (Asahi Shinbun, August 29 to September 19, 1911). In the article, Japanese schools were criticized for placing too great an emphasis on victory, some renowned intellectuals supporting these opinions. The criticism, however, had the opposite effect. Those who were concerned with school baseball became more closely united than ever and organized the Baseball Symposium on September 16, 1911, sponsored by *Yomiuri Shimbun*, one of the other influential national newspapers. Ironically, the baseball creed and ideology based on *Bushido* was further integrated and reinforced.

Isoo Abe was the key person in the creation of the internal ideology of college baseball. He was the senior manager of the baseball club and a professor in Waseda University. Being a cosmopolitan and pacifist, he believed in the character-building aspect of playing baseball with foreign teams. Headed by him, the Waseda team became the first Japanese group to make a tour of the United States from April 4 to June 29, 1905. Abe's rational approach to economic ideology was the driving force of the tour. He said: 'Fair play is vital to every sport' (Abe, 1931: 2) and that *Bushido* had 'the same spirit of fair play' (Abe, 1926: 3). Hence, he insisted: 'After all, fair play, which is a widespread concept among the Westerners, makes no difference to *Bushido*' (Abe, 1926: 3). He offered a reinterpretation of *Bushido*, which was, according to him, the equivalent of fair play in the West. On the other hand, he criticized excessive emphasis on victory, saying: 'The outcome, victory or defeat, is of course one aspect of sport, but not everything. Skilfulness is a large attraction of sport' (Abe, 1908: 3). He also related baseball to three important *Bushido* virtues of: wisdom, benevolence and courage. He argued that baseball needed the self-discipline of *Bushido*, which fostered baseball players who could master wisdom, benevolence and courage and become men of character (Abe, 1905a: 199–211). Playing games with foreign teams, according to him, would be a great opportunity for character building and international sports such as baseball could be a tool for eliminating prejudice between two countries. He advocated that games between countries should be intended to contribute to peace in the world (Abe, 1931b: 2–3). With this pacifist approach in mind, he tried to develop cultural exchanges with the United States by means of baseball.

Travelling abroad, however, was a luxury in the inter-war years. Abe commented: 'It costs a vast amount of money to go to the United States. We will charge for admissions to games held in the States and I wonder how much of the expenses can be covered by the profit' (Abe, 1905b). He also added that admissions for international games held in Japan could facilitate further participation in international games and championships overseas. He argued:

It would not be difficult to charge for admission to baseball games between Japanese and American teams. Each of us could invite the other by using the profit from the games. Moreover, if expenses can be covered by admission charges the Japanese people will have more opportunities to take part in all kinds of international sports competitions.

(Abe, 1936: 290–291)

Stoicism and frugality as well as dignity dovetailed well with the old Japanese saying, 'A *samurai* glories in honorable poverty'. This, then, rejected the idea of making money out of sport. This attitude in baseball, which Ichiko had originally developed, gradually declined. One of the main reasons was the increasing cost of playing baseball, due to purchases of expensive imported baseball equipment. This external and structural change was attributed to the baseball team's tour of the United States. A reliance on financial resources from third parties was inevitable, and this resulted in admission charges for spectators. The most significant factor for introducing admission charges, however, was probably Abe's influence. Abe, who initiated a new (Waseda group) ideology, attempted to remove the spirit of frugality from baseball and set a nobler aim, which was to organize international games, funded by admission charges. Through this process, the ideology of economic rationalism, which is typical of the West, was introduced to the baseball institution in Japan. The following games were the initial examples of games where admission charges were made and this system gradually spread throughout the country:

- October 31 1907: Keio University versus Saint Louis University of Hawaii (the first-ever game in Japan for which spectators paid admission);
- October 29 1911: Mita Club versus Tomon Club (the first game with admissions between Japanese teams);
- October 29 1914: The College Baseball League, among Waseda, Keio and Meiji universities (the first inter-college game with admissions);
- August 15 1924: The 10th Secondary School Baseball Championship (the first inter-school game with admissions) (Syono, 1931: 132–157).

## The establishment of the Japan Sports Association

Since Waseda and Keio played a major role in baseball, the rational economic ideology gained influence and led to the foundation of *Nippon Undo Kyoukai* (Japan Sports Association) as a form of limited partnership in 1921. It was the first professional baseball team sponsored by baseball players and their supporters, such as Atsushi Kono, Shin Hashido and Kiyoshi Oshikawa. They were all Waseda graduates who went on the first baseball tour to the United States, organized by Abe. The members of other university baseball clubs also joined the project. They suggested that sports should be more extensively played by all ages and classes and proposed the building of a baseball stadium for the citizens of

Tokyo (The Editorial Department of *Undo Kai*, 1921: 120). Their early financial records reveal that their first priority was the building of a home stadium modelled after the American Baseball League (The Editorial Department of *Undo Kai*, 1921: 121–122). Yet, even in the late 1980s, while baseball was still very popular in Japan, not all of the twelve professional teams owned their own home stadiums.

In hindsight, it was apparent that Kono and others, the founders of *Nippon Undo Kyoukai*, had a clear vision for managing a professional baseball team (Sato 1986: 17). Hashido, one of the founders, declared: 'We felt that it was necessary to make a strong baseball team, whose skills were higher than university clubs', so that it could lead the baseball scene in Japan and even compete against overseas teams. It was the reason why we started the plan to set up a model team by ourselves' (Hashido, 1921: 63). The *Nippon Undo Kyoukai* team became the 'first-ever professional baseball team in Japan' (Hashido 1921: 63) and the founders' expectation was that the team should take the lead, exceed university clubs in terms of skills as well as attitude, and challenge overseas teams. The team's commitment was to gain nationwide support and contribute to the development of baseball in Japan. Kono warned against materialism and not to indulge in show performances (Kono, 1922: 17–18). This implies that the commercial aspect of professional baseball was not the association's ideology. In order to realize their noble aim that a really professional team should be created both technically and psychologically, they carried out a very stoic and tough training camp for probationers (Kono, 1921: 17–18), and recruited only those players who had decent academic backgrounds and excellent personalities in addition to high levels of baseball skills (Kono, 1921: 48).

In a sense their concept was consistent with the then existing *Bushido* spirit of baseball, which aimed at victory in a context of nationalism. They tried to improve players' skills based on self-discipline and even elaborated the idea. On the other hand, the Western rational economic ideology was incorporated, as the club was a professional team funded by membership fees. The influence of the latter ideology, however, was not strong enough to co-exist successfully with the former *Bushido* ideology, especially in terms of the systematization of team management. Consequently, *Nippon Undo Kyoukai* and its baseball team disbanded in January 1924. Based on the ideology of *Nippon Undo Kyoukai*, it was impossible to introduce outside economic orders, or commercial sponsorship, and the aim of professionalization was to evolve as a spontaneous reform within the baseball institution. This type of professionalization can be tentatively called Ideology Type A, spontaneous internal reform.

Other professional baseball teams were formed at that time. The Tenkatsu Baseball Team was formed in February 1921 and also had university graduates as players. The aim and professional ideology of the founder, however, were ambiguous. Although they had skilful players, the game against *Nippon Undo Kyoukai*, which was held on August 30th, 1923, was bitterly criticized because of the insufficient training (The Editorial Department of *Undo Kai*, 1923: 85). Tenkatsu was a successful female magician and her niece succeeded to her name as Tenkatsu II. Shigeru Nakai, husband of Tenkatsu II, confessed:

> The *Tenkatsu* team was founded by *Tatsunosuke Noro*, husband of the original Tenkatsu. Wherever the magician troupe put on shows, the team played a baseball game with locals with the intention of promoting the troupe, which was the aim of the foundation.[5]

The Syokyokusai Tenkatsu and her troupe hired renowned university graduate baseball players and coaches at high salaries and used them for promoting their magic performances. Being the captain and having previously coached the team, Kantaro Suzuki provided an excuse for the team's involvement in 1923: 'We do nothing but baseball and aim to be professional. But we bear the same spirit of amateurism as baseball clubs at universities do. We have high respect for the spirit of baseball and intend to contribute to the development of baseball in this country' (Suzuki, 1923: 22–23). But the background and ideology of the team was unclear. This team can be categorized as the type that introduces and accepts outside economic orders and advances professionalization by using them and can be tentatively called Ideology Type B, institutional external reform.

The Daimai Baseball Team, was founded in 1920, and was exclusively sponsored by the *Osaka Mainichi Shinbun* (Newspaper Company). The team recruited not only well-known graduates from universities in the West of Japan (including Osaka, where the headquarters of the company were located), but also from the five universities in Tokyo, including Waseda and Keio, of which the baseball clubs were highly competitive. The team was ranked as the top company-run baseball team in the early twentieth century (Kizukuri, 1929: 22–26, Editorial of *Mainichi Shinbun* history 1952). It certainly contributed to the promotion and sales expansion of their newspapers. Their proclaimed ideology was 'our players are all journalists, but in their spare time they use their baseball skills to show our spirit of fair play' (Fukae, 1929: 59). In other words, they insisted that the team should play a role in propagating the sports spirit of the company and their players should not be professional but employees who played baseball in their spare time after work. The team tried to hang on to their amateur status. However, when the Far East Baseball Championship was held in 1923, it was debated whether the players of the Daimei team could represent Japan, as they should be regarded as professionals. Ryuzo Kizukuri, the then coach of the team, assured people that the team was by no means professional (Kizukuri, 1923: 63–64). This, he claimed, was for three reasons: the players were the employees of the company and performed their duties at the workplace, with the exception of some temporary employees; they did not receive any money for playing baseball; and, charges for admission to the games did not justify the argument that they were professional, as school baseball games also charged admission fees in this period.

According to Eiji Sugai, however, who was an outfielder of the team and said by the coach to be a sub-editor at the workplace:

I was assigned as a sub-editor in the Western region and also worked as a reporter for some local and sports news. But in fact, my main task was playing baseball. Our distributors from every part of Japan requested the team to visit their areas. After we had games with locals, the company increased their sales in the area.[6]

The baseball ideology of the Daimai Baseball Team is similar to Ideology Type B, as it encompasses the economic orders of the sponsoring company, but as it emphasizes its amateur team status, it can be tentatively called Ideology Type C, institutionally externally conservative.

Type A, derived from the Waseda ideology, was supported by the then two major baseball journals, *Yakyu Kai* ('Baseball World') and *Undo Kai* ('Sports World'). It was based on the economic ideology of Western rationalism, in which admissions, or making profit, was justified. A sense of guilt in making money by playing baseball was removed by the new ideology and the *Bushido* spirit in training and self-discipline was given priority. Furthermore, it was linked with the idea that fostering professional teams with professional players should lead to improved baseball techniques and retain a spiritual dimension. It was elaborated in the professional ideology in the baseball institution and initiated the foundation of the Japan Professional Baseball Team in February 1936.

## The baseball ideology for the establishment of Japan Professional Baseball League

Initially, attention needs to be given to the baseball creed of those who devoted themselves to founding the Japan Baseball Club team (currently the *Yomiuri* Giants) in 1934. The people involved included Yoshio Asanuma, Daisuke Miyake, and Tadao Ichioka. Their actions initiated the establishment of the Japan Professional Baseball League in 1936. Miyake was a *Keio* graduate, while others were Waseda graduates. In other words, they acquired the baseball creed of these two universities. Their baseball ideology also reflected the tradition and spirit that the two universities had developed thus far. Each of them publicized their opinions on professional baseball and the ideology behind it. Asanuma made known his argument in *Kyukai no Joka* (Clean-up Campaign of Baseball) (Asanuma, 1931: 6–8) and Miyake in *Yakyu Seishin* (Baseball Spirit) (Miyake, 1933: 46–50), while Ichioka refuted an article published in the *Asahi Shinbun*, *Kogyo Yakyu to Gakusei Yakyu* (Commercial Baseball and Student Baseball) by Tobita, which criticized the professionalization of baseball. The ideology underpinning the professionalization of baseball reflected their wish to: a) improve skills, b) fulfil the ideals of *Bushido* baseball through acquiring the American baseball spirit and nobleness of character, c) establish a self-supporting business system.

The concept was similar to the baseball ideology adopted by the *Nippon Undo Kyoukai*, but there was also one unique characteristic: they introduced investment from third parties. Miyake highlighted this point when he was interviewed for the journal *Beisuboru* (Baseball). He observed:

> Until now, baseball players like ourselves tried to establish a company which sponsors our own baseball team. But we had some financial problems due to the lack of business knowledge. Luckily, Sir *Okuma* and Mr *Shoriki*, the President of the *Yomiuri Shimbun* Company, had sympathy for us ... but I would like to make the point clear that our team is not owned by the *Yomiori Shimbun*. Mr *Shoriki* helped us to find sponsorship because he endorsed our project.
>
> (The Editorial Department of Baseball, 1934: 54–55)

Miyake denied that the team or the Japan Professional Baseball League, was organized as a sub-system of the company, following this intervention. For him, their professional ideology was formed as an autonomous spirit within the institution.

The professionalization of baseball was also supported by journals such as *Yakyu Kai* ('Baseball World') and 'Baseball' and formed an influential group which encouraged the establishment of the professional baseball league in Japan. Several advantages for professionalization were stated by the group. These included: a 'clean-up campaign for student baseball' (Naoki, 1935: 176–177, Naoki, 1936: 104–105), a 'clear distinction between amateurs and professionals' (Matsumoto, 1936: 192–194; Tsunematsu, 1935: 22–23; Hashido, 1935: 25–26), or 'professionalization as an extension of the baseball spirit' (Takasu, 1936: 17–18; Washizawa, 1931: 5–6; Azabu, 1937: 192–194; Ogikubo, 1936: 164–166).

The foundation assembly of the Japan Baseball Club was held on December 26, 1934. Ichioka was installed as the general manager, while Miyake and Asanuma took up the coaching positions (*Yomiuri Shimbun*, 1934). The professional ideology that they had insisted on was presented in 'The Outline of the Japan Professional Baseball League' as:

> We should demonstrate the real spirit of baseball and collaborate to create the sound spirit of our nation. We should preserve the spirit of fair play and set a good example in games. We should quickly contribute to the promotion of wholesome baseball in Japan and make as our target the hosting of world championship.
>
> (Japan Professional Baseball League Office, 1936: 4)

## Professionalism as the sports ethic in Japan

Here, I will consider the historical evolution of baseball beliefs, which are sources of the baseball ideology, as mentioned, using the framework of Figure 3.1 and which is represented in diagrammatic form in Figure 3.2. In the pre-Second World War era, the ideology of the *Bushido* baseball spirit (I) was transformed

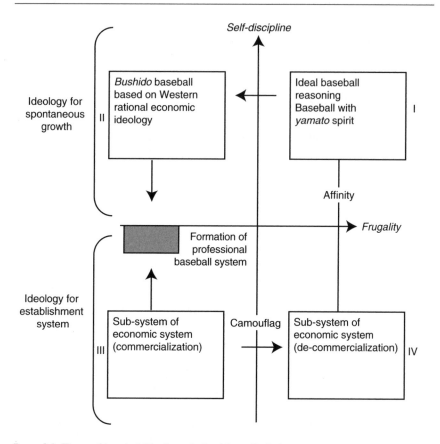

*Figure 3.2* Types of baseball ideology derived from *Bushido* spirit

into the ideology of Western rationalism (II). In the process of this transformation, making profits by playing baseball gradually became accepted. Consciously or unconsciously, it was finally accepted as part of the ideology as a sub-system of the economy (III), which prompted the professionalization of baseball.

As noted, there was an influential group which encouraged the professionalization of baseball and the ideal baseball spirit for the group was to establish baseball as a sound national sport and to advance players' techniques so that they could challenge US teams. This group, which can be called the ideologues, shared the ideology of pure amateurism. The ideologues were supported by the idea that both amateurs and professionals in Japan should retain the aspect of self-discipline based on the *Bushido* spirit. According to them, some people assumed that fair-play, high morals and sportsmanship were confined to amateur players (Glader, 1978: 24). As we have already seen in the baseball creed of *Nippon Undo Kyoukai* (The Japan Sports Association), professionalism was also sustained by the same moral code that permeated amateurism. Professional baseball players were even required to acquire higher morals, which became a characteristic of their existence.

Consequently, amateurism was not defined as the spirit for amateur players who did not belong to any professional teams. Whether amateur or professional, players should strive for spiritual elevation. The introduction of admissions and the emergence of professional players were evaluated as useful means for achieving this aim. The establishment of professional baseball, for the purpose of pursuing superior baseball skills, was inevitable and a matter of course from the spiritual and ideological points of view, let alone from the financial and behavioural ones (Glader, 1978: 23).

Today, considering the institutional and structural relationship between sports and commerce, the professionalization of amateur sports, such as the inauguration of the J-League or the Japanese professional football league, seems to be more and more unavoidable. Given this, we need to look at the mechanism of professionalization objectively and review the ideology possessed by those who take responsibilities for acknowledging and promoting professionalization within the institution.

Based on the development of baseball ideologies in Japan, we can infer a basic solution to the issue: it would be better not to attribute separate cultural values to amateur and professional sports. Rather, we should maintain common ethics and develop an autonomous value within the institution, which is characteristic of sports in general. In other words, while accepting the economic order in sports, we would do better to view the mechanism of professionalization objectively. By so doing, we will be able to establish professionalism as a cultural value within the sports institution and construct a system of ideology and a model for those who are concerned with sports. It could bring many advantages in the future. For example, it would be possible for a professional system to provide a lead for a hierarchical order that extends down to the grassroots sport supporters (Ushiki, 1976: 27–28). There would also be potential for players and others concerned with sports to realize their ideal while being financially sponsored by companies. The changes which led to the professionalization of baseball in the pre-Second World War era in Japan should provide a historical model. The model shows how all concerned with sports, including ideologues, can maintain their internal and psychological autonomy for their own benefit and ethos, how they can realize sports as pure values (Tatano, 1985: 24), as centred professionalism or professional ideology in opposition to the commercialism and de-civilizing processes within sport, and what they should do to achieve their aims.

## Conclusion

When baseball was first introduced into Japan during the late nineteenth century (the Meiji era), it was nothing more than the pursuit of pleasure and pride in playing baseball. During the period that Daiichi High School, or Ichiko, was dominant in baseball, from 1890 to 1903, there developed what can be called their 'baseball creed'. The creed was elaborated from the Japanese *Bushido* spirit of the medieval times, which had been mainly composed of three principles: frugality, self-discipline and victory supremacist. Among these principles, self-discipline and victory supremacist became more crucial than frugality in the process of developing the baseball ideology. In the early twentieth century (from the late Meiji era to the Taisho era), Isoo Abe, who was the manager of the baseball club in Waseda University, played an important role in developing the baseball spirit. He and the Waseda graduates promoted two critical baseball ideologies. First, their approach to professionalism was to build a team of individuals who were ready to devote themselves to baseball. In addition, they aimed to practice psychological training and self-discipline in baseball, emphasizing fair play and sportsmanship. The idea of the Waseda group influenced the baseball spirit in Japan, which generated the basic ideology leading to the launching of professional baseball teams in the 1930s (the early Showa era). It is noteworthy that amateurism and professionalism combined in the process of developing baseball in Japanese modern society.

## Notes

1  This contribution is based on the following papers: Kiku (1989), Introduction to Historical Sociological Study on the Development of Professionalism in Sports; focusing on the formation of baseball creed concerning professionalism before World War II, *Taiiku Spouts Syakaigaku Kenkyu* (The Sociological Journal of Physical Education and Sport) 8: 91–117, and Kiku (1993) '*Kindai Puro Spouts' no Rekishi Syakaigaku* (Historical Sociology of 'Modern Professional Sports'), Fumaido Publication, p. 283.

2  Gerth and Mills characterized institutional orders with four spheres: status, symbols, technology and education. By doing so, they extracted common components in each institution and indicated structural issues, sketching the social system and the whole picture of a human being. Symbols were defined as being visual or acoustic: they may be signs, signals, emblems, ceremonial, language, music or other arts. Without such symbols we could not understand the conduct of human actors, and normally, their belief in and use of these symbols operate to uphold or justify the institutional orders (Gerth and Mills, 1954: 29–30).

3  With regard to the relationships between institutional orders, Gerth and Mills argued that each institutional order and sphere should be related to every other order and sphere and it would be often convenient to examine these relationships in terms of ends and means. It implies that the activities that often fulfill one institutional order's ends serve as means to the dominant ends of another order. This phenomenon was called 'ramification', which was defined as those activities which are ends in one order may be used as the means of another institutional order (Gerth and Mills, 1954: 31–32).

4  This was very expensive at the time, in the Meija era of Japan.

5  An interview in the house of Shigeru Nakai (1-6-7 Yagumo, Meguro-ku, Tokyo) on August 10, 1986.

6  An interview in the house of Sugai Eiji who was an outfielder of Daimai Baseball Team (2-4 Yumoto-cho, Takarazuka-city, Hyogo) on February 5, 1986.

# References

Abe, I. (1905a) 'Yakyu no Santoku' (Three virtues of baseball), in S. Hasido (ed.) *Recent Baseball Skill* (Saikin Yakyu Jutsu), Tokyo: Hakubun Kan.

Abe, I. (1905b) 'Waseda Daigaku Yakyu Sensyu no Beikoku Yuki ni Tsuite' (Regarding the tour to America of Waseda University Baseball Player), *Yorozu Cho Ho* (Yorozu newspaper), 26 March, by extension photocopy of microfilm.

Abe, I. (1908) 'Kyogi Undo to Syohai no Kan-nen' (Competition sports and the concept of win-lose), *Undo Sekai* (Athletics World), 9: 3.

Abe, I. (1926) 'Undo no Seishin' (Spirit of sports), in T. Kitahara (ed.) *Arusu Dai Undo Koza* (Arusu Great Exercise Series), Tokyo: Als.

Abe, I. (1931a) 'Kohei naru Kyogi' (Fair competition), *Undo Sekai* (Athletics World), 12 (4): 2.

Abe, I. (1931b) 'Kokusai Kyogi no Jomaku' (Prologue of international competition), *Undo Sekai* (Athletics World), 12 (1): 2–3.

Abe, I. (1936) 'Yakyu to Tomoni San'jyu nen' (30 years in baseball), in I. Abe (ed.) *Seinen to Riso* (Ideal of Youth), Tokyo: Okakura Syobo.

Asahi newspaper (eds) (1911) 'Yakyu to Sono Gaidoku' (Baseball and negative influences), *Asahi Shinbun* (Asahi Newspaper), 29 August to 19 September [22 issues in total].

Asanuma, N. (1931) 'Kyukai no Jyoka' (Purification of the world of baseball), *Beisuboru* (Baseball), 2 (6): 6–8.

Azabu, Z. (1937) 'Syokugyo dan Tokyo League Zakkan' (Impressions of the professional team of Tokyo League), *Yakyu Kai* (Baseball World), 27 (1): 192–94.

Barion, J. (1971) *Was ist ideologie?*, trans. Makoto Tokunaga (1974), *Ideology toha Nanika*, Tokyo: Kodan Sya.

Daiichi High school alumni association (ed. and published) (1894) *Japanese, Daiichi Koto Gakko Koyukai Zasshi* (Daiichi High school alumni association magazine), Vol. 41, 28, November (in).

Daiichi High school alumni association (ed. and published) (1895) *Koyukai Zasshi Gogai: Yakyu Bushi fu Kisoku* (Extra edition of alumni association Magazine: additional regulation of history of baseball club), Tokyo.

Daiichi High school alumni association (ed.) (1972) 'Yakyu bushi: Meiji 36 nen' (History of baseball club: Meiji 36th year), in T. Kimura (ed.) *Meiji Bunka Shiryo Sosho Dai Jukkan Supotsu hen* (Meiji Culture data series Vol. 10 sports version), Tokyo: Kazama Syobo.

Daiichi High school alumni dormitory (ed. and published) (1930) *Koryo Shi* (Koryo history), Tokyo.

Editorial committee of Mainichi Shinbun history (ed. and published) (1952) *Mainichi Shinbun 70 nen* (Mainichi 70 years), Oosaka.

Editorial department of Undo Kai (1921) 'Nippon Undo Kyôkai Souritsu no Syui' (An objection to the establishment of Japan Sports Association), *Undo Kai*, 2 (4): 120–122.

Editorial department of Undo Kai (1923) 'Undo Kai Shôsoku' (Sports world tidings), *Undo Kai*, 4 (12): 85.

Editorial department (1934) 'Syokugyo Yakyudan Umareru' (Professional baseball is born), *Beisuboru* (Baseball), 5 (8): 54–55.

Fukae, H. (1929) 'Kansai Kyukai Nidai Myojo no Kinjyo' (Recent situation of two big stars in the baseball world of Kansai), *Yakyu Kai* (Baseball World), 19 (5): 59.

Furukawa, T. (1957) *Nippon Rinri Shiso Shi Kenkyu 2: Bushido no Shiso to Sono Syuhen* (Japan Ethics Idea History Research 2: Idea of Bushido and the peripheral conditions), Tokyo: Fukumura Syoten.

Gerth, H. and Mills, C. (1954) *Character and Social Structure*, London: Routledge & Kegan Paul Ltd.

Glader, E. A. (1978) *Amateurism and Athletics*, New York: Leisure Press.

Hashido, G. (1921) 'SyokugyoYakyudan Setsuritsu no Syusi' (Purpose of establishment of professional baseball team), *Yakyu Kai* (Baseball World), 11 (12): 63.

Hashido, G. (1935) 'Yakyu Konogoro Ki' (Baseball recent record), *Beisuboru* (Baseball), 6–8: 25–26.

Hirose, K. (1940) *Waseda-Keio Baseball History* (in Japanese, Sokei Yakyu Shi), Tokyo: Sanseido.

Ichioka, T. (1936) 'Kyukai no Boron wo Hakusu' (Counter argument against wild view of baseball world), *Yomiuri Shinbun* (Yomiuri Newspaper), 28 to 29 March.

Imamura, Y. (ed.) (1976) *Shinsyu Taiiku Daijiten* (New Physical Education Dictionary), Tokyo: Fumaido Shuppan.

Japan Professional Baseball League office (ed. and published) (1936) *Nippon Syoku Gyô Yakyu Renmei Koho Dai Ichi Go* (1st bulletin of Japan Professional Baseball League).

Kiku, K. (1984) 'Kindai Puro Spourtsu no Seritsu ni Kansuru Rekishi Syakaigaku Teki Kosatsu: Wagakuni ni Okeru Senzen no Puro Yakyu no Seritsu wo Tyushin' ni' (Historical sociological consideration of formation of modern professional sports: mainly formation of professional baseball in prewar Japan), *Taiiku Spoutsu Syakaigaku Kenkyu* (Sociological Journal of Physical Education and Sport), 3: 1–26.

Kiku, K. (1988) 'Puro Spourtsu no Seritsu ni taisuru Rekishi Syakaigaku teki Kenkyu no Kanosei to Sono Tenkai' (Possibility of historical sociological research into formation of professional sports and its development), *Taiikuka Kyoiku* (Monthly Journal of Physical Education), 36 (14): 73–75.

Kiku, K. (1993) *Kindai Puro Spouts' no Rekishi Syakaigaku* (The Historical Sociology of Modern Professional Sports), Tokyo: Fumaido Shuppan.

Kimura, K. (1960) 'Meiji Jidai ni Okeru Undo no Kachikan no Ichikosatsu (II): "Kofu Ronso" wo Tsujite Mita "Undo" no Nihonteki Doka no Ronri' (A consideration of theory of values as for exercise in Meiji era (II): theory of Japanese assimilation of 'exercise' seen through 'School tradition argument'), *Taiikugaku Kenkyu* (Japan Journal of Physical Education, Health and Sport Science), 5 (3): 69.

Kizukuri, R. (1923) 'Kyokuto Taikai wo Ki ni Daimai Yakyudan no Tachiba wo Akasu' (To clarify the Daimai baseball team's position using the opportunity of the Far-East competition), *Yakyu Kai* (Baseball World), 13 (9): 63–64.

Kizukuri, R. (1929) 'Daimai Yakyudan wo Nasu' (Wail Daimai Baseball Team), *Ykyu Kai* (Baseball World), 19 (9): 22–26.

Kono, A. (1921) 'Sensyu no Sensyutsu ha Genjyu ni Suru' (Select player strictly), *Yakyu Kai* (Baseball World), 11 (12): 48.

Kono, A. (1922) 'Syokugyo Sensyu no Nichijyo' (Everyday life of professional players)', *Yakyu Kai* (Baseball World), 12 (3): 17–18.

Kusaka, Y. (1985) 'Meijiki ni Okeru "Bushi", "Bushido" teki Yakyu Shinjyo ni Kansuru Bunka Syakaigaku teki Kenkyu' (Cultural sociological research into 'Bushi' and 'Bushido' baseball creed in Meiji Era), *Taiiku Spoutsu Syakaigaku Kenkyu* (Sociological Journal of Physical Education and Sport), 4: 26.

Matsumoto, T. (1936) 'Tetsudo Yakyu to Syokugyo Dan' (Railroad baseball and professional team), *Yakyu Kai (Baseball World)*, 26 (8): 192–194.

Mills, C. (1959) *The Sociological Imagination*, trans. Suzuki Hiroshi (1965) *Syakaigauteki Sozoryoku*, Tokyo: Kinokuniya Syoten.

Ministry of Education in Japan (1972) *Gakusei Hyakunen Shi: Shiryo Hen* (100 years history of the school system: data edition), Tokyo: Teikoku Chiho Gyoseikai.

Miyake, D. (1933) 'Yakyu Seshin' (Baseball spirit), *Beisuboru* (Baseball), 4 (6): 46–50.

Miyashita, H. (1985) 'Waimaru Kyowakoku to Rekishi Syakaigaku' (The republic of Weimar and historical sociology), *Shiso* (Thought), 736: 100.

Nakano, T. (1922) *Ichiko Shiki Yakyu* (Ichiko-style Baseball), Tokyo: Undo Sosyo Kanko Kai.

Nakazawa, F. (ed.) (1957) *Kyukai Hachi Junen no Ayumi* (80 years History of Baseball), Tokyo: Tokyo Shinbun Sya.

Naoki, F. (1935) 'Syokugyo Yakyu Dan no Doko' (Movement of professional baseball team), *Yakyu Kai* (Baseball World), 25 (11): 176–177.

Naoki, F. (1936) 'Syokugyo Yakyu Dan no Hamon' (Stir of professional baseball team), *Yakyu Kai* (Baseball World), 26 (5): 104–105.

Ogikubo, S. (1936) 'Syokugyo Yakyu Jidai Kuruka' (Will the time of professional baseball come?), *Yakyu Kai* (Baseball World), 26 (11): 164–166.

Oota, S. (1930) *Sokei Yakyu Senshi* (Baseball Game History of Waseda-Keio), Tokyo: Toei Sya.

Sato, M. (1986) *Mô Hitotsu no Puro Yakyu* (Another Professional Baseball), Tokyo: Asahi Shinbun Sya.

Shinbun Nippon (eds) (1896) 'Baseball no Raireki' (The origin of baseball), *Shinbun Nippon* (Japanese Newspaper), 20 July, by extension photocopy of microfilm.

Skocpol, T. (1984) 'Emerging agendas and recurrent strategies in historical sociology', in T. Skocpol (ed.), *Vision and Method in Historical Sociology*, New York: Cambridge University Press, pp. 362–386.

Strange, F. W. (1883) *Outdoor Games*, Tokyo: ZP Maruya & Co.

Suzuki, K. (1923) 'Shikai ni Yuhi Sento Suru Tenkatsu Yakyu Dan' (Tenkatsu Baseball Team launches into the world), *Yakyu Kai* (Baseball World), 13 (6): 22–23).

Syono, Y. (ed.) (1931) Rokudaigaku Zensyu: Jokan (Complete Series of Six Universities: the 1st volume ), Tokyo: Kaizo Sya.

Tahara, M. (1929) *Nippon Yakyu Shi* (History of Japanese Baseball), Tokyo: Kosekaku Syoten.

Tajima, T. (1905) *Yakyu Ben'yo* (Handbook of Baseball), Aichi: Aich Kenritsu Daiichi Tyugakko Gaku'yu Kai.

Takasu, K. (1936) 'Zuiso' (Random Thought), *Beisuboru* (Baseball), 7 (1): 17–18.

Tatano, H. (1985), 'Spouts no Taisyuka ni Okeru Kadai' (The problem of the popularization of sports), in M. Tokunaga (ed.) *Gendai Spoutsu no Syakai Shinri* (Social Pychology of Modern Sports), Tokyo: Yugi Sya.

Tobita, S. (1928) *Yakyu Seikatsu no Omoide* (Reminiscences of a Life in Baseball), Tokyo: Asahi Shinbun Sya.

Tsuboi, G. and Tanaka, S. (eds) (1895) *Kogai Yugi Ho – Kogai Undo Ho* (Way of Outdoor Play – Way of Outdoor Sports), Tokyo: Kinkodo.

Tsunematsu, Y. (1935) 'Gakusei Yakyu no Saiginmi' (Re-investigation of student baseball), *Beisuboru* (Baseball), 6 (7): 22–23.

Ushiki, M. (1976) 'Purofesyonaru Spouts: Sono Genjyo to Ninki no Himitsu' (Professional sports: the present situation and secret of popularity), *Taiiku no Kagaku* (Journal of Health, Physical Education, and Recreation), 26 (1): 27–28.

Washizawa, Y. (1931) 'Yakyugi no Shinpo to Gakusei Yakyu no Shimei' (Development of baseball skills and mission of student baseball), *Beisuboru* (Baseball), 2 (3): 5–6.

Yomiuri Shinbun (eds) (1934) *Yomiuri Shinbun* (Yomiuri Newspaper), 27 December.

# Part II

# Social reconstruction, reproduction and sport

# Chapter 4

# Economic development and the value aspect of sport

*Masayoshi Nakayama*

## Introduction

Studies into the values of sport have investigated the values peculiar to sport and the problems related to the ethical values of sport. In addition to those concerning attitudes and value-orientation, studies have also been concerned with arguments regarding 'sport involvement' or 'sport and socialization'. In Japan, there has been a tendency to focus on the Japanese view of sport, or value-orientation towards sport, rather than on the values of sport (Kawanabe, 1981; Kishino, 1968; Sugawara, 1976; Uesugi, 1982, 1990; Yamaguchi, 1988; Tatano, 1997). Tatano pointed out some problems, especially methodological ones, indicating that many of the arguments about Japanese sport reflect common images such as spirituality, the creeds of discipline, whole-hearted effort, and victory precedence. Yet, Tatano and Yamaguchi have argued that the Japanese view of sport does not preclude the characteristics of behaviour or value-orientation.

However, the situation of sport has changed greatly since the mid-1970s, and so have the concepts and the values of sport. This has not been limited to Japan. We can find similar trends in other countries through the descriptions provided by Eitzen and Sage (1989: 337–340), Defrance and Pociello (1998: 53), Digel (1995: 57–68). These trends may be consistent with the proposition that 'sport reflects and reinforces social values' (Snyder and Spreitzer 1978: 38; Edwards 1973: 90; Saeki, 1984: 263–264), as is frequently discussed. However, it may be too hasty simply to advocate that the 'values of sport reflect social values and they change according to the change in social values'. Rather, the values of sport should be regarded as a complex of dominant social values and value elements which underlie the dynamics of sport activities, groups and organizations, and it is necessary to investigate the process by which they change.

This chapter not only discusses the values of sport and the changing values of sport, but also investigates the meanings underlying the change in sport's value, especially in the context of Japan's economic revival and development after the Second World War. Sport was incorporated into the economic revival and development, along with social reconstruction, as this was an urgent economic priority for government policy in post-war Japan. Reinforcing these trends was an emphasis on values supporting the pursuit of wealth – values that came to occupy a central position in Japanese social values. We can see 'a structural and value similarity between sport and economy' as has been often suggested. We may also be able to sustain the belief that 'culture affects economic development' (Harrison and Huntington, 2000). Subsequently, the circumstances under which 'economic development affects culture' have in turn begun to emerge. This cultural change does not necessarily mean a transition from traditional culture to democratic culture. Sport is pervasive as a symbol of affluence in Japan, as Japanese society seems to have achieved the status of being a wealthy society. On the other hand, sport is likely to gradually lose the values that it symbolizes, or are peculiar to it. The spectacularization of sport, along with the advent of a highly consumerist society and/or a market-based society, ensures that this is the case.

Here, it is necessary briefly to clarify the concept of value. We can find two general uses of the word 'value'. One is 'the desired (thing)' such as an object of need. Another means 'an idea regarding importance and desirability', which is related to the selection of goals and actions. According to Mita (1974), value is the attribute of an object that satisfies the needs of a subject, and value orientation should be thought of as a strategically important variable. He argued that values integrated subjects and culture, desires and morality, and philosophy and experimental science, or mediated their products. However, as Sakuta (1993) stated, value is in existence infinitely if we refer to the attribute of an object that satisfies the need of a subject as value. Accordingly, it is inevitably difficult to use the word 'value'.[1] In this paper, the latter usage – the concept of value as desirability that influences the selection of goals and actions – is used. It is also considered an important element of culture.

## Democratic values and sport in social reconstruction

The priorities in post-war Japanese society were the amelioration of social confusion and the reconstruction of society on the basis of democratic values under the directives of the American Occupation authorities. Hence, democratic reorganization in the various spheres of society was pursued. The Japanese Government presented guidelines and specific measures in compliance with the policy of GHQ regarding education. In this educational reform, physical education was reorganized and aimed at cultivating a sound mind and body, as well as a social character supportive of the democratic values needed for the development of a democratic nation state. Therefore, directives and uniform instructions were restrained as far as possible, and group learning – which was a teaching method respecting the autonomy of children – was introduced in physical education. A natural consequence of this was to regard the participation of all pupils in sports meetings, the building of friendships among participants, and the cultivation of the spirit of sportsmanship and fair play through sporting experiences, as more important than the cultivation of athletes who were active in extramural activities.

The Ministry of Education came to see sports promotion as helping to build democratic attitudes through the experiences of sportsmanship, fair play and observance of rules, as well as a wholesome life bringing pleasure both within school and outside of it. In 1946, the ministry implemented measures to promote sports such as the placement of sport instructors, the holding of *Kokumin-Taiiku-Taikai* (the National Sports Festival), and the promotion of the *Shyakai-Taiiku*[2] (physical education in society), and so on. In the central course for sports instructors, which was promoted by the Bureau of Labour Management in the Ministry of Communications in June 1946, a lecturer advocated the need to change the pre-war sport system that had called for victory precedence, compulsion as well as excessive discipline and high esteem of athletes. In contrast, the idea that many people could enjoy sports spontaneously, moderately and in a scientific way was encouraged (Teishin-Sho Romu-Kyoku Hoken-Ka, 1948: 49–58).

The democratic way of sport and sports promotion for the masses was also supported through the *Nihon-Taiiku-Kyokai* (the Japan Amateur Sports Association), which was formed in place of the *Dai-Nihon-Taiiku-Kyokai*, and was considered to be the national body governing sport. In particular, it drew up the outlines of the 'badge' test for sport on the basis of: 'the skill level that even a person not endowed by nature with sports ability can attain' (*Nihon-Taiiku-Kyokai*, 1949: 4). This was designed to encourage sport among the population in 1949. In addition, the policy on sport was managed as part of the policy on social education: when the Social Education Act was enacted in 1949, it included regulations relating to the directives, 'no support and no control' of the Civil Information and Education Section regarding social education.

Thus, sport was introduced as the main domain of physical education in schools and school sports naturally became important extracurricular activities. That is, the activities of the *Undo-bu* (school sports club) assumed an educational significance in the democratization policy. Sport outside of school also had an educational role, in addition to its democratic one. Sport came to be promoted as part of social education. Also, the subsidization of sports bodies (including *Nihon-Taiiku-Kyokai*) that were regarded as social educational bodies, was prohibited. This was meant to avoid political control over them. The political neutrality of sports bodies was guaranteed and sport activities were based on educational values in this way.

Sports meetings revived one after another in the course of sport's reformation. In the summer of 1946, 745 schools participated in the Secondary Schools' Baseball Championship. The success of the National Sports Festival – *Kokumin-Taiiku-Taikai* – which was held in Kyoto and other areas, with about 5,000 participants, was said to have cast a bright ray of hope on the construction of a new Japanese society. Many Japanese people were also enthused by the activities of Huruhashi, who set a world record in the All Japan Swimming Championship of 1947 (despite it being an unofficial one) and broke several records thereafter. As Takenoshita (1950: 294) remarked with regard to the sports situation during the years after the war, the end of the war liberated a need for sport that had been repressed. Sport revived remarkably and the mass promotion of sports and the popularity of professional sports advanced further than ever before. This process occurred despite a shortage of food and facilities. During this process, Japan had an opportunity to participate in the 1952 Helsinki Olympic Games after regaining international approval with respect to sports from 1949 with the support of Gen. Douglas MacArthur, the Commander of the American Occupation authorities.

Even though minimal living standards were still beyond the reach of many people, and the need to resort to 'the black market' was sometimes necessary, the sense of liberation and/or the feelings of freedom from various forms of repression during wartime, encouraged people to play sports, as expressed by the desire to experience a 'joy in living and playing sports' (Sayama, 1988: 412–419). Children also seemed to gain 'the heroic feeling in a social situation of anomie' (Ooe, 1988: 439) and 'the recovery of life feeling' (Terayama, 1988: 379–385) through sports. It was freedom, liberation from repression and the joy of living – universal values of human existence – that supported sports at that time. At the same time, democracy could be understood as an embodiment of these values.

However, the revival and flourishing of sports caused serious problems, such as excessive emphasis on winning, adaptation for performance in sport, a threat to amateurism, school sports clubs monopolizing funds for extracurricular activities, the increased cost of school sports clubs, and a relative decline in the esteem of engaging in schoolwork. Voices of alarm concerning the situation were heard in the world of education, especially among those concerned with the physical education that was intended to promote democratic education. The Ministry of Education provided guidelines for schools in 1948 by establishing criteria regarding the extramural sports meetings for pupils so that they would not deviate from the intended educational purposes. As a result, the Japan Student Baseball Association established the Charter of Student Baseball in January 1950. Also, the Consulting Committee for Student and Pupil Sports, which was set up within Nihon-Taiiku-Kyokai, in 1952 prescribed a standard for the conduct of student sports. In 1953, Nihon-Taiiku-Kyokai laid down 'the General Principles for Sportsmen' which gave prominence to amateurism, fair play, and sportsmanship. On the other hand, Nihon-Taiiku-Kyokai and the National Federation of Sports each wanted to undergo organizational improvements and expansion, and aimed at the improvement of competitive abilities. In particular, some high ranking members of these groups had a strong desire to hold the Olympic Games in Japan, which had not been possible in the pre-war era. Therefore, as Seki (1997: 107–110) mentioned, the fundamental course of Nihon-Taiiku-Kyokai drifted toward the improvement of competitive abilities. Consequently, sports development, centring on athletic meetings, or events, was promoted. Many common people also could not afford to participate in sports because of a lack of sports facilities or their austere lifestyle.

Sport based on democratic values seems to have not only created the habitual conditions that helped cultivate 'personal freedom', namely spontaneity and sociability' (Matsushita 1960: 46), but also incorporated a spirit of the human lust for life. However, this effect of sport was undermined by problems that accompanied the increased emphasis on victory, which shaped the behavioural form of athletic meetings. In addition, major disturbances frequently occurred at professional bicycle races, becoming 'the outlet of the impatience of the masses and the indignation that smouldered in those who were struggling to make a living and were at their wit's end' (Ookochi, 1951: 25).

## Economic precedence and the values of sport

As the Japanese economy revived and, by 1955, surpassed pre-war levels with regard to both productive capacity and national income, there was a perception that 'the post-war period had ended'. The high economic growth rate, which continued for about twenty years thereafter, was maintained by national consensus. This represented a shift in the dominant social value system from freedom to wealth (Sakuta, 1975: 405).

### Sport as a corporate welfare

The Japanese version of pinball, Pachinko, became popular in cities at the beginning of the 1950s. Pachinko, which can be played alone, was 'the most suitable game for the 'lonely crowd' in metropolitan areas, with the element of gambling in addition to convenience and popularity' (Ishikawa, 1979: 76). Moreover, pervasive radio broadcasts took 'pleasure of radio plays and sports relays' (Ishikawa, 1979: 94) into sitting rooms throughout Japan. Television broadcasting began to hit its stride in 1952 and then commercial radio stations became increasingly numerous. Sumo and professional wrestling became popular and, by the late 1950s, professional baseball came into public favour. Also, mass leisure resulting from a mass production system based upon automation, and the rapid spread of household electrical appliances reduced the burden of housework. The values of privatism – a principle of precedence of the individual's private life – in turn was permeating people's lives. Okabe (1960: 59) noted a psychological problem, the need for an 'ethics of leisure' that would release people from the fetters of ascetic ethics and legitimize an orientation towards play and consumption. He indicated that this was presented as a rational attitude, 'play has a significance as play, and work has a significance as work' that was explored in 'The Study of Attitudes Towards Play and Work' which was conducted by the Tokyo University News Papers Institute in 1959. That is, in an age of leisure and consumption, traditional ideology would only increase a sense of guilt. In an age of consumption, it is psychologically necessary that the value of leisure, and the significance of play, be approved. The attitude that 'play is one thing, work is another thing though both are important' is to accept the external pressures of the leisure age. We can call it a rational attitude only in a very special interpretation, according to which it prepares the energy of people for the task of economic and social organizations.

The course and system of Japanese society were not entirely stable, however, regardless of symptoms indicating the coming of mass leisure. The Japanese Government found it necessary to suppress the radical political movement as well as the angry organized labour movement. At the same time, the Government pushed forward corporate rationalization to establish an independent, economically stable and superior society which would become part of the Western bloc. This was done in response to the urging of the United States Government. Both recreation in the workplace and corporate sport developed as countermeasures to the above political and labour pressures. An enhanced corporate consciousness and a focus on the welfare of employees were emphasized. The Ministry of Education already collected data, and supported the exchange of opinions, surveys and lectures for physical education supervisors in the workplace in co-operation with the Ministry of Labour. The Ministry of Education also regarded the promotion of physical education in the workplace as a management responsibility. The Japan Federation of Employer's Associations also launched a programme to support recreation in the workplace in co-operation with the Japan Recreation Association which was increasingly encouraged throughout the 1960s.

The 1960s was a period when many Japanese people were achieving a reasonable level of prosperity. It was also a time when there was an increasingly bitter debate regarding a revision of the Japan–US Security Treaty. The outcome of this debate was that many Japanese people concluded they wanted neither a revolutionary or anti-Establishment movement led by the Communist Party or the left-wing faction of the Socialist Party – nor a revision of post-war excess reform or reactionary reform by the Conservative Party. They preferred the more tranquil maintenance of the status quo.

The policy giving priority to economic growth, supported by the consensus of the Japanese people, prompted industrialization and the gravitation of population towards major cities. It also caused the population of agricultural villages to decrease rapidly. Recreation in the workplace was both a means of securing and retaining young workers in a corporation, and was part of the social support needed by workers exposed to the industrialization and urbanization processes. Moreover, for the corporations, the strong promotion of efficient production seemed to rely on the workers' will to work, more than on the potential improvement of the material environment that could be achieved through the provision of more machinery. Therefore, 'the significance of sport and recreation in the workplace came to be highly regarded, as the maintenance of the health of labourers and the adjustment in human relations among and between them and their superiors were needed first of all' (Ministry of Education 1964: 39). The social support provided for newcomers and employees was mostly based on the roles of the kinship group, the neighbourhood group and the local authority. However, many employees of major corporations tended to become estranged from the community because they lived in a company flat or house, in a company town, and received various company benefits needed to maintain their lives. The corporate community had been formed. Besides the company town, the large enterprises provided 'support extending to all aspects of regular workers' lives' (Hazama 1994: 66). Many medium-sized businesses also formed sports clubs in addition to providing for sport and the support systems for living. A survey by the Ministry of Education showed that large and medium-sized enterprises especially had improved their facilities and organization for sport in the workplace, while public facilities for sport were poorly equipped and the organization for sport in communities was undeveloped (Monbusyo, 1963b: 9).

'Enterprise-based welfare', including recreation in the workplace, is considered part of the Japanese style of management and is regarded as an important factor in Japanese industrial development. A somewhat opposing view is that mobility between jobs within an organization and on-the-job training have made the greatest contribution to Japanese industrial and enterprise development, and other factors have only partly contributed to the stabilization of labour-management relations (Murakami, 1985: 143). However, Murakami (1997: 157) remarks with respect to *Toyotism*, which is a prototype of Japanese Fordism, as follows:

> The life processes of labourers are totally assimilated into the dominant corporate system, as the human relations within the corporation extend to and penetrate into their personal domains. Thereby, a kind of 'corporate community relation' is formed. Actually on the basis of this 'community feeling', the conflicts of interests between worker and manager are absorbed into 'the corporate co-operative systems'. That is, they are neutralized by the exaltation of the corporate consciousness.

> In this way: ... labourers are pushed into positive participation in the work process 'spontaneously' ..., although their initiatives are limited, at best, only to spontaneity on the level of the device and the improvement in the working process at their job sites. It is suggested the fundamental characteristic of Toyotism is 'the corporate community consciousness'.

Corporate sport, or recreation in the workplace, was considered as important to the building and enhancement of the corporate community consciousness. With regard to this point, the case of Toyota Motor Co. has been studied (*Nihon Jinbun Kagaku-Kai*, 1963). In 1960, Toyota city had a population of about 47,000. Approximately 14,000 inhabitants were employees of the Toyota Motor Co. Toyota city's *Taïku-Kyokai* (sports governing body) consisted of 22 sports associations, many members of which were the employees of the Toyota Motor Co. or allied corporations, and 15 sport associations only comprised Toyota Motor Co. sport clubs of (Monbusyo, 1963a).

The trade union spontaneously initiated cultural and sports activities in the Toyota Motor Co. until about 1950, and these activities were considered quite remarkable. Management took a positive interest in cultural and sport activities from about 1951, while the union was weakened by a large-scale labour dispute which began with the strike of April 1950. In this situation, the company constructed tennis courts, a sports centre, and a boathouse for the rowing club in 1951, and then a swimming pool the following year. The Toyota General Sports Meeting, which included 10 companies allied to Toyota, was also held. The company constructed a general sports arena in 1957 and formed the Toyota Club, an integrated organization, in 1959. It has been reported that most of the members in the sports section of the Toyota Club were clerks, engineers and trained factory workers, while the participation of unskilled workers was low.

Many of these sport clubs were leaders in terms of athletic success within Aichi prefecture, or the Tokai district, where they are located. In addition, the Association of Physical Education in the Workplace held an internal company sports meeting about once a month. The company, at this time, gave priority to sports activities over cultural activities, and the promotion of sport activities for general employees over the development of sports clubs for athletes. The physical education in the workplace was expected to be a source of relaxation and diversion because automation was increasing the mental fatigue of employees. In addition, sport and recreation, as well as the public relations magazine and the company communication system 'play a most important role in uniting the various groups within the company' (Nihon Jinbun Kagaku-Kai, 1963: 116), which are functionally separate. Moreover, in the training of young people who have completed junior high school and are being trained to be factory workers, Toyota includes additional collective education 'life guidance' which has a value beyond the required subject matter and technical practices. The goal of this education is to develop a Toyota-man and build Toyota-spirit. Specifically, it is described as 'the training of talent that has the will to work and lives through with the corporation' (Nihon Jinbun Kagaku-Kai, 1963: 116).

Social studies and physical education are included as part of the life guidance provided to the trained worker. Teamwork is stressed and regarded as important in physical education. Morale, human nature and trust in the corporation are shaped on the basis of co-operative consciousness, and this co-operative consciousness is produced by teamwork. The teamwork that develops through physical education soon leads to a person's consciousness of being a Toyota team member. It is regarded as 'the human foundation of a stable productive system' (Nihon Jinbun Kagaku-Kai, 1963: 116). The organization of trained workers in active service, Hoyokai, also has a committee for physical education which organizes sports teams at each of 13 job sites, and participates in training as well as inter-job site matches.

The role of sport in the workplace has been to reproduce the energy for work of general employees who are separated according to their respective managerial function, bring them into a harmonious relationship, and cultivate a fellow feeling and a corporate consciousness. Also, a corporate sports club that represents the corporation naturally must strive to win, and its members need to avoid making any shameful action as corporate members in an inter-corporate sports match. In other words, to win games and improve the corporate image have become the main purposes. Since members of corporate sports clubs always participate in matches as members or representatives of their group, they endeavour to behave in a way that does not bring disgrace on the group, and for honour as well as victory. Corporate sport also has a value aspect much as school sports does. This is particularly valid for sport in the community.

According to Matsumaru (1955: 10), sport in rural communities is held in a form that further engenders initially strong regional feelings through inter-community matches within the village or town, and inter-village or inter-town matches within the county. He describes this as a negative influence, stating that it does nothing but lay the emphasis on 'the honour of village' as well as 'the honour of community'. As such, it has not been useful in promoting democratization or urging agricultural workers to stand up for agricultural development. Dan (1970: 111) also shows that the participation of the inhabitants in an inter-community match is, 'participation on the basis of the sense of obligation to a settlement or a group representing individuals, as it were, one that bears the honour of a group'. In doing so, he mentions that participation brings about a sense of compulsion among the inhabitants. Physical education outside school in the agricultural village is held in the form of a competition between representative athletes. Such an orientation towards athletics and victory grew in importance in Japanese sporting circles when Tokyo was approved as the host of the Eighteenth Olympic Games. In holding the games, a cherished wish among Japanese sporting circles was achieved and the preparations for it became extremely serious.

### Victory precedence and the Tokyo Olympics

Formally, efforts to bring the Olympic Games to Tokyo began with a statement by the Governor of Tokyo in 1952. The main purposes were that the games would lead to the provision of various facilities, including the reconstruction of the Tokyo Metropolitan area which was a pressing problem at that time. The Olympics would provide momentum for further economic development, and they would provide an opportunity to demonstrate the revival and development of post-war Japan to the world, raising Japan's international status (Nakayama, 1984: 204) and thus restore the pride and self-confidence of the nation. For several reasons, it seemed essential to obtain good results in the games.

The headquarters for the development of the abilities of Japanese athletes was founded as a sub-organization of the Japanese Olympic Committee in January 1960. Its goal was to improve the international competitiveness of Japanese athletes who had won only four gold medals in each of the Melbourne and Rome Olympics. The headquarters therefore introduced new methods of scientific training and development. In addition to improved physical fitness and technique, spiritual strength (i.e. 'guts' or 'Konjo') was considered important. The headquarters set about preparing a text for the building of Konjo, which has been defined as 'the intense will to achieve victory that has a high goal consciousness, as well as the mental concentration needed for goal attainment, and maintains it' (Nihon Taiiku Kyokai Tokyo Orinpikk Sensyukyooka Taisaku Honbu, 1962a: 2) by the Psychology Section of the Sport Science Research Committee. The contents of the text were arranged on the basis of results from studies done by the Psychology Section and interviews with former highly ranked athletes who had participated in Olympic Games or other high-level sports. The headquarters intended to organize its findings under two themes: 'knowledge for athletes' and 'knowledge for coaches'. The final text was decided upon through these investigations and extensive discussions at coaching staff meetings.

As part of the knowledge, each coach would need to train athletes capable of winning at the Tokyo Olympic Games, thus meeting the nation's expectations. The 'Text for the Building of *Konjo*' stressed that each coach should play a role both as an educator and a cultural pioneer, who would challenge the utmost limits together with the athletes. This document is indicative of the expected attitude and instruction of the coach, stating that each coach needed to cultivate character-building, scientific knowledge regarding technique and training, and related devices suitable for each individual athlete. Likewise, the ideal athlete that such a coach should develop is summarized as:

> an athlete with the self-control needed to suppress every desire and temptation of ordinary life; who recognized the significance of both the behaviour and the result in a competition; who was willing to rely on the coach; who had the pride and self-confidence needed to be a good representative; who was willing to practise with a device as well as an idea; who was able to overcome difficulties; who would fully devote all personal energies to training; who would make the utmost effort, and be willing to make sacrifices for the team as a member with a fair and fighting spirit.
>
> (Nihon Taiiku Kyokai Tokyo
> Orinpikk Sensyukyooka Taisaku Honbu, 1962b: 33)

These expectations of athletes and coaches did not seem particularly extreme, though we can find in this document clear value aspects such as victory precedence, and the creeds of self-discipline, asceticism and collectivism. However, this approach was limited to the pursuit of victory in the Olympic Games. The problem was that victory was quickly and carelessly attributed to *Konjo*. In contrast, the introduction of scientific training and frontier theories, the invited foreign coaches, the acquisition of knowledge and experience through participation in international matches (playing tours abroad as well as inspections overseas) tended to be forgotten.

Japanese athletes gained 16 gold medals, beyond the target number, in the Tokyo Olympics. Their performances excited many of the Japanese people. The volleyball final between the Russian team and the Japanese team – mainly made up of members who were *Nichibokaizuka* players – achieved a national telecast audience rating of 85 per cent of the population. As Seki stated: 'The match means little without winning for the athlete, one has to be strong to win, one needs hard training to be strong and strictly graded human relations are necessary for the accomplishment of hard training' (1997: 163). The victory precedence attitude to the Tokyo Olympics caused the fundamental schema for victory in Japanese sport circles to come to the fore. This behavioural schema for victory in sport was a parallel to the one by which the Japanese people devoted themselves to work, in those days, dreaming of doubling national income. These schemas have thus led people to believe that to co-operate with colleagues, make an earnest effort, and endure discipline based on hardship for achievement of a goal, developed human character. As a result, the connection between victory precedence, the creeds of self-discipline and educational values became stronger.

## Social re-organization and market-based values

Behavioural patterns such as those based on effort, endurance and co-operation – which were mythologized as Japanese virtues – began to decline as wealth, personal and national, was gained between the mid-1960s and mid-1970s. At the same time, wealth brought various social problems and people began to recognize that material wealth was not the most important goal. As a result, qualitative aspects of life began to draw their attention. Sport activities, and sometimes new sports, oriented toward freedom, self-realization, self-expression and socializing were on the rise from the latter half of the 1970s.

### Traditional values and community sport

The decision of Japanese society to give priority to economic development yielded material wealth, but it also led to social problems such as depopulation of rural villages, overpopulation of cities, environmental deterioration and inadequate welfare policies. Japanese society was eventually obliged to modify itself as concerted action taken by those living in various communities as well as members of the student movement spread, and as people became aware of the importance of their own lives and welfare, and the need to preserve the environment. This meant that the values approving the pursuit of wealth, which were the central values of Japanese society, lost some of their importance and there was an awakening of 'a value orientation towards quality of life' according to Aiba (1983: 128). However, Ootake (1999: 31) states, 'in Japan, that was seen only in limited groups and for a limited term, as in the student movement at the end of the 1960s and the concerted actions by residents from the end of the 1960s to the beginning of the 1970s', reflecting the appearance of post-materialist values such as participation and self-expression. He also indicates that 'most of the youth and the new middle class in the cities, rather, were inclined toward privatism in the sense of concentrating on their private life' (1999: 31). These phenomena can be called the 'paradox of wealth'. However, Japanese people, confronted by an economic crisis, due to the 1973 oil crisis, renewed their faith in the need for stable economic development. Japanese society gradually became able to maintain a relatively stable economic development through the demand management policy of the Central Government and through cost-cutting, cutbacks in personnel, inventory readjustment and so forth on the part of corporations, although the economic growth rate fell. The outcome was that the values orienting people towards quality of life did not replace economic wealth as the central value. Furthermore, the privatism that had permeated people's lives since the period of high economic growth represented no core value (Tanaka, 1985: 154).

As Miyajima (1985: 68–9) indicated, 'life under privatism as worth living did not necessarily offer an opportunity to pursue 'individuality', and it also failed to supply a basis for the essential image of life, *how an individual himself lives*, that is formed from the inside of individuals'. In the course of this process, the orientation toward pleasure became conspicuous, especially among young people, as often indicated. The situation was described as 'the direction that leads to the loss of what has been diagnosed as the permanent characteristics of Japanese society and culture by the people, who have a bias toward a static viewpoint and hence advocate that they are disitnctive' (Tominaga, 1988: 45).

In the first half of the 1970s, Japanese Government changed the policy that was centred on Olympic success and, for the first time, developed a substantial policy on sport for the nation. This occurred during a period when recreation in the workplace was stagnant because of the decline of traditional or dominant values and the pervasiveness of privatism. In 1973, in particular, a policy for the promotion of community sport came to the fore after it was proposed by the Economic Planning Agency, which supervised the general planning and adjustment of fundamental economic policies, rather than by the Ministry of Education which supervised sport administration. The purpose of this policy was to cope with the crisis of community collapse, especially in urban areas, which was caused by the social change attendant upon rapid economic growth; that is, to reconstruct the symbiosis and co-operative aspects of community that were being undermined because people's lives were confined within the spheres of work and home and family.

The advocacy of Community Sport was 'a clever scheme intended to create both fuller personal life and community solidarity through sport activities' (Nakayama, 2000: 192). Afterwards, sport for the citizen in Japanese society had

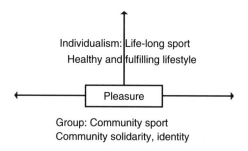

*Figure 4.1* Life-long sport for the community

the potential to follow the logic illustrated in the following figure, for life-long sports were advocated in the same way as life-long education in the 1980s (Nakayama, 2000: 52).

Sport activities by women, including housewives and the aged, also flourished, particularly from the mid-1970s through the 1980s, as seen in the popularity booms of jogging and tennis, the development of volleyball as a popular sport for housewives, and the pervasiveness or the invention of 'new sport'. Jogging and new sport do not place top priority on victory. People became more oriented toward self-realization, self-expression, sociability and social exchanges on the basis of pleasure by participation. As a result, these activities showed that the values of modern sport or the value prior to victory were relative. As it were, this was part of the spread of value relativism in society. Also, the number of people who could enjoy sport activities personally or in small groups, free from the competition of regional or organizational sport meetings, increased. In particular, young people living in city areas tended to be fond of novel or unusual sports such as surfing, skiing, roller-skating, and skateboarding.

Inoue (1977) considered youth culture to be a breakaway culture which had the characteristics of a counter-culture. He argued that one of the main reactive forms available to young people living in the contemporary controlled society was to try to experience the actual feeling of freedom by way of breakaway and that this was 'free from', or personal freedom and also freedom as an experience. He indicated that such a desire for freedom led young people to the world of play that, relatively speaking, was not 'serious'.

The serious issues for sport in the latter half of the 1970s were related to political neutrality, amateurism, and commercialism. The myth of the political neutrality of sport was destroyed by the boycott of the Moscow Olympics, and this made people aware of the reality that sport was affected by serious problems and related to important goals in society. As leading athletes went far beyond the rules governing amateurism, the gap between the ideal and the reality widened. Eligibility rules and the form of sport meetings changed drastically with appearance money, prize money and rewards being approved, the participation of professionals after the Olympic Charter being revised in 1974, and with sports meetings being named after a sponsoring company, or its products, Title Sponsorship Meetings such as 'Toyota Cup' and 'Kirin Cup'.

Title Sponsorship Meetings differed greatly from sports meetings that were simply financially supported by companies. They were organized by advertising agencies which cast the sponsor in the leading and the sports organization in the supporting roles. The number of Title Sponsorship Meetings reached 58 in 1980 (Komuku, 1984: 230) and then rose to above 100 a year (Taniguchi, 1997: 81). These meetings also included meetings for boys and girls, as well as for housewives. Moreover, the jogging boom from the mid-1970s led to a flood of civil marathon races and the organization of many running groups. National and international women's marathon and distance relay races were frequently organized, and then developed for men as the running boom grew. Companies realized that a runner could act as a human advertising tower, as marathon and distant relay races were frequently telecast. Companies increasingly sponsored distance runners because of the relatively low investment cost. In 1982, *Nihon-Taiiku-Kyokai* also began a project to support Japan's Olympic campaign, which was intended to promote famous athletes as commercial talents and gain the resultant profits. Moreover, it laid down the 1986 Sport Charter, which repealed the rules regarding amateurs and made each national sport governing body responsible for regulating those eligible to register as athletes.

### Commercialization – sport and business

The vagueness of the boundary between amateur and professional and the trend towards commercialism greatly changed sport during the 1980s. In particular, the influences of TV and corporate sponsorship upon sport became stronger and transmuted sport into a spectacle. Sport as a spectacle meant reorganizing it to make it more exciting for spectators and viewers, rather than for participants, and sporting encounters presented by the media as being significant and exciting events. Thus, the values of sport have been replaced by something other than victory. The spectacularization of sport progressed rapidly during the 1980s when society itself became more spectacular in nature.

The symbolic order of culture seems to be replaced by a commodity code in a spectacle market of which the market is the arbiter (Saeki, 1995: 179–273). The market reforms the value hierarchy in society through 'the money vote' as seen in fashion, celebrity, and best-selling books. Formerly, the market owed its spirit, which sustained structural stability and developmental dynamics, to domains outside the market i.e., the value hierarchy and lofty idealism in culture as well as religious spirit. The market's values simply reflect supply and demand and are modified by circumstances. Neither original normality nor abnormality exists there. What anchored fluctuating prices to a fixed point was custom and the feeling of normality established by custom. Therefore, the market floats when the customary order collapses.

Post-modernism had a hand in that collapse, from the viewpoint of ideology. Because what post-modernists hated most was 'metaphysics', such as any sort of 'essential value' (Saeki, 1995: 271–2). The value hierarchy in society fluctuated throughout the 1980s, and this was relative to the activation of the market economy from the 1980s. Policies expressed as Reaganism (Reaganomics) and Thatcherism, resulting in what could be called 'a social reorganization based on the market principle' were adopted in Europe and America. In Japan, the Nakasone Cabinet intensified market competition, reformed the administrative structure and promoted privatization from the mid 1980s. The ideology supporting this enhancement of the market economy was neo-liberalism. It liberated individual desire as far as possible while preserving individual responsibility. Individual desire conflicts with existing order and custom everywhere it is liberated, and neo-liberalism contributed to the destruction of the existing order under the name of freedom of individual activity.

The answer to the problem faced by advanced industrial countries from the 1970s to 1980s – what values should people rely on while the destruction of values is in progress? – was to entrust matters to the market. At the same time, freer global movement of capital raised funds in international money markets, which intensified the interdependence of industrialized countries remarkably from the mid-1980s. Thus K. Saeki (1995: 272–3) indicates that this development of global money markets rapidly led to Japan's bubble economy.

The flood of Title Sponsorship Meetings, the full financial support of athletic clubs by companies for promotional purposes, and the subsequent rapid increase in the number of company sports clubs, can be understood as parts of a corporate strategy in the spectacle society. The number of health and fitness clubs with training gyms, studios, pools, and so on, also increased rapidly from the mid-1980s. The health and fitness industry provided pleasurable and comfortable programmes as well as other services for people on the basis of their orientation towards health. People increasingly saw their bodies as personal capital, just as an object that yields the profit of corporate capital. In addition, the enactment of the Resort Act in 1987 was regarded as a policy aimed at increasing domestic demand as part of negotiations between the Japanese and American governments. The Act created a resort boom that coincided with a perceived need to open up new markets at a time when corporations had ample funds, while locals looked forward to enjoying the beneficial effects of the boom, i.e., the revitalization of declining communities.

Many of the resorts developed combined golf courses, marinas and ski slopes with resort condominiums under a membership scheme. Memberships became an object of speculation, especially in the case of golf and this helped heighten the popularity of golf. Golf seemed to be the first sport that suited the habitus of the wealthy and the elite. It gradually developed as a means of association with superiors that combined the work place and entertainment, and came to be a form of enterprise-culture. On one hand, as Ben-Ari (1998) argued, skill at golf is recognized as a suitable accomplishment for business people and a strategy for promotion; however, young people also enjoyed playing golf as a sport and seem to have enhanced the popularity of golf. The main point, here, was that the golf course became more than an object for the pursuit of profit, but also a place for engaging in bribery regarding development permission or approval, illegitimate trade practices, various other forms of corruption and entertainment shared by the political, governmental and economic worlds. The golf course became a point of contact and a hinge between the macro-alchemy of the Japanese economy and the micro-alchemy of golf course construction (Tanaka, 1992: 204).

Furthermore, subjective actions of both self-governing bodies as well as local inhabitants were necessary to encourage development of local communities that had been in decline since the 1970s. In particular, many self-governing bodies were not only the subcontract agencies of the state, but also subjective bodies that made their own policy in the 1980s, thus obtaining the participation and consent of local inhabitants. In the course of this process, regional initiatives founded on sport were also launched: the holding or introduction of national, international or unique sport events; the provision of comfortable sports facilities such as roofed stadiums and other structures; the provision of training camps for sport groups: the enhancement of athletic talent and the spread of specific sport events throughout the region; and the invention of new sports in addition to the provision of sport facilities related to resort and sport development as a focus of regional solidarity. Some communities aimed at rejuvenation as essentially 'sport towns'.

The policies regarding regional revitalization through sport were not often closely connected with the attraction and the self-sustenance of communities, though 'the rise of sport or viewing sport as a means of improving one's life and making it richer' was promoted in this process (Nakayama, 2000: 196). Also, it seems that many of the initiatives were not closely linked to enhancing local inhabitants' health and enriching their lives. At the same time, criticism as well as general dissatisfaction regarding the decline of Japanese athletes' performances in international sports meetings arose, particularly from the world of politics (Oono, 1996: 176–7; Murata, 1988: 14–21). The failures of Japanese athletes and the successes of both Chinese and Korean athletes injured Japanese pride, even while Japan sang in praise of its economic prosperity and took pride in its national superiority regarding its social system compared with the economically distressed circumstances of other advanced countries. In 1987, measures to improve athletic performance were part of the educational reform launched by Prime Minister Nakasone and were linked to the interests of the persons concerned with sport at that time. The improvement of athletic performance was considered an important and positive measure, along with the promotion of life-long sport, in Japanese sport policy. It was also, as Watts (1998: 191) argued with respect to the establishment and development of J League soccer, a manifestation of 'frustration that national identity was being seen merely in terms of economics and the promotion of Japanese cultural exhibitions abroad'.

## Conclusion

In Japan, sport has been adopted by business so that it can contribute to corporate interests in a process initiated in the social democratic reformation and led to the era of economic priority. Values of victory precedence and contribution to the group were reinforced by the Tokyo Olympic Games. These values conformed with the values of Japanese industrial society; that is, sport assumed characteristics that reflected the dominant social values and reinforced them. However, various social problems arose and Japanese society encountered a paradox where economic wealth was increasingly seen as not the most important goal, just when Japanese society began to achieve it. In this paradoxical situation, the permeation of privatism coincided with the decline of traditional values. Under a modification of governmental policy, sport came to be regarded as important not just as a counter-measure to social problems, but also as a means of enabling a full personal life. Thus, sports or sport activities that differed from those oriented towards victory and group contribution became more popular. Practically speaking, it was difficult to overcome the contradictions caused by the economic priority and construct a workspace that allows people to recover their affluent human qualities. It is undeniable that people wished to recover these human qualities and this found expression in sport and leisure after modification of government policy, as Okada stated (1982: 141–2).

These reinforced the values of freedom, self-realization, self-expression and sociability, and then lowered the contributive value to the group and the value of victory precedence as a result. These sports activities and the relativization of sports values were also connected to the adjustment of social values, which economic wealth itself brought forth, and a diversity of values in the process of becoming a mature industrial society. That is, they represented one aspect of how the values of sport changed according to the change in social values. Consequently, economic development affects culture.

In a highly industrialized society such as Japan, even sport and leisure are involved in socio-economic dynamics. Traditional values declined further and the value formation of the market advanced as the market extended its influence rapidly in an environment of globalization. In this way, on one hand, sport that was seen as a symbol of qualitative wealth became an important form of human expression; while on the other, the value of sport as spectacle was replaced by something other than the value of victory. Sport began to lose its peculiar symbolic values and assumed diverse values from social life expressed by sport.

## Notes

1   Sakuta (1993) takes an approach that starts from the experience of being alive itself and theorizes about social phenomenon. He also proposes a distinct use of the word value.
2   The words, 'physical education', have been used as indicating organized activities including sport and physical recreation with an educational significance in Japan. This is related to the way in which sport has developed in school. Simultaneously, the word is modified by the name of social context or group within which it is practised, thus home physical education, workplace physical education, social physical education, or nation's physical education were coined. In particular social physical education or physical education in society (*Shakai Taiiku*) indicates all the activities of sport and physical recreation practised by citizens, corresponding to the term 'social education'.

## References

Aiba, J. (1983) *Chiiki Seiji no Shakaigaku* (Sociology of Community Politics), Kyoto: Sekaishiso-Sha.

Ben-Ari, E. (1998) 'Golf, organization, and "body projects": Japanese business executives in Singapore', in S. Linhart and S. S. Frühstück (eds) *The Culture of Japan as Seen through Its Leisure*, Albany: State University of New York Press, pp. 131–161.

Dan, T. (1970) 'Noson no Hendo to Shakaitaiiku' (Change of farm village and physical education in society), in A. Asai (ed.) *Taiiku Ronso* (Second Collection of Treatises on Physical Education), Osaka: Nihonjisyo, pp. 96–113.

Defrance, J. and Pociello, C. H. (1998) 'Structure and evolution of the field of sports in France (1960–1990): 'A "functional", historical and prospective analytical essay', in Nihon Supōtsu Shakaigakkai (ed.) *Henyo suru Gendai Shakai to Supōtsu* (Changing Contemporary Society and Sport), Kyoto: Sekaishiso-Sha, pp. 43–61.

Digel, H. (1995) *Sport Science Studies 7: Sport in a Changing Society, (ICSPE)* Schorndorf: Karl Hofmann.

Edwards, H. (1973) *Sociology of Sport*, Homewood: The Dorsey Press.

Eitzen, D. S. and Sage, G. H. (1989) *Sociology of North American Sport* (fourth edition), Dubuque: Wm. C. Brown Publishers.

Harrison, L. E. and Huntington, S. P. (eds) (2000) *Culture Matters: How Values Shape Human Progress*, New York: Basic Books.

Hazama, H. (1994) *Kodo Keizai Seicho-ka no Seikatsu Sekai* (Life-world under the High Growth of Economy), Tokyo: Bunshindo.

Inoue, S. (1977) *Asobi no Shakaigaku* (Sociology of Play), Kyoto: Sekaisiso-Sha.

Ishikawa, H. (1979) *Yoka no Sengo Shi* (Postwar History of Leisure), Tokyo: Tokyo Syoseki.

Kawanabe, H. (1981) 'Nihon Shakai no Kachi Taikei to Nihonjin no Supōtsu-Kan' (Value system of Japanese society and Japanese view of sport), *Taiiku Shakaigaku Kenkyu* (Sociological Journal of Physical Education), 10: 149–167.

Kishino, Y. (1968) 'Nihon no Supōtsu to Nihonjin no Supōtsu-Kan' (Japanese sport and Japanese view of sport), *Taiiku no Kagaku* (*Journal of Health, Physical Education and Recreation*), 18 (1): 12–15.

Komuku, H. (1984) 'Supōtsu to Keizai' (Sport and economy), in R. Sugawara (ed.) *Supōtsu Shakaigaku no Kiso Riron* (Basic Theory of Sport Sociology), Tokyo: Fumaido-Shuppan, pp. 208–234.

Matsumaru, S. (1955) 'Noson Taiiku Zuiso' (Essays of physical education in the farm village), *Taiikuka Kyoiku* 3 (9): 8–12.

Matsushita, K. (1960) 'Taishu Goraku to Konnichi no Shiso Jokyo' (Mass entertainment and a situation of present thoughts), *Shiso*, 431: 19–50.

Mita, M. (1974) *Gendai Nihon no Seishin Kozo* (Structure of Contemporary Japanese Ethos), Tokyo: Kobundo.

Miyajima, T. (1985) 'Shakai Ishiki no Henka' (Change of social consciousness), in M. Mita, Y. Yamamoto and K. Sato (eds) *Nihon no Shakaigaku 12: Bunka to Shakai Ishiki* (Japanese Sociology Vol. 12: Culture and Social Consciousness): 55–75. Tokyo: Tokyo Daigaku Shuppankai.

Monbusyo (Ministry of Education) (1963a) *Shakai Taiiku Jittai Chosa Dai Isshu* (The Survey on the Real Condition of Physical Education in Society, First Series), unpublished papers.

Monbusyo (1963b) *Shakai Taiiku Jittai Chosa Dai NI-Shu* (The Survey on the Real Condition of Physical Education in Society, Second Series), unpublished papers.

Monbusyo (1964) *Nihon Supōtus no Genjo* (The Present Situation of Japanese Sport), Tokyo: Kyoiku Tosyo.

Murakami, T. (1985) *Shin Chukan Taishu no Jidai* (The Time of a New Middle Class), Tokyo: Chuokoron-Sha.

Murakami, K. (1997) 'Gendai Nihon Shakai to Kaishashugi' (Contemporary Japanese society and companism), in Y. Tudumigutchi and H. Ohama. (eds) *Gendai Nihon*

*Shakai no Genjo Bunseki* (An Analysis of the Situation of Contemporary Japanese Society), Tokyo: Keibundo.

Murata, T. (1988) *Yureugoku Supo⁻tsu-Kan* (Fluctuating View of Sport), Tokyo: Shinsen-Sha.

Nakayama, M. (1984) 'Seiji no Supōtsu Riyo' (The Political Use of Sport), in R. Sugawara (ed.) *Supōtsu Shakaigaku no Kiso Riron*, Tokyo: Fumaido Syuppan.

Nakayama, M. (2000) *Chiiki no Supōtsu to Seisaku* (Sport in Community and Policy), Okayama: Daigaku Kyoiku Shuppan.

Nihon Jinbun Kagaku-Kai (1963) *Gijutsu Kakushin no Syakaiteki Eikyo: Toyota Jidosha Toyo Koatsu no Baai* (Social Influences on Technological Innovation: The Cases of Toyota Motor Co. and Toyo-Koatsu Industry), Tokyo: Tokyo Daigaku Shuppankai.

Nihon-Taiiku-Kyokai (Japan Amateur Sport Association) (1949) 'Supōtsu Bajjitest Yoko' (The important points on sport badge test), in H. Kinoshita (ed.) (1995) *Sengo Taiiku Kihon Shiryo-Shu Dai Juichi-Kan*. Tokyo: Oozora-Sha, 1995.

Nihon Taiiku Kyokai Tokyo Orinpikk Sensyukyooka Taisaku Honbu (Japan Sport Association and Headquarters for Development of Athlete's Abilities toward the Tokyo Olympics) (1962a) 'On the subject of so-called "Konjo": Part one', *Olympia*, 26: 2–10.

Nihon Taiiku Kyokai Tokyo Orinpikku Senshukyoka Taisaku Honbu (Japan Sport Association and Headquarters for Development of Athlete's Abilities toward the Tokyo Olympics) (1962b) 'Text for building of Konjo', *Olympia*, 27: 33.

Okabe, K. (1960) 'Goraku Shiko to Seikatsu Yoshiki no Henka' (An orientation towards entertainment and the change of lifestyle), *Shiso*, 431: 51–59.

Okada, S. (1982) *Rejā Shakaigaku* (Leisure Sociology), Kyoto: Sekaishiso-Sha.

Ooe, K. (1988) 'Tama no Wakare' (Parting from ball), in Bungeishunju (ed.) (1988) *Bungeishunju ni miru Supōtsu Showa-Shi Dai Ichi-Kan* (A History of Sport in the Showa Period as Seen in Bungeishunju Vol. 1.), Tokyo: Bungeishunju-Sha, 439–443.

Ookochi, K. (1951) 'Kokumin Seikatsu to Taishu Goraku' (National Life and Mass Entertainment), *Shiso*, 326: 21–28.

Oono, A. (1996) *Gendai Supōtsu Hihan* (Critique of Contemporary Sport), Tokyo: Taishukan-Shoten.

Ootake, H. (1999) *Nihon Seiji no Tairitsu Jiku* (*Opposing Axes of Japanese Politics*), Tokyo: Chuo Koron-Shinsha.

Saeki, K. (1995) *Gendai Shakai Ron* (Theory of Contemporary Society), Tokyo: Kodan-Sha

Saeki, T. (1984) 'Supōtsu to Shakaiteki Kachi' (Sport and social value), in R. Sugawara (ed.) *Supōtsu Shakaigaku no Kiso Riron*.

Sakuta, K. (1975) *Kachi no ShakaiGaku* (Sociology of Value),Tokyo: Iwanami-Shoten.

Sakuta, K. (1993) *Seisei no Shakaigaku wo Mezashite* (Aiming at the Sociology of Being), Tokyo: Yuhikaku.

Sayama, I. (1988) 'Showa Niju Nen Juichi Gatsu Futsuka no Kikku Ofu' (Kick off in the second day September 1946), in Bungeishunju (1988) (ed.) *Bungeishunju ni miru Showa Supōtsu Shi Dai Ichi Kan.*

Seki, H. (1997) *Sengo Nihon no Supōtsu Seisaku* (Sport Policy in Postwar Japan), Tokyo: Taishukan-Shoten.

Snyder, E. E. and Spreitzer, E. (1978) *Social Aspects of Sport*, Englewood Cliffs: Prentice-Hall.

Sugawara, R. (1976) 'Nihonteki Supōtsu Fudo no Shakaigakuteki Kosatsu' (A sociological investigation of Japanese sport climate), *Shin Taiiku* (New Physical Education), 46 (4): 276–279.

Takenoshita, K. (1950) Taiiku Goju-Nen (Fifty Years of Physical Education), in H. Kinoshita (ed.) (1995) *Sengo Taiiku Kihon Shiryo-Shu Dai Ju-Yon-Kan*, Tokyo: Oozorasha.

Tanaka, Y. (1985) 'Shiseikatsu Shugi Hihan' (Critique of Privatism), in M. Mita, Y. Yamamoto, and K. Sato (eds) *Nihon no Shakaigaku 12: Bunka to Shakai Ishiki*. Tokyo: Tokyo Daigaku Shuppankai.

Tanaka, Y. (1992) *Gorufu to Nihonjin* (Golf and Japanese), Tokyo: Iwanami-Shoten.

Taniguchi, G. (1997) *Hinomaru to Orinpikku* (The Sun Flag and the Olympics), Tokyo: Bungeishunju.

Tatano, H. (1997) *Supōtsu Shakaigaku no Chosa to Riron* (Research and Theory of Sport Sociology), Tokyo: Fumaido.

Teishin-Sho Romu-Kyoku Hoken-Ka (the Health Section of the Bureau of Labour Management in the Ministry of Communications) (ed.) (1948) Taiiku Koza (Lecture on Physical Education), in H. Kinoshita (ed.) (1995), *Sengo Taiiku Kihon Shiryo-Shu, Dai Ni-Kan*, Tokyo: Oozorasya.

Terayama, S. (1988) 'Yakyu no Jidai ha owatta' (The period of baseball has ended), in Bungeishunju (1988) *Bungeishunju ni miru Spōtsu Showa Shi Dai NI-Kan*, pp. 379–385.

Tominaga, K. (1988) *Nihon Sangyo Shakai no Tenki* (A Turning Point of Japanese Industrial Society), Tokyo: Tokyo Daigaku Shuppannkai.

Uesugi, M. (1982) 'Nihonjin no Supōtsu Kachi-Ishiki to Do Shugyo no Shiso' (Japanese value consciousness towards sport and thoughts of morality), *Taiiku Supōtsu Shakaigaku Kenkyu* (Sociological Research of Physical Education and Sport), 1: 39–57.

Uesugi, M. (1990) 'Supōtsu Kachi Ishiki no Patān to Sono Kanren-Yoin no Bunseki' (An analysis of the patterns of value consciousness towards sport and its relational factors), *Taiiku Supōtsu Shakaigaku Kenkyu*, 9: 1–21.

Watts, J. (1998) 'Soccer Shinhatubai: What are Japanese consumers making of the J. League?', in D. P. Martinez (ed.) (1998) *The Worlds of Japanese Popular Culture: Gender, Shifting Boundaries and Global Cultures*, Cambridge: Cambridge University Press, pp. 181–201.

Yamaguchi, Y. (1988) 'Nihonjin no Supōtsu-Kan' (Japanese view of sport), in S. Morikawa and T. Saeki (eds) *Supōtsu Shakaigaku Kogi* (Lecture on Sport Sociology), Tokyo: Taisyuukan-shoten.

# Chapter 5

# Sustainable sport and environmental problems

## The E-boat movement as a social experiment in Green Sport

*Kanji Kotani*

## Introduction

Many sports new to Japan exploit the opportunities provided by its natural assets, mountains, rivers and coasts. Large supplies of water and electricity are needed for modern industrial production, and for that reason almost all rivers have been dammed. Dams have been used to solve the problem of depopulation in certain regions, as well as to provide better rivers and irrigation. This has led to the development of a range of new activities including the use of boats and mountain-biking. These attempts first progressed with the help of the regions that own the dams and rivers and then with that of the Ministry of Construction. In 2001, the Ministry of Construction became the Ministry of Land, Infrastructure and Transport and now administers these facilities, with the help of special consultants. This marked the beginning of E-boat movement which I shall describe later.

Since the 1870s sport has been encouraged by the Ministry of Education but, with the help of the Ministry of Construction, quests for new sports using dams and river resources began. Modern sport is said to be the product of the modern industrial society (Taki, 1986: 94–101). If this is true, then these new sports, represented by the 'E-boat' movement, must reflect Japanese society. Almost forty years ago children stopped playing in rivers or on waterfronts: now, both adults and children are returning to them.

The evolution of sport in Japan can be classified provisionally into three stages: the first stage, competitive Sport; the second stage, Sport for All and the third stage, Green Sport.[1] Sport in the first stage is achievement sport, recognizing scores, winning and losing, and scores or results have value in the public domain as information (Taki, 1995: 114–130). It also has the characteristics of a spectator sport. Sport in the second stage has the features of popular sport, being aimed at the health of the individual. These two have been positioned at the apex and the base of a pyramid model. They are in interrelation. The bigger the population of the second stage sport gets, the bigger the population of elites in competitive sports will be and the higher achievement the first stage sport will reach. On the other hand, sport in the third stage is quite different from these urbanized sports. It includes liberation of the body and festivity. It is closely

| First stage sport | Second stage sport |
|---|---|
| Competitive sport<br>Achievement sport<br>Plus/minus as a code<br>Results as records<br>Spectator sport | Sport for all<br>Not achievement oriented<br>Health or physical fitness<br>Competition records not recorded<br>Winning subordinated to participation |

(The two types of sport above have been shaped into an inverted pyramid model.)

Third stage sport

| Green Sport<br>Alternative to the first and second stage sport<br>Healing and liberation of bodies, festivity<br>Close connections with nature |
|---|

*Figure 5.1*  A proposal for Green Sport

associated with the natural environment. I use the term 'green' to refer to the environment or ecology and so name the third stage sport 'Green Sport'. Henning Eichberg (Eichberg, 1989, translated by Shimizu, 1997: 24–38), a sport sociologist in Denmark, named these three types of sport, elite sport, popular sport and folk sport.

The 'E-boat' symbolizes third stage sport, and it has resulted in the appearance of people who make their own sport. The E-boat movement came into being after repeating social experiments in rivers and dammed lakes which are the natural environments familiar to most Japanese people. Over the past decade, E-boat exchange meetings which even the old, the young, the handicapped and foreigners can enjoy, have been held all over Japan. By collaborating and accumulating social experiments and conventions, an 'exchange' between the upper, middle and lower reaches of a river has been achieved. From this exchange a certain movement towards protection of the natural environment, such as rivers, mountains, forests, sky and oceans, has been seen. Following this, the issue of protection of the natural environment of mountains and oceans has become apparent. As a result, these directional changes have offered opportunities for environmental education. Schools and citizens of NPO[2] have been co-operating closely, adding to the partnership of the government and the people.

Sport in Japan since the 1870s has advanced along the line 'government-leading-public-nature', as it has in under-developed countries. However, it has recently shifted to 'citizens-leading-public-nature': something which is not imposed by an authority or a school. Citizens living in areas and communities that are almost collapsing, are seeking means for their survival, thinking for themselves, repeating suggestions, agreements, experiments and inspections, besides getting aid from the outside. In these processes, and, for the first time, they realized that the natural environment is a priceless public treasure and thus made way for the promotion of environmental health, for green, sustainable sport.

When modern sport was introduced, Japan was underdeveloped and thus its development was shaped in a government-led, school-centred way and, initially, the thoughts or the ideas of those who created modern sport were not always accepted. But the present post-modern sport movement has taken root in Japan at almost the same time as in other developed countries. It entails body healing or liberation, festivity, and also has the power to bond a community and create a social network. Furthermore it focuses on the world environment beyond the framework of the economy and the nations that are the features of the modern era. We can see that the culture of sport reflects society.

In this chapter I shall first analyse the practice and the attempts of the E-boat movement and at the same time examine the methodology of social experiments. Next, I would like to discuss the impact of new sport on public owned land such as mountains or oceans, and present the background, potential, and problems in forming open public space and self-organizing communities.

## The E-boat movement as a social experiment

What I wish to show in this section is the E-boat movement as a case study for Green Sport. In Japan especially, sport on rivers had declined because of water pollution and serious accidents. Children no longer regarded rivers and the riverside as a playground. Now, however, people are looking again at dammed bodies of water, rivers and seas, and are trying to regain possession of them. This is related to green, ecological, agricultural, marine tourism. Dam water sports meetings and E-boat meetings on rivers have already been held. This kind of sport is closely connected with the revitalization of farming, mountain and fishing villages – connecting communities up and down the rivers by social exchange and learning about water and the natural environment. When sporting activities that take place on mountains, rivers and seas are regarded as business, how can it be possible to maintain the environment?

## Birth of the E-boat movement

The E-boat movement as a social experiment for Green Sport stems from several factors and these include:

1   Since 1868, with the birth of Japan as a modern state, the country's rivers have been used mainly for hydroelectricity and water for industry and irrigation. Rivers were once main transportation routes and supported thriving communities where children and adults lived, worked and had fun. But

fewer and fewer boats and people were seen on the rivers, and when the rapid growth of the Japanese economy led to water pollution, people began to reject them. Many river banks were concreted and lost their natural appeal. However, river authorities are now undertaking measures to make rivers more 'people friendly'.

2   In mountainous regions, on the upper reaches of rivers, populations had aged and declined. Local governments hoped that by making use of dam lakes and rivers such areas could be revitalized. They needed a way to foster exchange or interchange with communities further downstream. Tourism would be one of the desirable outcomes.

3   In Japan, most sports as institutions were introduced from Europe and the United States, and have been promoted mainly through school education. This means that Japanese sports culture is rather poor. In the latter half of the 1970s, the 'Sport for All' movement rose, modelled after the sport for all, slimming and fitness movements in Europe and the Unites States. The E-boat movement embodies three ideas:

(i)   Revitalization of depopulated areas;
(ii)  The invention of a 'tool' that people living along rivers could identify with;
(iii) Development of sport based on Japanese people's lives and culture.

Figure 5.2  An 'E-boat' meeting

*Figure 5.3* An 'E-boat'

'E-boat' is an abbreviation of 'Exchange-boat' and the letter E in the word E-boat stands for 'Ecology', 'Environment', 'Enjoyment', 'Earth', and 'Education', as well as exchange. It emerged from the practical use of dam lakes by people living near or around lakes in 1988. They gathered, argued, came up with ideas, did some experiments and tried to reach a consensus. Through discussion, and experimentation they developed the original boat as a 'tool' for the revitalization of farming or mountain villages. They aimed at exchange – more contact between communities up and down the rivers and learning about the natural environment. They named their boat 'E-boat' and attached many meanings to it.

Today, national E-boat meetings are held everywhere in Japan. Many people, regardless of age or sex, including handicapped people, are enjoying E-boat activities. In this way Japanese people are trying to regain what they lost through modernization and industrialization. The E-boat movement provides opportunities for social gatherings, festivity, and for rediscovering Japanese culture and Japan's natural heritage.

Until recently, activities on the water had been governed by rules framed by sports institutions. The production of boats or canoes had been authorized by each sport association and only boats designed for races had been available and these are difficult for ordinary people to balance and row. The E-boat is easy to row, and it does not need special training. Everybody can enjoy rowing an E-boat.

## Aims and hypotheses of social experiments

Now that society's values have become increasingly diversified and complex, 'social experimentation' has become a valid way of promoting social activities. Thus we can establish several hypotheses, examine them through on-the-spot investigations and try to reach agreements. Experimental events are organized for the purpose of answering a research question. The procedure is as follows. In a particular society, on a certain fixed theme, and within a certain period of time, the participants in the experiments set up some device that will create a certain phenomenon, and are present to collect data. A social experiment is a series of steps – devizing hypotheses, investigating them and reaching a consensus among the people concerned. The following elements are prerequisites for social experiments (Tanaka, 1996: 154–169):

1   Devizing a hypothetical event that tests points at issue
2   Field experience
3   Limited period of investigation
4   Community participation and experience
5   Practical neutrality
6   Public access to information
7   Reproducibility

There are two social experiment methodologies:

1   Programming first method: defining the period – for instance, over a month
    Idea ➡ Hypotheses ➡ Consensus ➡ Explanation ➡ Experiment
2   Field work first method: done over two days like event
    Idea ➡ Hypotheses ➡ Experiment ➡ Inspection ➡ Consensus ➡ Programming ➡ Experiment

The first type of social experiment is carried out daily over a defined period. In the second type, where social experiments take the form of an event, the non-daily repetition makes the festival's function clearer, which keeps authorities such as the police department, the fire station and the health centre from pointing out aspects that may contravene official regulations. Interference by the authorities might destroy the jubilant, festival atmosphere of the event.

Experiments are to be carried out in more than two spots at the same time for comparison, and they should be repeated and accumulated.

## Characteristics of E-boat social experiments

E-boat experiments use the second 'Field Work First' method. While a festival-like atmosphere is an essential condition for the experiment, the aspects of the event that the experiment is intended to examine should be defined so data relating to them, as well as any incidental problems arising during the course of the event, can be recorded and considered objectively.

The steps necessary in the creation of a successful experiment, referred to earlier, are now considered in more detail.

Next, a careful examination of the features of social experiments is made.

### 1 First making the hypothesis, and then entering into experiments

If the hypothesis that we want to investigate is attractive enough, it becomes like an actual event. As a result, the contents of the social experiment becomes richer and stimulates more people to participate.

### 2 Having fields for inspection

Field experience is crucial to social experiments. The field is where real information can be found. With the involvement of ordinary people, the information becomes compounded and concrete. The armchair theory tends to make the information flat and unrealistic. When verifying something, the quality of social experiments depends upon whether the fieldwork was good or bad.

### 3 Limiting the period of inspection

Without defining the period or deciding when the experiment will end, there could be no set time for assessing the outcome. By limiting its duration, the experiment can temporarily liberate participants from the existing restrictions and can give them a new open space. It leads to the promotion of festivity and 'non-ordinariness'.

### 4 Having a need for the residents' participation and experience

An important factor of social experiments is the participation of those who actually live in the community. Their experience of what the investigators want to inspect is an indispensable asset. Understanding deepens and changes with activities and experiences, and contributes to the forming of a consensus.

### 5 Participants being positioned in a neutral standpoint

The more serious and wider the influence of the experiment, which destroys the barriers of customs and conventions, the more people will feel antipathetic towards it. Neutrality, which excludes arbitrariness of those who are in particular positions, is indispensable for both those who carry out experiments and those who participate in them.

### 6 Information being open to the public

Social experiments tend to lose their neutrality or meaning because of their proponents' subjective views, personalities, or political intentions. It is essential that experiments be pushed forward from an objective standpoint; disclosure of the information is essential in order to guarantee neutrality.

### 7 Having a reproducible nature

Experimental results should be reproducible. That is, the experiments might lose much of their meaning if they indicate entirely different outcomes when they are carried out in different situations. But some differences are unavoidable because of the differences among communities.

### 8 Being able to call off experiments

'Experiments' can be called off.

## E-boat social experiments in practice

The E-boat was invented as a 'tool' that people in the upper and lower river-basins could use for social exchanges. As I mentioned before, the letter E has many implied meanings such as Ecology, Environment, Enjoyment, Earth, Education as well as Exchange. The flowchart (Figure 5.4) shows the concept of a social experiment.

This chart shows that the people in the river basins developed the E-boat as a tool in their lives and are working out a new type of sport. In the next section, I will outline each step of the E-boat experiment, including management, involvement, budget and preparation (Kotani, 1999: 181–7).

## I The use of the dam lake surface

The E-boat movement started with the use of the dam lakes themselves. In 1988, landscapes surrounding these lakes began to be maintained as parks under the lake resorts plan. Rivers, dam lakes and ordinary lakes were originally open to individuals but they were not open for organized events. Administrative regulations prevented local people from having fun on rivers and lakes. The dams in Japan are under the administration of either the electric power companies or the Ministry of Construction or the Ministry of Agriculture, Forestry and Fisheries. Several years ago, the Ministry of Construction began to make its dams available for events but the municipalities which have dam lakes did not know how to use them. In 1988, about sixty people in charge of dams from sixteen municipalities, and those concerned with sport, assembled for the first time at Aimata Dam, Gunma Prefecture, and discussed how to carry out a new dam water sport. Their

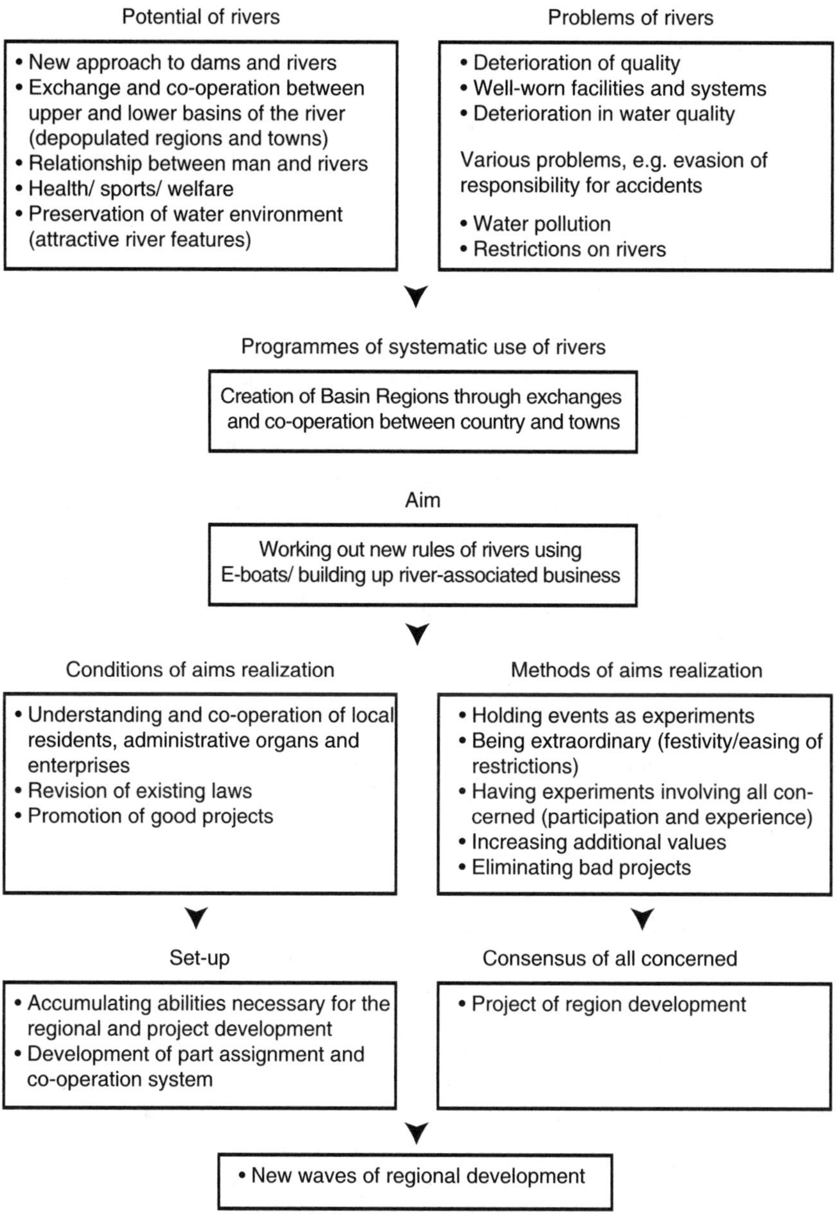

Potential of rivers

- New approach to dams and rivers
- Exchange and co-operation between upper and lower basins of the river (depopulated regions and towns)
- Relationship between man and rivers
- Health/ sports/ welfare
- Preservation of water environment (attractive river features)

Problems of rivers

- Deterioration of quality
- Well-worn facilities and systems
- Deterioration in water quality

Various problems, e.g. evasion of responsibility for accidents

- Water pollution
- Restrictions on rivers

Programmes of systematic use of rivers

Creation of Basin Regions through exchanges and co-operation between country and towns

Aim

Working out new rules of rivers using E-boats/ building up river-associated business

Conditions of aims realization

- Understanding and co-operation of local residents, administrative organs and enterprises
- Revision of existing laws
- Promotion of good projects

Methods of aims realization

- Holding events as experiments
- Being extraordinary (festivity/easing of restrictions)
- Having experiments involving all concerned (participation and experience)
- Increasing additional values
- Eliminating bad projects

Set-up

- Accumulating abilities necessary for the regional and project development
- Development of part assignment and co-operation system

Consensus of all concerned

- Project of region development

- New waves of regional development

*Figure 5.4* Flowchart of an E-boat social experiment

meeting resulted in games using ordinary canoes and canoe-polo. This demonstrated that such lakes can be used for on-the-water leisure activities.

## 2 Organization

In 1991, twenty-five municipalities founded 'The Dam-Water Sport Conference' with their own money and began social experiments on the use of huge facilities. This organization constituted the second step of social experimentation. The Dam-Water Sport Conference consisted of a symposium and a sports meeting. It was held over two days: one day was for the symposium and the other for the sports meeting. The symposium consisted of a keynote lecture, case study presentations, a panel discussion and subcommittee meetings. The sports meeting had a great many participants in commonly used boats such as canoes, 'knucklefore' or dragon-boats. Since then, five national conferences have been held with the Boat Association and the Canoe Association assisting with management tasks.

The sport facilities seen here were built before the first social experiments were carried out. They are in accordance with the precedents, and therefore they are within a paradigm of modern sport: for example, a swimming pool, a soccer court, a tennis court, a cycling course, an auto campsite, a horse riding course, and so on. These are all built for modern sport but, sited in depopulated villages, there would not be many people to use them and they would soon be abandoned.

## 3 Development of E-boat as a tool

At the fourth Dam-Water Sport Conference, the name was changed to 'The National Exchange Conference in Dam-Water Areas' and the following aims were defined:

1   To get more familiar with water
2   To promote exchange among the districts along the river
3   To make the movement easier for anyone to join
4   To have some original 'tool' symbolizing the uniqueness of the movement.

From the fourth aim, a new type of boat was developed. Until then the meetings were held with the great help of the Boat Association and the Canoe Association. The boats rented from these associations were used, and they are of course used for races and are therefore neither stable nor easy for beginners to row. Since then the meetings have been run by the local residents. The necessity for a new type of boat was stressed at the third conference whose working party I co-ordinated, and a new boat which is stable and easy to handle was developed. It was given the name 'E-boat' and came into use at the fourth meeting. The E-boat development as a tool was the third stage in the social experiments. Among water sports such as canoeing, dragon-boating, rowing and so on, the dragon-boat is the easiest and has the most simple rules. The E-boat was made in the image of a dragon-boat. In order to develop the movement nationwide, the standardized E-boat tool was essential.

The E-boat is a ten-man, 8.5 metre-long boat that is very stable and easy to row, so that anyone – the aged, the handicapped, or children – can easily handle it. The concept of the E-boat can be defined for now as follows: 'The E-boat is a new tool for promoting exchange [communication] between the upper and lower reaches of a river and creating a new ecologically acceptable river culture'.

## 4 The foundation of the co-operative association

Looking at the geographical features of Japan, we can trace a river from the Pacific Ocean, through towns, up a stream, through villages on the upper reaches, past dam lakes, to its source; and then go over a mountain and trace another river from its source, past a dam lake, through villages on the upper reaches, through towns down stream to the Sea of Japan. In other words, there is here the potential for 'Watershed/Urban Regeneration in Accord with Nature' (Yoshikawa, 2003: 247–250).

In 1997, The National E-boat Co-operative Association was founded. This comprised the fourth stage of the social experiment. The association saw that it was very important for cities, towns and villages in a river basin to communicate, collaborate and promote Green Sport.

Local inhabitants were thus encouraged to participate in a survey of their local facilities and needs, and to communicate these to adjacent communities in the river basins. In this way resources could be shared, complemented or supplemented and local knowledge, wisdom and creativity could be engaged. (Experience showed that where such local surveys were delegated to consultants they most often ended in failure.)

At this point the E-boat idea was conceived and grew, and over time with much labour came into being.

Several virtues of the E-boat project can be identified:

1   An E-boat is easy to row and women, children and old people can take part in E-boat activities and such meetings provide opportunities to make new friends and contacts. In the Kuma River, Sakamoto Village, Kumamoto Prefecture, a group of blind people joined the meeting. Even handicapped people can enjoy rowing E-boats and participate in the meetings.
2   Holding regular E-boat events makes people take more interest in rivers and means that more people get to know the rivers well. They provide the impetus behind the call for a sustainable sport.
3   Local people can easily run the meetings and therefore there are many opportunities for social exchange along the river between communities both above and below them in the river basin.

4   People gathering along the river means that toilets and resting places are needed. This leads to the provision of open spaces with suitable facilities providing meeting places for the communities.
5   A framework for the study and training of life-savers and rules for safe river usage can be established, institutionalizing 'E-boat instructors', 'E-boat co-ordinators' and so on. This leads to the training of 'river masters'.
6   E-boats provide the potential for creating a new river culture, as whole districts along the river develop a sense of unity and begin the new Exchange habit through E-boat events.

Future aims for the E-boat project are:

1   Provision of centres for exchange and co-operation on rivers
2   River maintenance and welfare
3   Training of river masters.

Facilities such as the proposed exchange spaces on rivers, should not have a single function but compound and multiple functions: possibly including facilities for health, welfare, education and information centres besides toilets and rest areas. The question of how best to use the land around the river, the municipalities concerned should work together with the residents. Both the river administration bureau and the municipality should share the expenses of operating exchange centres. The E-boat movement also suggests that rivers and waterfronts could be very effective in maintaining, improving or recovering health, and that roads and facilities should be equipped with consideration for the special needs of elderly and handicapped people.

## Green Sport: liberation from modern sport

I am concerned about what modern sport lacks: healing, liberation of the body, festivity and so on. One of the characteristics of modern sport is the generalization of 'sport culture' in order to popularize it to the world. In it, universality has been eagerly pursued with socially regulated and normative rules. By contrast the new Sport for All movement has gained popularity. One of its important aims is to improve health or develop physical fitness. It does not require special facilities such as fields, stadiums or arenas; it is independent of associations or leagues; free from official rules; and free from pressure to compete and break records or for victory. But it does not have festivity. Figure 5.5 shows what the E-boat movement means and its possibilities.

We will now consider the 'E-boat movement for Green Sport' and clarify its meanings and potential. I myself, as a member of the committee, have been concerned with the development of the E-boat and its promotion from the beginning. Up to now, I have always asked myself what this movement is. Various phenomena have been appearing not only in rivers but in mountains, forests and oceans.

For example, both the fishing industry and marine sports lovers are boat users and have been creating rules necessary for successful co-existence. No winter Olympic Games can be held in the mountains if enviroment protection issues are ignored, and the number of those who love skiing while coexisting with nature rather than skiing on artificial slopes is growing. The next section draws on reports on new sport experiences in the mountains and on the oceans.

## Green Sport in the mountains

While rivers and dam lakes are providing opportunities for new sports, so too are the mountains. Many lessons have been learned from the experiences of the Hakuba Skiing Village after the Nagano Olympic Games in 1998. Popular wisdom maintains that a large town or city gains from assocation with the skiing industry. Hakuba Village, however, proved that a local small colony could establish community land ownership under its own leadership. It was unaware that it had become a skiing village. Now, however, the number of skiing visitors has decreased to half that at its peak, and the structure of the village has changed. The Nagano Olympic Games in 1998 was a transient factor but economically, individuals as well as the village itself, remained in debt. However, the environmental preservation experience of the inhabitants from children to elderly people, has an enduring value. Through this experience, village people were made aware of their environmental assets. Hakuba saw that there was no alternative to maintaining a healthy natural environment and that tourism would also decline if the natural environment was not protected. Out of consideration for a healthy natural environment, cross-country skiing tourism, rather than conventional down-hill skiing was encouraged. This was the origin of 'sustainable sport'. Niseko Town ('Experience Kingdom Niseko') in Hokkaido is attempting to develop the same type of tourism.

It is becoming more understood that the old order has changed, people must be prepared to accept that old customs will not necessarily serve them well in the future. Nothing will happen unless all the villagers including those who have come back from *Soto* (the outer world), and new residents including foreigners, stand together and overcome this crisis, as was done in Yufuin, Oita Prefecture. It follows therefore that:

1 Communities can no longer be exclusive,
2 The barrier between the old and new residents, and the barrier between *Uchi* (the inter world) and *Soto* must be removed,
3 The power of *Soto* should be used positively,
4 The natural environment, which is the only asset of Hakuba Village, must be respected and protected, and
5 As a technique for pursuing this idea, a social experiment (proposal → discussion → agreement → experiment → verification → proposal → discussion) should be adopted.

---

The situation of rivers in Japan

Flood control and supply of water for power generation, for industry, for irrigation

River pollution, environmental education

---

Aspects of Japanese society today

Depopulation, ageing communities, low birth rate, diversity of values

Disruption of the family or a community exchange or interchange

---

The situation of sport promotion in Japan

Introduction of modern sport through schools

Competitive sport, sport for all, community sport culture

People's own sport culture, new sport culture, Green Sport

---

E-boat movement

New sport culture, social experiments, consensus of all those concerned

Rivers, festivity, revitalization of depopulated areas through exchange

---

E-boat invented in citizens' new movement

Sustainable sport, natural environmental health, public sphere, community organization

*Figure 5.5* Framework of the E-boat movement

Social experiments challenge people to seek alternatives to conventional skiing in the interest of a healthy, natural four-season green tourism and Green Sport. What strategy would a former skiing village now adopt to ensure its survival? While surveying the conditions existing in Hakuba Village and introducing the techniques of a social experiment, I offered suggestions on a policy for skiing promotion, alternatives to skiing and the promotion of tourism (Kotani, 2002).

## Green Sport on the oceans

There has also been a change in attitude towards the sea. Cultures related to the sea declined under the policy of national seclusion in the Edo Period (1603–1867). Japanese have been poor in creating devices enabling them to benefit from using seas or rivers. They were merely an economic means for transportation or production, so they were easily given up when they were no longer required. Furthermore, conflicts of opinions over sport accidents during school classes and water pollution by factories led to irreparable damage. It is very hard to maintain marine resorts in such circumstances, even if a great deal of money was once invested. In the past, the number of people who enjoyed marine sports was very small, although this has been increasing recently and creating some areas of conflict between them and fishermen. The Ministry of Agriculture, Forestry and Fisheries is now trying to work out rules to prevent such conflicts.

Here, I would like to introduce 'the order formation enterprise in the use of the sea surface' towards 'the formation of opened sea under the rules in the use of the sea surface' by the Fisheries Agency (Nomura Research Institute, 1994–97). It is predicted that the rules governing the use of the sea surface will greatly change the marine culture in Japan. So far, the sea has mainly been regarded as a fishery resource and the preserve of the fishing industry. Now people wish to be part of the equation. As mentioned above, the number of marine sport lovers is increasing every year and consequently more and more trouble is arising between them and fishermen. Establishing rules for mariners has been a matter of great urgency. Taking into consideration the security of fishery activities while providing facilities nationally for marine leisure activities, the report of the Fisheries Agency aims to 'prevent trouble and create an environment where it is easy to enjoy marine abundance'. Three years (fiscal years 1994–97) were spent on the investigation. The general flowchart was as follows:

1  The subject is connected to the use of sea surface.
2  Problems exist and generating factors will be confirmed.
3  The basic idea and its management will be discussed by all concerned.
4  The present situation of system formation will be confirmed.
5  A system of communication will be established.
6  A venue for negotiation on rules will be offered.
7  Certain procedures and rules will be applied to disputes.
8  All concerned will participate in the rule drafting process.

From calculations based on the annual total frequency of sea surface use, the annual total number of marine recreation sport participants is estimated at about 35–40 million, while that of the fisheries is estimated at about 45–47 million. It cannot be said that there is a big difference in the sea surface usage between these two. Although Japan is surrounded by sea and is called a seafaring nation, concern over marine accidents is grave, and hazard warning and sea rescue capability are inadequate. Historically, Japanese people have tended to keep away from the sea and therefore are unfamiliar with it. In consequence, ordinary people's knowledge and understanding of the sea and fisheries are inadequate, and the report pointed out that this makes it difficult to form rules to prevent trouble. Most marine sport lovers do not know how to use the sea surface and some perform illegal acts, which cause distrust among fishermen who then try to keep marine sport lovers out. After this investigation, the traditional meetings held by the fishing industry alone have changed to include coastal residents, the local municipality and people of learning and experience.

## The alternative to modern sport

Guttmann (1978) observed the characteristics of modern sport very accurately and these also apply to sport in Japan. Here, we shall look at it in a Japanese context and we shall discuss it concretely and try to seek alternatives. Modern sport which originated in Britain, reflects British people's thoughts, nature and feelings (Nakamura, 1977: 14–28), and is a very social occurrence for participants and spectators alike. Sport does not only mean a game where victory or record-breaking is sought. That is why it is said to be a mirror which reflects society, and why the word 'sport' has been accepted in the modernized world. Japan, which was late to modernize, strove to catch up with developed countries and absorbed much of their culture. Modern sport was, of course, introduced at the dawn of Japanese modernization in the 1870s. As with other under-developed countries, schools played an important role.

The promotion of sport through school education was very effective. Sport culture was soon diffused all over Japan, and good results were achieved. Japan achieved parity with the rest of the world but the so-called Japanese cultural lag remained. Indeed, while there have been 'effective' government-led projects such as school education, 'voluntary' or 'citizen-led' initiatives have not been fostered. In the 1970s Sport for All as an alternative to the old 'competitive sport', was promoted in Japan at about the same time as in Europe and the United States. This Sport for All movement has also been adopted by the government and administrations have offered its programmes, content, leaders and club services.

Let us consider modern sport and its universality. Modern sport is characterized by a generalizing of sports culture to diffuse it all over the world. It is the flow of chronic culture rather than that of synchronic culture. We have succeeded in positioning sport in the school curriculum, and it also became a subject in school education around the world. The persistent pursuit of universality has been served by socially controlled and normative rules. But, on the other hand, it has also produced abnormal athletes in an excessive pursuit of victory and records. Doping cases symbolize this. Traditional games and physical activities which included an element of festivity were forced into an enclosure, or stadium. That is how modern sport originated. We can understand the nature of modern sport by observing its movement towards record breaking, achieving victory, or accomplishment; we also see its tenacity in pursuit of victory through great skill, such as that displayed at the Olympic Games, or at the World Cup. Modern sport also reveals itself in rule production through attaching great importance to the media and doping cases which reflect contemporary values.

While some traditional sports involved a form of fighting, one of the features of modern sports is that the level of violence has been reduced and controlled by rules. In the case of rugby football, for example, the Rugby Public School principal Thomas Arnold succeeded in taking sports into the educational system and the rules of this public school soon turned into standardized rules at Cambridge University. As transportation developed, the common rules were institutionalized and with colonialism and prosperity of worldwide games they spread all over the world.

In public boarding schools, sport helped students to release energy and was encouraged to prevent homosexuality in dormitories. In France, it was expected to cultivate tough, masculine youths. Coubertin established the Olympic Games from this background. However, although the nature of domestic politics remained non-violent, violent wars continued internationally. In sport, as typically seen at the Olympic Games, the contradiction has arisen that athletes originally trained for sport are later institutionalized by competitive pressures and directed toward the breaking of records, winning and bureaucracy, with the result that some fall victim to the lure of performance-enhancing drugs which can lead to abnormal physical development and ill health. Thus, modern sport has not liberated the body any more than the army does when it enforces physical fitness training. On the other hand, modern sport was successfully integrated into the school curriculum and became physical education, a school subject common throughout the world. In PE, universality has been eagerly pursued through socially regulated and normative rules.

In opposition to modern sport, Sport for All is now increasingly popular. However, it is also a product of urbanization, that is, modernization. This question is taken up in the following section.

As in Sport for All, some people do sport for health; however, sport was not originally for health. It was born out of culture. Sport for health should be good for the health. It is better to forget the myth that we will be healthy by doing sport. Moreover, the concept of being healthy is itself a very ambiguous one. When someone says that something is good for health, Japanese people have a tendency to be very thankful, and take it for granted. Today in Japan, authorities have been building the old type of sport institution, that is, competitive sport institutions such as tennis courts, soccer courts, baseball fields and so on, even in depopulated districts, saying that they would serve to improve health and physical fitness. But people came to know that they do not serve to improve fitness. In urban districts there are those who enjoy competitive sports and use them, while in rural districts there are few. Some facilities on rivers, dam lakes or the seashore are already abandoned and covered with weeds If future physical activities are taken into consideration, then the 'liberation of the body' or 'healing' should become a key concept.

As Satoshi Shimizu (1993) says, young men who enjoy in-line skating, skateboarding, performing on bicycles, or three-on-three-basketball on the city street, are dancing in designer clothing to hip-hop rhythms and showing off to passersby. Their clothes are not at all functional for sport activities. A new type of sport performance quite different from that gone before has appeared. Young men say that they feel the wind on the body, become one with the wind and often surrender themselves to the eye of a wind, when they enjoy hang gliding or windsurfing. Those who love scuba diving begin to be conscious of the natural environment, and try to make sure that their fins do not disturb the seabed. It should be concluded, from what has been said above, that such alternatives to modern sport will surpass it in popularity and be related to nature.

## The body liberated from the brain's dominion

Japanese society is one where the intellect is of pre-eminent importance. As Takeshi Yoro (1989) says, the history of human beings has been that of penetration of the brain into nature. People call it 'progress'. Modern society thoroughly controls human beings. Why? The brain is an organ which regulates and dominates the body. It is the organ which receives information but does not process it, merely transmits it through executive powers. Therefore, it hates incoherence. In the brain, everything has to work as if there were a manual in order to avoid incoherence. But, in nature, no one can tell what the results will be. Nature is not to be controlled. Nevertheless, the brain strives to control, regulate or dominate nature. It tries to regulate and dominate the body, for the body is nature itself. Brain dominion often makes us forget about it. What is called freedom is freedom within the brain. The brain restrains the body. Sex and violence obviously violate this freedom; the brain strives to control these two but sometimes in vain.

Natural environmental health is, in fact, a problem of the brain. It is the problem of how far penetration of the brain into nature can be allowed. Perfect penetration will result in thorough control of sex and violence. The society which regards the brain as superior, hates the body, because the brain is unfailingly betrayed by it. Nature exists in our body; the body is nature itself. Our existence in the brain is what is defined by society. We can find ourselves only through our bodies, not through our brains. We often neglect the body. Through the body, we can feel a togetherness with the wind or the waves and the warmth or coolness of the atmosphere. We can realize how wonderful it is to experience these sensations through our bodies. Self-realization, self-research or self-discovery can be achieved in such circumstances. Many people are now attracted by fantasy worlds and theme parks which stimulate them by dizzying the senses, but they will not be popular for long. Instead of these theme parks, creative spaces where various opportunities for learning are presented will be required. We can experience self-realization or self-development in nature such as mountains, rivers and seas where we play and can enjoy true liberation.

## Urbanization and sustainability

In the modern era the farming population has decreased and has become a labouring one. People left their lands and came to work in cities. Most people live in an urbanized space. According to Yoro (1989), people today live in the city dominated by the brain. The body, or nature, has been long neglected. Now our present situation appears to be in deadlock. Sustainability of everything: the natural environment, natural resources, our lives, our existence itself, are in danger. As mentioned above, it can be said that we are able to regain ourselves through the body, for example, by playing Green Sport. The first requirement is that we should come back to our own bodies and realize that the body is nature. We will then realize that the natural environment is vital to us. Without environmental health, we cannot exist. For our own psychological well-being we must face nature and do our best to conserve it. In an urbanized space, it is difficult to find nature. In Japan, a river runs through many villages, towns or cities. It is the most familiar and probably the only kind of nature available to Japanese people.

When we face nature we find numerous and various roles. The word 'farmer', which expresses a hundred family names in Chinese characters, originally meant an agricultural worker who did everything required for himself or herself in agriculture, with the one hundred family names standing for one hundred vocations. Farmers could not survive, unless they did everything for themselves, for their partner was nature. The same thing can be said when we face nature. When facing nature, people's roles multiply so that they can regain themselves, their bodies and their identities in nature.

It is here that the meaning of experience learning can be found. We can give young boys and girls various roles and their identities through it. The importance of experience learning has won wide recognition, but it is very difficult for teachers to provide it successfully. Experience learning is always accompanied by the fear of serious accidents, while there is no system to ensure safety. Therefore, teachers are not willing to put experience learning into practice. It is necessary to encourage and train leaders who will help us enjoy ourselves in seas and rivers. Some measures for the promotion of learning in seas and rivers are needed.

Thus, we see that modern sport has extended the logic of the city, civilization and artificiality. Games became sport with artificially framed rules. Even at schools in the mountains, the domain of sport came to be the playground and swimming pool. The construction of swimming pools is symbolic of this. Even schools standing near rivers have built swimming pools and it is in these, and not in the rivers, that schoolchildren have learned to swim. Therefore, it is very important and meaningful for villagers who live along the river to work in close co-operation and promote a new type of sport, Green Sport, which will also revitalize rural communities.

## Conclusion: two contexts for sustainable sport

When we think of the alternative to 'modern' from the viewpoint of sport culture, we see two contexts: 'liberation of the body as nature' and 'creation of sport culture as counter culture'. As stated before, new types of sport in the natural environment such as wind surfing and the E-boat bring about liberation of the body. For the creation of a counter culture, an academic approach leaves much to be desired. The E-boat movement is being formed with the aid of consultants or think tanks, but they often hinder its development unconsciously. Although in practice the E-boat movement has the potential to surpass current thinking in Japanese academic circles, there is a considerable danger that such a possibility will be denied with 'modern institutions' that the academic congress or armchair theories have a tendency to graft on to it. In Japan, especially, great danger is perceived because the modern era has not been fully experienced and therefore the view-point distinguishing 'modern' from 'that which surpasses modern' has not been fully formed. The following problem arises: some consultants or think tanks often monopolize or lead the meetings to make money and consequently they hinder the local people's self-organization and formation of their own sport culture, and this has brought about stagnation. Here, we see *The Need for a Green Games Ethic* (Chernushenko, 1994: 65–70). Furthermore, it must be noted that, at this turning point, researchers should play an active and key role. In Japan some researchers still introduce foreign literature alone and criticize the current sport situation of Japan. Some develop armchair theories, ignoring the field. They tend to criticize 'that which surpasses modern' by the paradigm of 'modern'. It has pleased me greatly to see these new movements appearing in Japan, especially as I have been able to participate in and observe them from the beginning, and confirm that sport is changing along with society; sport is a mirror of society.

## Notes

1   In this sense Chernushenko also uses the term 'green' and its derivatives. See Chernushenko (1994: 10).
2   NPO is the abbreviation for non-profit organization. NPOs act to benefit society in addition to their normal business activities. In 1998 corporate status was given to NPOs, and approval was given to the non-profit activity promotion law (NPO Law) which aims to support such activity. NPOs work in the public interest and earnings cannot be expected for social action work.

# References

Chernushenko, D. (1994) *Greening our Games*, Ottawa: Centurion Publishing & Marketing, trans. K. Kono, K. Kotani, H. Komuku, M. Tobo, S. Jung, M. Hashimoto, K. Matsumura and W. Yasaki (1994) *Olimpic ha Kawaruka: Gurin Supotsu heno Michi*, Tokyo: Dowashoin.

Eichberg, H. (1989) 'Body culture as paradigm: the Danish sociology of sport', trans. S. Shimizu (1997), *Shintaibunka no Imajineishon*, Tokyo: Shinhyoronsya.

Guttmann (1978) *From Ritual to Record: The Nature of Modern Sports*, New York: Columbia University Press, trans. T. Shimizu (1981), *Supotsu to Gendai America*, Tokyo: TBS Buritanika.

Kotani, K. (1999) 'Kasen Ryuiki ni okeru E-boat Shakai Jikken' (E-boat social Experiment in the use of river basins), in K. Yamazaki (ed.), *Syakai Jikken: Shimin Kyodo no Machi Zukuri Syuho* (Social Experiment: Technique of Town Making in Collaboration with Citizens), Tokyo: Toyo Keizai Shinposha.

Kotani, K. (2002) 'Hakuba-Mura ni okeru Teiju-Joken toshiteno Shizen heno Kodawari to Foh Shi'zun Tsurizumu heno Chyousen' (Environmental integrity and four season tourism as settlement conditions in Hakuba Village), in K. Matsumura (ed.) *Tohki Gorin gono Teiju-Joken to Kankyo-Hozen no Shakaigakuteki Jissho Kenkyu, Monbukagaku-sho Kenkyu-Seika Hohkokusho* (the Report on the Studies of the Ministry of Education, Culture, Sports, Science and Technology), (Kiban-Kenkyu(B)(1)), Tokyo.

Nakamura, T. (1977) *Kindai Spotsu Hihan* (Criticism on Modern Sport), Tokyo; Sanseido.

Nomura Research Institute (1995) Heisei 6nendo 'Kaimen Riyou Chitsujo Keisei Sokushin Jigyo' Chosa Hohkokusyo (The 1st Report of the Project for Promotion of Systematic Use of Sea Surface), presented at the Fisheries Agency Consignment Enterprise, Tokyo.

Nomura Research Institute (1996) Heisei 7nendo 'Kaimen Riyou Chitsujo Keisei Sokushin Jigyo'Chosa Hohkokusho (The 2nd Report of the Project for Promotion of Systematic Use of Sea Surface), presented at the Fisheries Agency Consignment Enterprise, Tokyo.

Nomura Research Institute (1997) Heisei 8nendo 'Kaimen Riyou Chitsujo Keisei Sokushin Jigyo' Chosa Hohkokusyo (The 3rd Data-Investigation Report of the Project for Promotion of Systematic Use of Sea Surface), presented at the Fisheries Agency Consignment Enterprise, Tokyo.

Shimizu, S. (1993) 'Safin Suru Shintai: Datsu Kindai no Shintai to Shizen' (A surfing body), *Taiiku no Kagaku*, 43 (7): 535–538.

Taki, K. (1986) 'Shihonsyugi no Moderu toshiteno Sports' (Sports as a capitalism model), *Gendai-Shisou*, 14 (5): 94–101, Tokyo.

Taki, K. (1995) *Supotsu wo Kangaeru* (Think about Sports), Tokyo: Chikumashobo.

Tanaka, E. (1996) *Chiikirenkei no Giho* (Techniques for Partnerships of Regions), Tokyo; Imaishoten.

Yoshikawa, K. (2003) *Shizen Kyouseigata Ryuikiken: Toshi no Saisei ni mukete* (River Basins in Harmony with Nature: Towards an urban reformation), Tokyo: Kokudo-Seisaku-Sogo-Kenkyusho.

Yoro, T. (1989) *Yuinouron* (Brainism), Tokyo: Seidosha.

# Chapter 6

# Voluntary associations formed through sport spectatorship

## A case study of professional baseball fan clubs

*Hidesato Takahashi*

## Introduction

At professional baseball games in Japan, stadium spectatorship consists of three segments: members of private fan clubs, people who join in the cheering around the fan clubs, and people who do not participate in the cheering. The private fan clubs organize and lead the cheering in the stadium during the game. They usually occupy blocks of seats in the outfield bleachers. We assume that private fan clubs have a subculture of cheering. This study is based on participant observation that I conducted with an organized group of fans who support one of Japan's twelve professional baseball teams, the Hiroshima Toyo Carp. The fan club is a member organization of the National League of Hiroshima Toyo Carp Private Fan Clubs which was founded in 1997. It has thirty fan club members. In addition, there are several other fan clubs that support the Hiroshima Toyo Carp.

Although each fan club has its own official flag and the uniform (*happi* coats), the way of cheering is almost the same in all Japanese stadiums, and is negotiated on the basis of the relative power of the fan clubs. Fieldwork has shown how the clubs have been maintained, and are constantly being re-created and revised through people's interactions. This case study demonstrates the completely spontaneous formation of fan clubs by making new networks that are concerned with the subculture of cheering.

## Definition of a private fan club

### Voluntary associations of mass-sport fans

The origin of this collective cheering in professional baseball can be traced back to the cheering style of student baseball (Kiku, 1993: 238–242; Ariyama, 1997: 29–31; Shimizu, 1998: 212–146; Sakaue, 2001: 37–39). When baseball started to become popular among students in the Meiji era, cheering took the so-called *Ichikoh* form which was rough and uncouth. The game between Waseda and Keioh in 1906 was marked by collective cheering by spectators for the first time. At the game, spectators synchronously sang and shouted with small flags and megaphones in their hands (Nagai and Hashizume, 2003: 107). We can also see this type of cheering with clapping and shouting to drums, whistles and trumpets in the National Intercity non-Pro Baseball Championship Series. The cheering parties in student baseball or inter-city baseball consist of people concerned with the school or the company that the team is affiliated to. In Japanese professional baseball, in corporate identy teams (Sugimoto, 1990: 32–34), the company owning/sponsoring the team organize a cheering party like Hankyu (Nagai and Hashizume, 2003: 116). But the cheering activity of private pro baseball fan clubs is strictly voluntary. They are quite different from the fan clubs run by the baseball teams and are really private groups of team devotees.

Kornhauser (1959: 74–102) states that every society has three levels of social relationship. The first level is a very basic, individual relationship like a family. At the opposite end, the third level is the relationship shared by the entire population, and the significant example of this is a nation. In between these two levels is the second level and its role is to tie these levels together. Various intermediate relationships are lacking in mass society, while individual primary relationships connect directly with the nation and national organizations. Kornhauser says the typical mass society is characterized by a weakness of intermediate relationships, and a pluralistic society is characterized by the strength of such relationships. According to Kornhauser's theory, Fujiwara (1975: 109–114) regards community sports clubs as intermediate groups. 'The comprehensive sports club' which is needed to organize and promote community sport in Japan is ideally equivalent to a voluntary association among intermediate groups.

In this situation, how should we describe the pro baseball fan clubs examined in this study? Large sport events have produced mass-sport audiences and sport fans who gather in stadiums. A private fan club is neither an occupational group, nor a fan club managed by the baseball team. It consists of members who associate for a common goal, cheering, based on free will. So the private fan club is a voluntary association which evolves from mass-sports fans. Generally the private fan clubs are neither organized within the company, nor sponsored by it. They are utterly spontaneous associations. In this chapter, I would like to examine how private fan clubs develop from mass-sports fans who previously have had a tenuous relationship.

### Subculture of private fan clubs

In some cases, subculture takes the meaning of 'back' culture, one that is strange and extraordinary (Ina, 1999: 2). Surely, the sight of Japanese fan club members waving flags and pounding drums while wearing long livery coats (*happi*) gives an impression of a group of fanatics who differ from the generality of spectators. The fan clubs may have their own subculture. Although Hata (1991), Sugimoto (1997) and Kelly (1997) dealt with the private fan clubs in Japanese pro baseball, they didn't explain the fan clubs from a subcultural perspective.

On the other hand, according to Donnelly's theory (1981, 1985), there are three levels concerning cultural products: one is subculture, and the others are dominant culture and parent culture. Dominant culture means the most widely shared cultural productions, values and norms, while parent culture refers to the culture of groups based on ascribed characteristics such as social class, gender, race and age. By using these concepts, sporting subcultures should be placed in relation to the parent culture and dominant culture, not merely reported as a unique phenomenon. The methodology of studying sport subculture presented in Donnelly's paper is seen to be useful in investigating the subculture of fan clubs. When we examine this subculture it is important to relate the parent culture to that of the fan clubs, as well as indicate and emphasize what is peculiar to the fan clubs as subcultural contexts.

Furthermore, Donnelly argues that 'as cultural units which share in the dominant culture and maintain and produce a number of alternative cultural forms and ideologies, subcultures provide an ideal model with which to explore dominant, residual, and emergent aspects of culture' (Donnelly, 1993: 121). He explores the sport subcultures of rugby, climbing and boxing as residual culture providing both a resistance and an alternative to the dominant sport culture, and he shows that sport subcultures have a transformative effect on the dominant sport culture and his work draws on the results of the Centre for Cultural Studies at the University of Birmingham (Andrews and Loy, 1993). Considered from this perspective, sport subcultures resist or reproduce the dominant sport cultures. For example, Beal describes how skateboarders resist amateur contests or authoritarian-controlled sports, and argues that the subculture of skateboarding as popular culture is a form of resistance to the values and norms associated with corporate bureaucracies (Beal, 1995). Crosset and Beal criticize this cultural studies approach that insists that there is 'a tendency to exaggerate the oppositional qualities of sport without producing evidence of causal connections between the activities of a subculture and its parent culture' (Crosset and Beal, 1997: 77).

The sight of Japanese fan club members waving flags and pounding drums while wearing long livery coats gives an impression of a fanatic unit who differ from the generality of spectators. Their clothes and behaviour seemingly express resistance. For example, Hebdige describes the appearance of young people such as punks, and argues that their culture crosses the boundary of class and race in the context of British society, and is a form of symbolic resistance (Hebdige, 1979). It is also possible to explain the subculture of the cheering fan club as a style borrowed from a part of the peripheral parent culture. But it is not adequate to assume that fan club fashion implies resistance to Japanese dominant culture, because Japanese social class relations are different from the British system that Hebdige refers to. It is also inconsistent to regard a fan club as an oppressed group if we accept that a private fan club is a voluntary association derived from mass-sport fans. Accordingly, in this study I would like to focus attention on what the parent culture of the private fan club subculture is, and how the subculture is formed by the processes of borrowing and domestication.

## Fan club formation

In 1999, I became a member of Kobe *Chuoukai*, one of the fan clubs of Hiroshima Carp. As a rule, Kobe *Chuoukai* has a regular meeting on the evening of the last Sunday of every month. The meeting starts around 6:00 pm. Members talk about several issues: the opening game, arrangements for a tour to Hiroshima; a report from the National League of Hiroshima Toyo Carp Private Fan Clubs (which is abbreviated as the National League) and the Kansai Branch; securing tickets, assigning of cheering role and the cheering method. Afterwards, they dine together. The members sometimes watch videos of baseball games and tours. The main topic is about cheering Carp, but sometimes they talk about their jobs and families. This time and space is comfortable and the occasion emotionally satisfying.

The members have various social attributes. There are men and women within an age range of 20–50. Some have graduated from junior high, some from university. As for their occupations, there are students, housewives, salesmen of big companies and labourers. Their only common point is that they are Carp fans. When the Carp visits the Koshien Stadium, the fan club always occupies the same places in the lower sections of so-called Alps seats. Spectators around the fan club use megaphones or shout encouragement in stylized patterns. Collective cheering behaviour in Alps seats is developed at the level of mass behaviour. There seem to be three stages in this collective behaviour: the established order is taken up by fans, *then* the atmosphere can be absorbed, and *then* it becomes easy to join in the mass behaviour even if participants don't know each other.

Interpersonal relationships among the official cheering members are based on primary relations. Close relationships are formed based on respect for each other's character, and the participants interact as unique, whole persons. By contrast, the standardized mass cheering activity of the group in the Alps seats is based upon secondary human relationships. These relations are limited in scope and can easily be transferred to other persons. I asked Mr Nakakubo of the trumpet party how he came to join. He told me that a member of Kobe *Chuoukai* said to him: 'You always come to cheer, would you like to join us?' At the time he was a spectator sitting in the benches. For eighteen of the twenty-five official cheering members who are active in cheering, occupation of Alps seats gave them the chance to join. People who have never met before find kindred spirits in the Alps seats and are persuaded to join.

The collective cheering behaviours correspond to 'a focused gathering' that Goffman indicated as 'one type of social arrangement that occurs when persons are in one another's immediate physical presence' (Goffman, 1961: 2). This gathering is enclosed within a membrane, existing under different rules from the outside and forming a peculiar reality within the stadiums. When participants can spontaneously maintain the authorized rules and become unselfconsciously engrossed with others, they feel at ease or natural and the interaction will be euphoric for them. This situation results from the standardization of action of cheering members and spectators. This enables close communication and the group develops the characteristic of a primary relationship where the possibility of personal involvement forms.

## The conflict between two vice-presidents

### Mr Wakamiya's restaurant Koikoi

On April 22, 2000, around ten members of Kobe *Chuoukai* gathered to celebrate the opening of Mr Wakamiya's restaurant, *Koikoi*. *Koi* means a carp and is the team's symbol. The restaurant was reserved exclusively for the celebration and the shutters were half-closed on the day. Mr Wakamiya was a vice president of the club. A regular meeting had been held at his home, but after he opened his restaurant it was held there on the 2nd floor. Mr Sone, a chief secretary, and Mr Sumiyoshi, a vice leader, collected money from members. The restaurant has eight seats at the counter and twelve Japanese style seats. On the wall are ten autograph signs of the Carp players and photos of more than ten players taken by Mr Sone. There is also a bat autographed by a player and a group photo of a bus tour to Hiroshima. *Koikoi* is, so to speak, Carp Restaurant.

*Koikoi* is only closed on Tuesdays usually, so it was hard for Mr Wakamiya to go to the stadium on any other day. He often went back to work within 30 minutes

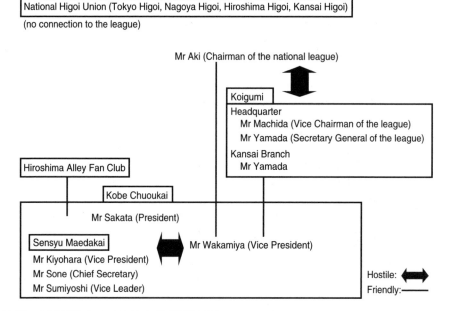

*Figure 6.1* The key persons and the fan clubs

even if he did come to the stadium. Cheering tools such as flags, drums, poles, and a stepladder on which a leader stands, were transferred by Mr Sone, Mr Kaichi and Mr Sumiyoshi in turn using Mr Wakamiya's car to travel back and forth between *Koikoi* and Koshien stadium.

### Mr Kiyohara's sub-group Sensyu Maeda-kai

The individual flag of the player Maeda was shown in *Koshien* Stadium on July 2, 1999. Maeda's name and his number '1' were written in big red letters in the centre of a white flag. Beneath the name and number were the words Kobe *Chuoukai Sensyu Maeda-kai*. *Sensyu Maeda-kai* was represented by Mr Kiyohara, the vice president. Mr Kiyohara did not wear the Kobe *Chuoukai* uniform in the Alps stand. Mr Kiyohara, Mr Sone and Mr Sumiyoshi started to wear Sensyu Maeda-kai T-shirts from June 2, 2000. The T-shirts were deep red with the words 'Sensyu Maeda-kai' written in white on the back.

Mr Kiyohara became a key person when Mr Wakamiya was absent. On July 29, Mr Jittani, vice chairman of the Kansai Branch, brought the executive of the Okayama Branch with Mr Yamada, the office manager of the National League, to the meeting. It was decided that a meeting of the national league would be planned for Okayama in November of that year and that the Okayama Branch would organize it. Mr Kiyohara dealt with the executives of the Okayama Branch. A cheering style called *Ichiku* was performed between the announcement of starting members and the commencement of the game. This was put to theme music for each player and generally began from the fan clubs in the Left Stand together with Kobe *Chuoukai* on the Alps Stand. On August 27, 2000, Mr Kiyohara said: 'let's start *Ichiku* before the Left Stand starts it' and everyone followed his wish. Kobe Chuoukai kept on calling a left fielder's name, 'Kanemoto', every time he took his position on the left in the first innings until he answered by raising his hand. But, on the day, Mr Kiyohara called: 'Work better, Kanemoto' instead of just his name and the leader, Mr Sumiyoshi, followed suit. This call came as a result of Kanemoto's play on the previous night when he had missed a catch close to the left pole even though he had touched the ball with his glove. Of course, Mr Kanemoto could not respond to the call. In the first fielding innings, Mr Kiyohara went to greet the fan clubs in the Left Stand with Mr Sumiyoshi. Coming and going between the Left Stand and the Alps Stand was usually made in the fourth, fifth and sixth innings. Starting *Ichiku* earlier than the Left Stand and going to greet in the first inning meant Kobe *Chuoukai* looked stronger than the fan clubs in the Kansai Branch. By changing the collective call from 'Kanemoto' to 'Work better, Kanemoto', this altered the usual way of cheering and showed the power of Mr Kiyohara in the group.

### Year-end Party

The opportunities for Mr Kiyohara to take the lead in the stadium increased after Mr Wakamiya started his *Koikoi* restaurant business in the 2000 season. On the other hand, Mr Wakamiya, by opening the restaurant, strengthened the relationship with *Koigumi* which has its head office in Hiroshima. Mr Yamada of the Kansai Branch of *Koigumi* brought a catcher of Carp to *Koikoi* on June 19, 2000. The Koigumi has strong ties to the baseball team. They organized a Gala party with players in Hiroshima city during the off season. The annual 'Fine Noodle Event' was held in the park near Koshien Stadium on August 26, 2001. This annual event is held on a Sunday lunch time in July or August before the evening game is played and people eat noodles outside. They enjoy drinking beer, waving flags and blowing trumpets. Mr Aki, the chairman of the national league, and the executives of *Koigumi* in Hiroshima, were invited to the event by Mr Wakamiya. Mr Sone, Mr Nakayoshi and Mr Kaichi, who were middle ranking members in Kobe *Chuoukai*, did not try to talk to the guests and did not show a friendly attitude towards them.

Mr Yamada of the *Koigumi* Kansai Branch attended the regular meeting of Kobe *Chuoukai* in November 2001, when he announced that he would bring three active young players to the year-end party on December 16. He gave instructions on how to behave towards the players: requests for autographs and photo taking should be done within a fixed time; no questions concerning their yearly income should be asked and no request for them to autograph the uniform of another player should be made. He also said that the National League was thinking that Kobe *Chuoukai* would develop through inviting players and the players would recognize the existence of Kobe *Chuoukai*. The meeting also discussed whether Kobe *Chuoukai* should attain independence from the Kansai Branch and organize the Hyogo Branch through Mr Wakamiya. Mr Yamada said that if they attain independence, they wouldn't have to ask the league head office permission through the Kansai Branch.

On December 16, after 1:00 pm, the executives of Kobe *Chuoukai*, players and guests (Mr Machida, *Koigumi* leader, Mr Yamada, secretary of *Koigumi* and Mr Yamada, *Koigumi* Kansai Branch) came to the party. After that, Mr Sakata, the president of Kobe Chuoukai made a speech in which he said that they wanted to have the annual general meeting of the national league in Amagasaki where Kobe *Chuoukai* is located. Mr Machida, the *Koigumi* leader, made a speech as a representative. Mr Yamada of *Koigumi* Kansai Branch proposed a toast. They enjoyed the interviews with players, party games with players, and the performance of a Japanese ballad singer. In addition, they played a game in which they could win players' used equipment, and there was a demonstration of cheering. The party ended and the players moved to *Koikoi* at around 4:30 pm. After the players and the guests left, a fiery dispute about independence from the Kansai Branch arose between Mr Wakamiya and other members. Different factions of Kobe *Chuoukai* were splitting apart.

The beginning of the conflict inside Kobe *Chuoukai* signalled the decline in numbers cheering in the stadium under the vice president, Mr Wakamiya, who was the key person of the fan club. Then, leadership in the stadium was taken by Mr Kiyohara, the other vice-chairman. Mr Wakamiya invited the young players to the Kobe *Chuoukai* year-end party using his connections with *Koigumi* in order to turn the tables. Having thus attained independence from the Kansai branch, he started the Hyogo branch. It is inferred from these consecutive events mentioned above that demonstrative commitment in a stadium is an important way of attaining social power in the fan club, and that closeness to players can be a power resource.

## Power relationship among the fan clubs

### Flag-waving

The organizing of a new fan club is called *Hata-age* (Raise the Flag, meaning the start of an enterprise) and a fan club has its own team flag. Other than the team flag there are individual flags which carry a player's name. These flags are waved before each batting innings, just after each hit and after winning the game. There are two main ways to wave the flag. One is tracing the shape of a recumbent 8, the other is to trace the letter 'c' lying on its back. The latter is more common and sometimes flags are waved on the bottom line and intentionally pass a nearby spectator's head. Kobe *Chuoukai* supplied canned beer and snacks to other spectators when they made a new team flag under the name of *Hata-biraki* (start new flag) in the opening game of March 21, 1999. It was confirmed that members contributed ¥50,000 (US $460) to make a new bigger flag at the regular meeting in August 2000. Then they bought a flag 1.8m high by 2.5m wide which they started to use from the 2001 season. They took the flag to games played at other stadiums besides Koshien Stadium. On September 11, 2003, when they were cheering using the flag in the Saga prefecture stadium, Mr Nakamura, chairman of Kansai Carp Club, who was there had a call to his mobile from Mr Jittani of Osaka *Kawachi Nankokai* who was watching the game on satellite TV and he asked Mr Nakamura to say hello to Kobe *Chuoukai*.

There are nine fan clubs in Hiroshima Citizen Stadium and the stadium rules limit the number of flags that can be used by each fan club to two. When Kobe *Chuoukai* goes to Hiroshima, they cheer in the place of Hiroshima Alley Fan Club, and use one of their own flags as one of the two allocated to the Alley Fan Club. The first time they waved their own flag in the Hiroshima Alley Fan Club position, another Hiroshima based fan club made a complaint: 'Why does the Alley Fan Club allow an outside fan club to use its flag?' but Mr Wakamiya said that members of the Alley Fan Club stood by them. We can see the relationship and closeness between home fan clubs and outside fan clubs by the way an outside group is allowed to wave its own flag.

Kobe *Chuoukai* has never waved its flag in the Tokyo area. This is due to the fact that Tokyo fan clubs do not belong to the National League and are not close to them. On December 5, 2002, when they asked Mr Edo, the previous chairman of the private fan club 'red army' based in Kanto area if they could cheer in Tokyo Dome or not, he said: 'You don't have to give a name card, but you should greet first. We will lose our place if you don't greet. You can use trumpets, but you shouldn't use a flag. I recommend you to contact Mr Matsuda of Kanto Carp Club which belongs to the National League'. The flag ceremony is a means by which one fan club appeals visually to another as well as for showing support for the players.

Since the National League was established, fan clubs which belong to the National League have been required to buy a league flag for ¥17,000 (US $150 dollars) and wave it in the seventh innings. They are not allowed to wave another flag in the seventh innings. That they should 'use only the league flag in the lucky seventh batting (seventh innings)' was printed in the cheering rules supplied to fan clubs in Kansai Branch on April 1, 1988. At the general meeting of the national league in November 2001 it was decided that each stadium could decide how to deal with the league flag. Only Hiroshima Citizen Stadium and Koshien Stadium stated requirements for the use of the league flag, and then Koshien was permitted use of the Carp pennant in the Alps Stand in the seventh innings, in addition to the league flag, in the meeting of the Kansai Branch. The decline of social control over affiliated clubs and the cohesiveness of the National League was shown in the flexible application of the rule that limits flag usage in the seventh innings to the league flag.

*Figure 6.2* Flag-waving

### Leadership

Leadership means to take the lead in the player's theme song by controlling the beat and sometimes shouting humorous slogans to spectators supporting each batting side. If there are several fan clubs in the same block, the rotation is fixed before the game. Table 1 shows which fan club took the lead in each innings. There is a tendency for the home fan club to take charge in the odd number innings and the fan club from another area to lead the even. There is also a tendency for the home fan club to lead the seventh innings. The way of cheering differs from stadium to stadium and a fan club from another area has to follow the local rules. In Nagasaki Citizen Stadium (September 10, 2002) which does not

*Table 6.1* The fan clubs that took a lead

| Place | Sapporo Dome | Sapporo Dome | Osaka Dome (1st floor)* | Nagasaki Citizen Stadium | Saga Prefecture Stadium | Koushien Stadium |
|---|---|---|---|---|---|---|
| Inning | 2002/7/20 | 2002/7/21 | 2002/8/21 | 2002/9/10 | 2002/9/11 | 2002/9/21 |
| 1 | ☆ Sapporo Nekkyou | ☆ Sapporo Nekkyou | ☆ Osaka Carp Club | ★ National Higoi Union | ★ National Higoi Union | ☆ Osaka Nankoukai |
| 2 | Hiroshima Carp Club | ★ Tokyo Higoi Kai | Hiroshima Alley Club | ★ National Higoi Union | Hiroshima Carp Club | ☆ Kansai Higoi Kai |
| 3 | ★ Tokyo Higoi Kai | ☆ Hokkaido Koirei Kai | ☆ Kobe Tyuoukai | ★ National Higoi Union | ★ Hiroshima Higoi Kai | ☆ Osaka Carp Club |
| 4 | ★ Tokyo Higoi Kai | ★ National Higoi Union | ☆ Kyouri Kai | Hiroshima Alley Club | Hiroshima Alley Club | ★ Hiroshima Higoi Kai |
| 5 | Koigumi Headquarter | ☆ Hokkaido Koirei Kai | ☆ Osaka Nakoukai | ★ National Higoi Union | ★ Nagoya Higoi Kai | ☆ Osaka Carp Club |
| 6 | Hiroshima Carp Club | ★ Tokyo Higoi Kai | ☆ Osaka Nakoukai | Osaka Carp Club | Hiroshima Carp Club | ★ Tokyo Higoi Kai |
| 7 | ☆ Sapporo Nekkyou | ☆ Hokkaido Koirei Kai | ☆ Osaka Nakoukai | ★ Hiroshima Higoi Kai | ★ National Higoi Union | ☆ Osaka Nankoukai |
| 8 | ★ Tokyo Higoi Kai | ★ Hiroshima Higoi Kai | ☆ Kyouri Kai | ★ National Higoi Union | ★ Tokyo Higoi Kai | ★ Tokyo Higoi Kai |
| 9 | ☆ Hokkaido Koirei Kai | ☆ Sapporo Nekkyou | ☆ Osaka Nakoukai | ★ National Higoi Union | ★ Nagoya Higoi Kai | ☆ Osaka Carp Club |
| 10 | Koigumi Headquarter | | | | | Hiroshima Carp Club |
| 11 | ★ National Higoi Union | | | | | |
| 12 | ☆ Sapporo Nekkyou | | | | | |

☆ Home Fan Club
★ National; Higoi Union (no joining to the league)
* Higio cheered on 2nd floor in Osaka Dome

have a home fan club, the fourth innings was run by Hiroshima Alley Fan Club, the sixth innings by the Osaka Carp Club, and the other innings were all *Higoikai* (the National Higoi Union) which is not a member of the National League. In the Saga Prefecture Stadium the next day where there is no home fan club, the second innings was led by Hiroshima Carp Club, the fourth innings was led by the Hiroshima Alley Fan Club, the sixth innings by the Osaka Carp Club, and again the other innings were all *Higoikai*. Thus, *Higoikai* took the lead for odd numbered innings, and the way of cheering such as the out call, the pitcher's theme song, the fanfare for a home run followed the style of the National Higoi Union.

The National Higoi Union consists of four groups: Tokyo *Higoikai*, Nagoya *Higoikai*, Hiroshima *Higoikai* and Kansai *Higoikai*. The members are teenagers and young men in their twenties. The four groups co-operate with each other, and they cheer at all 140 games a year. In every stadium where Carp plays, we can see them waving the same big death's-head flag of *Higoikai*. They complained to the national league that they could not wave their own flag during the seventh innings. Pressure from the National Higoi Union is one of the factors in the movement for non-enforcement of the use of the national league flag. The power relationship among the fan clubs is evident in the cheering behaviours such as flag-waving and lead-taking, and we can see a struggle for power between the National Higoi Union and the National League through demonstrative cheering performances.

## Bureaucracy as parent culture

Fan club organization is hierarchial and where position and role are fixed depending on duty. Kobe *Chuoukai* is densely structured. In 1999 a staff list was submitted to the National League, which itemized the positions including president, counsellor, manager, vice president, accountant, chief secretary, fan club leader, vice fan club leader, foreign affairs, lead party, trumpet party, ladies' section, and district members. Each fan club pays the league an annual membership fee of ¥10,000 . The Kansai Branch of the league which Kobe *Chuoukai* belonged to until 2002, also provides positions such as president, vice president, chief secretary, manager and counsellor. It has its own constitution consisting of twenty-five articles. The members of fan clubs have visiting cards on which their positions or job descriptions are written, and they exchange cards in the stadiums and at parties.

The memorial party of the establishment of the National League of Hiroshima Toyo Carp Private Fan Clubs was held on November 24, 1997, at the Hotel Granvia, Hiroshima, with more than forty fan clubs from all over Japan participating. Mr Tatsukawa, head coach of the farm team, and twelve players came to the party.

However, six fan clubs of the Kanto branch (National *Koikoigumi*, Red Army, *Tokyohigoikai*, Tokyo *Syourikai*, Tokyo *Shitamachi Etokai*, Tokyo *Lefutokai*) withdrew around May the following year. According to Mr Edo, the previous head of the Red Army, the reasons for these resignations were threefold: first, there was displeasure with the structure that had Hiroshima as the head office and Kanto as a branch; second, the top-down system was controlled by *Koigumi*, and the third was the compulsory waving of the league flag in the seventh innings. When representatives of the Kanto branch claimed for travelling expenses to attend the national general meeting of the league, the claim was rejected as it was felt that the branch should pay its own expenses. After that, some fan clubs resigned and some others joined, so there were thirty fan clubs in the national league in November 2002.

The general meeting of the National League is held in November every year according to Rule 14 of the League's constitution. The second general meeting was held in the Kansai branch in 1998, the third in Hokuriku branch in 1999, the fourth was held by the Okayama branch in 2000, and the fifth was held at the Hiroshima head office in 2001. The sixth general meeting of league was held in the Fukuoka branch on November 10, 2003. When we arrived at Fukuoka Airport, Mr Sakata, the president of Kobe *Chuoukai* answered a cell phone from Mr Aki, the national league chairman. He told us to come to see him in an ante-room before the general assembly began. The Nagoya Branch might have been planning to submit a motion of no confidence in Mr Aki and this would have been a bad mark of disrespect for him. So to prevent it, we were told to say nothing as he would announce his resignation as a chairman of the league for reasons of health although he had one more year of his term to run. Mr Shindo, the executive head, would become the acting-chairman and Mr Kunimi of Hiroshima Carp Club would become the executive head upon Mr Aki's accession to the role of honorary president. The Nagoya branch belongs to the Chubu Liaison Council which consists of the fan clubs of several baseball teams. The reason for

*Figure 6.3* The establishment of the National League

the motion of no confidence was a blunder in that a telegram of condolence to the late chairman of the Council was sent under the name of the *Koigumi* chairman, not the National League of Hiroshima Toyo Carp Private Fan Club. This was the hidden reason why Mr Aki had to lose his position.

The sixth general meeting was held in the hall of the Hotel Seahawk. The league flag was placed at the front of the hall and all participants wore suits and ties. The league chairman and vice chairman, the chief secretary and office manager took seats on the stage. The meeting chairman and the minutes signer were elected. The agenda was presented and personnel changes were announced. Finally, the meeting chairman and the minutes signer were recalled and the closing address was made. The meeting was stiff and formal, similar to the regular convention of a political party.

Weber mentioned rational-legal authority as one of three ideal types of legitimate authority with the most ideal type being bureaucratic authority (Weber, 1956: Japanese 32–59). He states the principle of the bureaucratic system includes the management of the organization and performance of one's duty based on rules, hierarchy within the organization, documentation of order, specialization of duty etc. (Weber, 1956: Japanese 60–63). The structure of a fan club involves not only specialized roles such as leading flag-waving, trumpet-blowing and drumming, but also shows the centralization of power in the order of chairman of national league, branch leader, and leaders of each party. Activity is based on rules and is formally documented. Thus the structure of an organization under a bureaucratic system can be seen in big organizations such as companies and universities as well as administrative organizations. We can see the organization of the fan clubs is based on a bureaucratic system and reflects the parent culture of bureaucracy.

## Conclusion

Sports events in modern society have created mass-sports fans. In this chapter I have clarified how a voluntary association for cheering was formed among mass-sports fans and how the group that had a cheering subculture was maintained. Members of the Kobe *Chuoukai* gain emotional satisfaction through their close and frank communication. This group can be formed around primary relations from a mass behaviour level based on standardized collective cheering patterns. That is, the primary group dynamics emerge from the secondary relations of these collective cheering behaviours which are easily transferred to others and involve only a segment of the personality. However, the behaviours consist of emotional interactions and evocative presentation styles. The spectators follow a certain pattern while adjusting their voices and movements to match those of other people. Through these ritual acts, the excitement is palpable, and a collective effervescent emotion is created among spectators. In the stylization and presentational staging, collective cheering behaviours deflect questions and doubts, while encouraging people to abandon their self-consciousness and feel a 'flow' to the participants is created (Moore and Myerhoff, 1977: 7–8). Their cheering serves not only as opportunities for recruiting new members for Kobe *Chuoukai*, but also as the cultural apparatus by which the fan club's sense of community is sustained and the organization of fan clubs is maintained.

Naturally enough, a demonstrative commitment in the stadium is necessary to keep and increase social power among fan club members. Therefore, a decrease in numbers of Mr Wakamiya's cheering in the stadium caused conflict in Kobe *Chuoukai*. For this reason, Mr Wakamiya planned to invite some baseball players to their end-of-year party, because increased power can flow from the closeness of the fan club to the players and team. By using his own achievement of bringing players to the party, he aimed to promote the fan club and achieve branch status and thus move up the hierarchy of the national league. As shown in the rise of *Koigumi* and *Higoikai*, demonstrative commitment in the stadium and close relationships with team and players increases the private fan club's powers.

Fan club organization also has a relationship to parent culture based on bureaucracy. Ritualistic actions such as flag-waving and cheer leading in behaviours symbolize social power and maintain the order of the organization. The national league demonstrates its power in that it requires the national league flag to be waved in the seventh innings. As for individual fan clubs, they can demonstrate their power through taking the lead in the main innings. So cheering behaviours have the function of rituals, not only because they cause a collective quasi-religious explosion of energy, but also because they justify the order in the organization of fan clubs. Expansion of size of management organization in modern society inevitably generated rational and functional groups and organizations. We can say that the bureaucratic system demonstrates an extreme functional rational nature and it is the main parent culture in modern society. Therefore, it seems that when mass cheering fans get together to form a nation-wide organization, they need to utilize the bureaucratic system as part of the parent culture in order to conduct cheering action rationally. Not only for reasons of functional rationality, but bureaucratic principles may have been required by the fan clubs in order to obtain affirmative social recognition through involvement in the main culture of modern society, and thus avoid the image of social outcasts.

## References

Ariyama, T. (1997) *Kohshien Yakyuh to Nihonjin* (Koshien Baseball and Japanese), Tokyo: Yoshikawakohbunkan.

Andrews, D. L. and Loy, J. W. (1993) 'British cultural studies and sport: Past encounters and future possibilities', *Quest*, 45: 255–276.

Beal, B. (1995) 'Disqualifying the official: An exploration of social resistance through the subculture of skateboarding' , *Sociology of Sport Journal*, 12: 252–267.

Crosset, T. and Beal, B. (1997) 'The use of "subculture" and "subworld" in ethnographic works on sport: A discussion of definitional distinctions', *Sociology of Sport Journal*, 14: 73–85.

Donnelly, P. (1981) 'Toward a definition of sport subcultures', in M. Hart and S. Birrell (eds) *Sport in the Sociocultural Process* (3rd edn), Dubuque: WC Brown Co. Publishers.

Donnelly, P. (1985) 'Sport subcultures', *Exercise and Sport Science Review*, 13: 539–578.

Donnelly, P. (1993) 'Subcultures in sport: Resilience and transformation', in A. G. Ingham and J. W. Loy (eds) *Sport in Social Development*, Illinois: Human Kinetics Publishers.

Fujiwara, K. (1975) 'Chuhkan Syuhdan to Komyunitih Spohtsu Shi' (Intermediate Group and Community Sport Press), *Taiiku Shakaigaku Kenkyu*, 4: 109–129.

Goffman, E. (1961) *Encounter: Two Studies in the Sociology of Interaction*, New York: Bobbs-Merrill Company.

Hata, H. (1991) 'Supekuteitah Supotsu no Syakai Bunkateki Seikaku to Mondai (Socio-Cultural features of Spectator Sports), unpublished thesis, Naruto University of Education.

Hebdige, D. (1979) *Subculture: The Meaning of Style*, London: Methuen & Co Ltd.

Ina, M. (1999) *Sabukarucyah no Syakaigaku* (Sociology of Subculture), Kyoto: Sekai Shisoh Sya.

Kornhauser, W. (1959) *The Politics of Mass Society*, London: Free Press.

Kelly, W. (1997) 'An anthropologist in the bleachers', *Japan Quarterly*, 44 (4): 66–79.

Kiku, K. (1993) *Kindai Puro Supohtsu no Rekishi Syakaigaku* (Historical Sociology of Modern Professional Sport), Tokyo: Fumaidoh Shuppan.

Moore, F. and Myerhoff, G.(eds) (1977), *Secular Ritual*, Assen: Van Gorcum.

Nagai, Y. and Hashizume, S. (2003) *Nankai Hohkusu ga atta koro: Yakyu Fuan to PaRihgu no Bunkashi* (When There were Nankai Hawks: Cultural History of Baseball Fans and Pacific League), Tokyo: Kinokuniya Shoten.

Sakaue, Y. (2001) *Nippon Yakyuh no Keifugaku* (Genealogy of Japanese Baseball), Tokyo: Seidosya.

Shimizu. S. (1998) *Kohshien Yakyuh no Arukeorogih* (Archaeology of Kohshien Baseball), Tokyo: Shin Hyohron.

Sugimoto, A. (1997) 'Supotsu fan no kohfun to chinsei' (Excitement and tranquility of sport fans), in A. Sugimoto (ed.) *Supotsu Fan no Syakaigaku* (Sociology of Sport Fans), Kyoto: Sekai Shisohsya.

Sugimoto, N. (1990) *Behsu Bohru Shitih* (Baseball City), Tokyo: Fukutake Shoten.

Weber, M. (1956) *Wirtschaft und Gesellschaft, Grundriss der verstehenden Soziologie* (Vierte, neu herausgegebene Auflage), besorgt von Winckelmann, J., Tübingen: Mohr (Kapitel IX. Soziologie der Herrschaft, S.541–632); trans. in T. Sera (1960) *Shihai no Syakaigaku I* (Sociology of Authority I), Tokyo: Shobun-Sya.

# Chapter 7

# Playfulness and gender in modern Japanese society

*Keiji Matsuda*

## Introduction

Gender role theory states that the behavioural pattern or role of an individual is determined by the individual's gender, according to societal positions. For example, in the field of women's studies, gender role refers to the feminine psychology, attitude, lifestyle customs and activity range that are expected in females by society and that are perpetually practised by females themselves. While a masculine gender role 'naturally' exists for men, with modern society as the scriptwriter, the discriminatory role that has constrained women and the losses suffered have been examined to date and clearly revealed.

The existing division of labour views cooking and cleaning as women's work and thus indicates the specific details of the theatrical performance imposed on the female role. The range of activities generally referred to as caring, such as housekeeping and child rearing, are left to the female who is expected to give a performance filled with gentleness, softness and smiles. Gender role theory attempts to rewrite the gender-related script of a society that brings forth such role discrimination. As the anthropologist Margaret Mead (1949) discovered with regard to tribes in the South Pacific, in which women took partial responsibility for the fishing and men for the housework, the theatrical performance imposed on a person by gender roles is arbitrarily created by culture and society. That is, gender role theory has associated the gender roles arbitrarily created in a society with the principles that make up that society. While criticizing the discriminatory nature of that society, theorists have sought societal reform and more desirable male and female role distribution. Today, gender role theory is moving toward research that addresses both the asymmetrical power relationship between men and women and the organization of modern day society.

In Japan gender role theory was actively discussed in the 1970s. Informed by such discussions, feminism and women's studies began to increase their influence in the academic community. In sports studies in Japan, full-scale incorporation of feministic research started in the 1990s, with most of the research focusing on gender bias in sports, aiming towards liberation from gender discrimination. In the process of the importation and the spread of sports in Japan, the opportunities for women to play sports, whether in school or in society, was markedly restricted. In schools, gender-specific curriculums were established and sports as an extracurricular activity was male dominated. Furthermore, in society and in the workplace, for a long time women were not assured a place to enjoy sports. In such an atmosphere, the sports in which housewives participated came to fulfil a critical role in local regions. With the gold medal achievements of Japan in the Tokyo Olympics, for instance, volleyball quickly made its way into the everyday lives of housewives under the name *Mama-san Volley*. This seemed to give women something to live for while they were confined to the house, and aided social integration. Research into this type of oppression and social function of women's sports was later established. The general gender role related research of Japan conducted in the 1970s therefore created a foundation for such research.

This chapter argues that the attempt to understand genders by comparing men and women roles in play is not significant just because it draws a new boundary between men and women. Although it has not drawn much attention to date, the dramaturgical view of explaining gender using a theatrical stage metaphor also indicates new potential for us to escape from gender restraints. This, then, also points to new potential in the culture of sports with the social reality of gender. The chapter argues that Japan is one case in which this potential has been socially manifested. In making this case, the chapter first discusses the work of Erving Goffman (1959) who employed the theatrical stage as a metaphor to explain social lifestyles.

## Theatrical performance and the body

When we sit down in front of a lover, we are more or less conscious of the fact that we are being watched. At this time, we normally behave a certain way since we would like to leave a certain impression as a man or woman. However, because we know that behaviour becomes interactive in this scene, we also know how to check for 'weaknesses' in behaviour. By conversely calculating and intentionally revealing such weaknesses, we can skilfully manage the impression we make. In this way, the strategy for impression management is mutually driven. And, to this effect, our behaviour in a social scene shows aspects of a type of 'information game'.

Goffman highlights the dramatic impression of a social scene that is likened to a 'theatrical performance'. He refers to the person offering an impression and presenting him or her self in an everyday face-to-face life scene as the performer, the recipient of this presentation as the audience, and the contents of the performance as the part or routine. This terminology, which is not customary in descriptions of social life, is fitting since it always includes the perception that our social life is being watched and that we have to more or less take on a performance strategy to counter this watching and express the self.

Recall, again, the scene in which you are sitting in front of a lover. If you are a woman, you may take care to make the conversation flow smoothly by continually smiling or making agreeable responses. If you are a man, perhaps you take on a bold or determined attitude or lead the conversation. Of all the role performances in social life, the one performance presented by everyone from the earliest stages involves the part of gender. Human life, which cannot survive with men or women alone, must continue strategic performances of gender before the eyes of others. The use of the body in the gender performance is critical. The various players are humans who can make full use of the body as a tool of expression. From clothing to makeup; the way one walks, sits, crosses his or her legs; one's posture; the placement of one's gaze; the way one drinks coffee … Humans use the body to such an extent that it can virtually be said that the entire body has been provided for the purpose of performing the role of gender. That is, the body is a system of signals that expresses gender. Or, in other words, our body in social life is merely a body created and enacted as man or woman.

## The body as a mask

Why is it that our bodies must continuously perform a role? From Goffman's perspective the way our social life depends on some type of performance stems from two concerns. First, there is the altruistic concern in a broad sense, such as when a woman wears an elegant dress to a party, i.e. the concern to maintain order in a social scene. Second, is the selfish concern in a broad sense, such as when a woman wears feminine clothing to an employment interview, i.e. the concern for strategy regarding impression management. With everyday life supported by this gender performance, gender is continuously intrinsically reproduced by the performance. With the parts established, failure to perform the parts results in failure of communication.

Yet, to perform is also an attempt to simultaneously project self as another. The self that is projected as another is a mask of the self. In this way, gender performance requires the preparation of one more self, i.e. a mask. Thus, it becomes evident that our body is actually a mask. It is well known that the word personality derives from the word persona, i.e. a mask that an actor puts on in a play. Taking this into consideration, gender performance involves the simultaneous splitting of the body into the body of the mask used for persona behaviour and the body of the true self. This state, in the end, is a disguise of the body. The attempt to behave in a more feminine or masculine way is aggressive and self-defensive, and with the disguise, results in a certain type of strain. This is an issue of the gap between persona and the self. When this gap widens under such strain, the person undoubtedly finds him or herself facing the trap of alienation. Persons who are slaves to a diet of excess and deteriorate in health are exemplary cases. Goffman felt that the splitting of persona and the self was our unique modality of self in a modern consumption-oriented society. Behind the mask of Goffman's performer is not the true self. The performer is constantly changing his or her mask according to social circumstance and role. Behind the mask, another mask appropriate for the next set of circumstances is already prepared. In other words, no matter how many masks are removed, the true self does not appear. Goffman asserts that the mask itself is the pluralistic true self.

From this standpoint, this perspective is appropriate for today's consumption-oriented Japanese society that is dominated by types who are constantly concerned about the appearance of themselves and others. With the constant taking off and putting on of different masks under different circumstances, like a switch assigned too many functions, this modality of the pluralistic self undoubtedly results in exhaustion. Exhausted, the performer is released from his or her performance and, in search of the carefree self, removes mask after mask only to find yet another mask underneath, in fact a multiplicity of selves similar to a Japanese scallion, or a performance of comic faces. However, given that this is all that the self is, the strain felt when a person feels obliged to cling to a persona when the mask (persona) and self are split is understandable. Why? Underneath that persona there is truly nothing.

The real reason the body must perform a gender role lies here: we have come to believe that, in general, we have a separate true body that is different from the body that acts as a mask. Given that the mask body that performs the gender role is referred to as gender, the true body underneath that mask is the body referred to as sex. However, this is, as Goffman predicted, our misunderstanding of ours as we live in a modern society dominated by awareness. We are not normally aware or perplexed by the fact that we each, for example, possess a body. However, this is a curious phenomenon. Why? In principle, we cannot recognize our own bodies. What does this mean? For example, we cannot look directly at our own faces or the back of our heads. Even so, we believe unhesitatingly that these bodies that we have never seen exist.

In phenomenological body related discussions, this is explained as an issue of body ambiguity, i.e. the idea that the body is an object as well as an existence. For example, Merieau-Ponty (1945) states the following:

> The body is not an object. For the same reason the awareness of it is not a thought. That is to say, it is not something I can take to pieces and put together again to form a clear idea of it. Think of it this way. For example, let us say that an artist attempts faithfully to render the world he sees before him in a painting. However, when he tries to do so, there is one thing that he can never render no matter how hard he tries. That is, the artist himself who is painting that world. Even if the artist quickly adds 'the artist who is painting the world' to his canvas, the issue is not resolved. Why? The painter who painted the artist who is painting the world has not been painted. This is due to the fact that the object (or non-ego) attempting to paint the painting is also the subject being painted.

That is, for us, the body always has this type of existence. In principle, recognition of one's own body is not possible since the object recognizing the body is one's own body. This is a great aporia that the awareness-oriented modern day society must face.

The fact that the body is something that cannot be recognized in modern day society leaves us with the insecurity that the body is something that we do not know. For this reason, a mask must be placed on the body. The body must always continue to perform based on gender and role. The critical point here is that the body that performs gender is borne of the emergence of the awareness-oriented modern day society that attempts to process the body as a single object of recognition, as described above. In other words, the body as gender was first created by the era referred to as the modern age. As is generally understood, there is not a gender body of ancient times, a gender body of the Middle Ages nor a gender body of early modern times. The gender body is the product of the modern age.

The information presented thus far can be summarized as follows. First, from Goffman's view of social life as a part in a performance based on a theatrical stage metaphor, masculine and feminine gender roles must always be performed. In addition, this gender performance is two-fold: it must embrace the awareness-oriented principles of modern day society and have the effect of countering insecurities with respect to the body. These requirements indicate well how deep-rooted the gender problem is in modern society. With this in mind, the modernization of Japan which began in the Meiji era also brought forth the formation of the gender body. And the most critical player in this development was a culture that spread by means of the new aspect of the modern school education system: the culture of sports.

## The role of physical education

I would like to first define the term 'sports' as a universal human activity relating to the physical and play, ignoring any such distinctions as nationality, ethnicity and environmental factors. When I use the word sports in this manner, I am not referring to the well-known popularization and spread of modern sports of Western cultures which began in the nineteenth century or the remarkable globalization of sports which ushered in the twenty-first century. Rather, I use this term as defined to more clearly refer to the sports which exist as popular culture in Asian countries, i.e. sports which are completely different from those 'modern sports' of Western culture, which have been positively received in Asian countries through modernization. I use the term, therefore, with nearly the same meaning as 'play' as defined by Huizinga (1938) and Caillois (1958).

In Japan, the first time the body was regarded as a subject of education was around 1840, when exercise was introduced from Western Europe. Naturally, training such as that for martial arts existed in Japan as well. However, martial arts and equestrian arts are first and foremost 'art' lessons. Physical training, on the other hand, requires attention to points of which one is not normally aware. Nevertheless, although the new school education system offered physical education as a subject derived from Western Europe, without knowledge of how to teach it, the instructors taught the course based on a translation of a French physical education handbook.

Preparation of a military force similar to that possessed by the modern states of Western Europe was the prime task of the Meiji government. The army, for this reason, intensively researched and practised methods of physical training. At this time, the physical movement of farmers in Japan was based on *Nanba*, which did not produce the quickness required in battle. *Nanba* refers to a way of walking in which the right foot and right hand, and left foot and left hand are brought forward simultaneously. It is virtually impossible to move quickly when alternately moving the entire left and right sides of the body. That is, the body movements of the Japanese who were mainly from agricultural backgrounds did not involve quick movement such as running.

Movement was not the only body-related difference in the two cultures at that time. Awareness with respect to the body was also quite different. For example, as is seen in Japanese phrases such as *hara ga ookii* (big-hearted), *hara ga tatsu* (to get angry) and *hara wo yomu* (to read a person's thoughts), it is well known that the Japanese do not consider the head as the centre of the body as does Western Europe, but rather the *hara* or stomach. For this reason, with the Westernization of clothing in Japan, there was understandable resistance to the idea of giving up the *obi* (sash) unique to Japanese clothing.

In the formation of a modern nation, the Japanese body had to be transformed. To this end, the government at the time placed much emphasis on the physical education system. In the society of Japan in which there was no custom of getting the body into shape, the physical education system was not well received. The Meiji government who perceived this as a big problem paid attention to the culture of sports that was first introduced as a special school activity. Sports, with its elements of play, was received as a new form of play from a foreign country without much resistance by the people of Japan who were not accustomed to physical training. The government determined it was best to use such sports as part of the physical education curriculum. Thus, due to the Meiji government which thought this way, sports spread throughout Japanese society. It is through sports that the Japanese first began acquiring modern physical techniques, body awareness and, at the same time, the gender body.

In 1900, the compulsory education attendance rate exceeded 90 per cent in Japanese society and the establishment of gyms was virtually widespread. Along with the spread of school education and sports, the transformation of body awareness in society emerged in a number of forms. The cutting off of the topknot proceeded at a somewhat rapid pace among the former *bushido* class, and the Westernization of clothing such as shirts, undergarments, socks, shoes and hats spread among the common people. The Japanese custom of mixed bathing started to fade away. At the time, Japanese bathing customs were regarded as extremely peculiar. For example, one Englishman who visited Japan noted in a description of his stay in Fukui Prefecture that he was shocked when a Japanese woman entered the bath fully naked without the slightest embarrassment in front of him.

It is bewildering that a country where one normally did not see clothing that revealed the chest, as in the West, a person revealed his or her entire naked body in front of another in the bath alone. The custom of mixed bathing in Japan began in the Edo era, enjoying popularity among the common people who referred to such baths as *iregomiyu* (general admission hot bath). However, the Meiji government often attempted to regulate mixed bathing, which was criticized as indecent by foreigners. Although Norbert Elias (1969) identified such manners related to the body as socially and historically regulated behaviours, Japan clearly had a different habitus than the modern day habitus of shame for the body, which was formed in Western Europe. However, with the spread of education and sports, this body unique to the Japanese began to disappear. And, from this time, the gender body began to spread throughout Japanese society as well. That is, Japan acquired the body perspective and body performing gender unique to the modern day society that perceives the heart and body in the framework of the spiritual and material. To this effect, sports became an effective medium for communicating gender. Our energetic performance of the gender roles written by the scriptwriter of modern day society, along with the use of power games, forms the foundation of everyday life. In the attempt to research and discuss sports as a symbol of gender today, we see traces of the large role the culture of sports has played in gender formation.

## Play and performing a gender body

This is not to say that, as a matter of course, performing a gender role is always anguishing. Take, for example a scene related to sexuality. A person looks to sexuality to find eroticism, which is a part of love. However, while often misunderstood, this eroticism is not the animal instinct incorporated in the desire to reproduce. Eroticism involves a certain excess beyond the purpose of reproduction. The meaning of this excess is explained by Georges Batailles (1976) as follows: A transgression of masculinity on femininity as the intentionally fabricated 'taboo' and 'beautiful' – in other words, the violation of everyday forbidden actions such as 'do not touch' or 'do not do' through the behaviour of sexuality. Batailles thinks that the human-originated erotic behaviour is established only in the opposing relationship of the roles of the fabricated taboo and its transgression. Here, even more critical than the details of the gender roles is the opposing nature of gender. In this case, there is no anguish in the gender roles that are produced under the premise of a split persona and self. Man and woman do not stand face to face in a relationship of performer and audience or the watched and watching. The genders are co-actors who together combine their strengths on the stage.

The performance of gender sometimes brings about excitement. This is not because we are in the secular world of selfish and altruistic interests nor, for that matter, because we are in the sacred world of eroticism. We select shirts, put on skirts and pants, adorn ourselves with accessories and choose hairstyles. We are all aware of our preoccupation with processing our bodies as masks. For some reason or another, we find putting on and off different masks (bodies) interesting. Perhaps the fun lies in the transformation. By changing our masks, we get to enjoy a transformation into another body. Here, a body that promotes self-image management through calculation and strategy, as Goffman wrote, does not exist. Roger Caillois (1958) labelled this type of behaviour 'mimicry' and argued that such behaviour is performed in an area of individual significance that is different from the secular or sacred world: that is, the world of play. Gender performance, therefore, opens the door to play.

The trend toward play in the body performing gender is particularly evident in women in the society of Japan today. Take, for example, television programmes. *Aishiteiru to Ittekure* ('Say you love me') was a hit TV drama that was broadcast in Japan during the first half of 1995. (According to video research data, the programme registered a viewer rate in excess of 20 per cent.) The drama is a love story of a painter who lost his sense of hearing at the age of seven and an aspiring young actress. The message of the series is the pursuit of new communication styles symbolized by sign language and the dash towards the finish. The gender roles performed included a tough woman with a diverse self, and a man who is perplexed by this woman. The leading female character oscillates between the painter and a male childhood friend. That is, she 'plays' with the two men. However, the leading female character realizes that oscillation between the two helps her to grow up. She then tries to accept the oscillating self as is. The male painter is continually perplexed by the woman. The last scene of the drama seems to be a happy ending with the oscillation at last at an end, but one wonders if this is just lip service to the audience.

The same message of a tough woman with a diverse self, and a man who is perplexed by this woman, can also often be found in the pop culture of the time, such as in hit songs. For example, the popular pop group Sharan Q in their great hit of the first half of 1995 *Zurui Onna* (Sly Woman) sings *Baibai arigatou sayounara / Itoshii koibito yo / Anta chotto ii onna datta yo / sonobun zurui onna da ne* (Bye-bye, thank you, sayonara / My love, my cherie / You were nice, sure / But just the same you were a sly woman). The man did everything he could for a certain woman. Yet, the woman did not consider a world with that man alone important enough. To this effect, the man was toyed (played) with by the woman. Yet, in the feeling of the language or the feeling of the song, there is no darkness such as blame. The lack of darkness reveals the perplexed state of the man, a certain resignation as if he met that other person, in the true sense of the word, and is standing paralysed like a deer in front of the headlights.

The 'perplexity' and 'resignation' seen in this man is due to the man not seeing a disguise strategy in the woman performing the diverse self, but rather a playful spirit. The word play here also means performance. In Japanese society, playing a body performing gender is certainly prevalent in women. Women have become tougher and stronger to the extent that they know how to diversify and proliferate the female gender body. In comparison, men have become weaker, as is evident, for example, even in sports: the activities in Japan that have reached a world-class level include the marathon, volleyball, judo and synchronized swimming, nearly all of which are female events. That is, women are playing sports well. In this sense, perhaps it can be said that gender performance in sports for women has reproduced the existing gender body and, through gender play, has resulted in a momentum that has reached areas outside the world of sports.

Shiki Masaoka, a well-known writer with an active literary career in the Meiji period, wrote in an essay that while Japan had various forms of play, none was as interesting as the play called sports that was imported from the West. In other words, the importation of sports in Japan conveyed the principles of modern day society, such as awareness-oriented philosophies, the system called the nation state, and power, and – at the same time – spread a very new form of play in the world of the everyday. For this reason, the word *supo-tsu* in Japan has a much broader meaning and scope of significance than the English word sport from which it derived. This is because the element of play is strongly imported as culture. Against the culture of sports that became the medium in which gender was strengthened and reproduced, play with the meaning to have fun was practised at the same time, bringing with it an aspect of gender relativization. Gender is perceived as performative. Judith Butler (1990) also strongly points out the possibility of breaking free from gender where gender is performed as parody. This specific phenomenon can be seen in parts of the sports phenomenon of Japan.

## Potentiality of playfulness on gender issues

With this in mind, the perspective of the body performing gender seems to involve the potential for escaping from gender restraints. The word potential used here does not refer to seriously ripping apart the gender issue, but rather playing with the issue and, through play, shifting the restraints. As mentioned in the beginning of the chapter, gender role theory is premised on the notion of drawing a new boundary between male and female roles. Yet, separate from the 'serious' activities involved in finding this new boundary line, and in order to prevent any gender research from becoming a new authority, perhaps it is possible for us to keep a critical perspective on the concept of gender itself, based on the case of Japan in which gender consideration from a play perspective has been manifested due to the country's later modernization.

At the beginning of the twentieth century, the famous Japanese philosopher Shuzo Kuki (1991), who studied under Bergson and Heidegger in Paris, discussed the differences between Western and Japanese cultures from the viewpoints of inevitability and chance. In his works, Kuki identified respect for ambiguity – or unclarity – and efforts to accept facts that contradict human will or reason as natural as a special characteristic of Japanese culture. Western culture, in contrast, has a strong tendency to try to build personal lives by understanding the world through the concept of human will or reason without recognizing contradictions. I believe this cultural mentality will surely draw out the potentiality of playfulness on gender issues.

## Conclusion

This paper considered new aspects of signifigance in the issues of sports and gender in Japanese society from the viewpoint of 'role', 'body' and 'playfulness', based mainly on a phenomenological perspective. Our face-to-face social life is like a the-atrical performance, as Goffman states, and we must perform the existing masculine and feminine roles precipitated in society. The same holds true for sports. In an awareness-oriented society, we cannot help but have the basic insecurity of perceiv-ing the body as something that we do not know, and it is the genderization of the body that counters that insecurity. From this viewpoint as well, the genderization of sports, which directly involves the body, is in line with the inevitable demands in the everyday life of each individual. And it is here where the foundation on which modern day power acts is born. This is because modern day power is based on a rela-tionship of complicity in crime between power from above and power from below.

However, in Japan which has imported sports with the viewpoint of play, an attribute of play that is present in performance has been brought forth, resulting in a 'shifting' effect on the existing gender structure. Perhaps this is one answer that will resolve the issue of sports and gender as viewed from the world of the everyday. From this viewpoint a change in the relationship between sports, gen-der and society is, at present, eagerly sought.

## References

Bataille, G. (1976) *L'histoire de l'érotisme, Oeuvres complètes de Bataille*, tome 8, Gallimard; trans. K. Sakai (2004) *Erotishizumu*, Tokyo: Tikuma Syobou.

Butler, J. (1990) *Gender Trouble*, New York: Routledge.

Caillois, R. (1958) *Les Leux et Les Hommes*, Gallomard, trans. M. Tada, M. Shinozuka (1990) *Asobi to Ningen*, Tokyo: Koudansha.

Elias, N. (1969) *Über den Prozeß der Zivilisation*, Bern and Munich: Francke, trans. K. Akai *et al.*, 1977, Bunmeika no Katei, Tokyo: Housei Daigaku Syuppank Kyoku.

Goffman, E. (1959) *The Presentation of Self in Everyday Life*, New York: Doubleday Anchor/Harmondsworth: Penguin.

Goffman, E. (1974) *Frame Analysis: An Essay on the Organisation of Experience*, New York: Harper & Row.

Goffman, E. (1979) *Gender Advertisements*, London: Macmillan.

Huizinga, J. (1938) *Homo Ludens: Proeve eener bepaling van het spel-element der cultuur*, Tjeenk Willink & Zoon (trans. H. Takahashi, 1973, *Homo Rudensu*, Tokyo: Tyuoukouron Shinsha).

Kuki, S. (1991) *Kuki Syuzou Daizensyu Dai-ni-kan* (The Complete Works of Kuki Syuzou, vol. 2), Tokyo: Iwanami Syoten.

Mead, M. (1949) *Male and Female: A Study of the Sexes in a Changing World*, New York: W. Morrow.

Merieau-Ponty, M. (1945) *Phénoménologie de la perception*, Gallimard, trans. M. Nakajima(1982) *Chikaku no Gensyougaku*, Tokyo: Housei Daigaku Syuppank Kyoku.

# Part III

# Modernization, globalization and sport

## A critical examination

# Chapter 8

# FIFA 2002 World Cup in Japan

## The Japanese football phenomenon in cultural contexts

*Hitoshi Ebishima and Rieko Yamashita*

## Introduction

Japan has often been regarded as being incompatible with Western societies. This is mainly due to a mutual lack of communication. Japan, which closed its doors to foreigners in its feudal era, possibly had fewer cross-cultural contacts in the past than any of the European nations whose citizens ventured all over the world. However, due to globalization, Japanese people have been aware that they are absorbing foreign cultures. The Japanese have been seeking ways of achieving global recognition. Sports are perceived as having a role to play in this process. The Japan League, or J-League, is a professional football league that was formed in 1993. It followed the model of European football clubs in being based on community level organizations. The Japanese organizers called the plan 'The Hundred Year Construction'. Japan had fallen behind European football standards and this long-term plan was the way it would catch up. Although football had been imported into Japan around a hundred years ago, clubs in Japan did not develop in the way they did in Europe. The best footballers belonged to elite sports schools or club teams sponsored by large enterprises. The popularity of football was therefore restricted to certain spheres. The ordinary people, who had nothing to do with such schools or company clubs, were ignored. It was intended that the J-League would fill the 'hundred year' gap since football was first introduced into Japan. It wanted to make football one of the most popular sports among the public as a whole.

The Japanese football team won a bronze medal at the 1968 Mexico Olympic Games. After this victory, however, the national team became less competitive and did not qualify for the FIFA World Cup, let alone any Olympics, for more than twenty years. In 1965, a non-professional football league, the JSL, consisting of company club teams, was launched. The maximum number of spectators, which was recorded in the year of the Mexico Olympic Games, was 7,491. In 1977, the highest number of spectators had dropped to 1,733. Its popularity was on the wane. The organizer even made a secret agreement that the number of spectators should be misrepresented as being three times more than the actual figure (Hiratsuka, 2002: 30).

In such a situation it seemed to be out of the question to establish a professional football league in Japan. However, the professionalizing of football was on the agenda from 1988. The organizer, the JSL's committee for promoting soccer in Japan, finally decided that the introduction of a professional league was needed and this was based on the assumption that footballers would play better if more supporters came to cheer them on in a professional environment. It also set as its target the hosting of the FIFA 2002 World Cup (Hiratsuka, 2002: 145–148).

The Japan Football Association (JFA), under which the J-League is organized, successfully launched the league in 1993. Some community-based teams, such as the Kashima Antlers in Ibaragi, were very popular with local residents. The J-League games started to attract attention. They also succeeded in Japan being selected as the venue for 2002 FIFA World Cup, as co-hosts with South Korea. The World Cup is not only one of the biggest sporting events in the world, but is also an opportunity for intercultural communications. Japan, as the newcomer to the football world, and one of the first-ever hosts of the World Cup in Asia, exposed itself to the world. Thus, in this chapter, four phenomena which were highlighted during the FIFA 2002 World Cup will be considered: regionalism, nationalism, conflict with a foreign coach and conspicuous female football supporters. These issues may not be unique to Japan, but they do provide key insights into the cultural context of Japanese society.

## Regionalism in Japan

The government of the modern state of Japan concentrated on centralizing its power in Tokyo, the capital city, which means basically that the regional governments do not have financial autonomy. Constantly looking to Tokyo, they gradually lost their distinctive local cultures, which had been many in the feudal era, and these cultures lost their appeal for their communities. Consequently, rural districts in Japan often suffer from declining populations. Boosting the popularity of under-populated towns or villages is an urgent mission for many regional governments. The World Cup was highlighted as an opportunity for them to do this. They saw a possibility of regional revitalization by means of football, as the matches were held not only in large cities like Tokyo or Osaka, but also in many medium-size cities, and even smaller towns and villages were to be used as training camps. Around one hundred regional governments applied for training camp status hosting overseas teams. Eighty-four venues were officially approved, but only twenty-eight venues were actually used by any of the teams.

Those who were not selected as training camp venues still enjoyed indirect benefits. Because their football facilities were regarded as guaranteed by the authority, domestic football teams started to play on these grounds and the number of local football fans also increased. *Kuriyamacho* in Hokkaido (the northern island), for example, entirely renewed the pitch in its stadium at a cost of £314,00.[1] Kuriyamacho's stadium was not used for training by World Cup footballers, but applications to use the venue increased significantly after the World

Cup. The town also attracted large donations for promoting *Kuriyamacho* as a training camp venue. This was not wasted. The money was eventually used to establish a foundation to promote local sporting and cultural activities for children (*Asahi Shimbun*: December 30, 2002).

In addition, local people who lived in camp venues experienced real cross-cultural communications. Among them, was Nakatsuemura, which is located in the mountainous interior of Kyushu (the southern island). It had a population of around 1,360 residents, of whom one quarter were sixty-five years old or over and had never played, or probably seen, football. One of the reasons why the village decided to apply for training camp status was to attract domestic (not foreign) tourists who would spend money in their village. In fact, the facility had been recently refurbished with financial aid from the central government, but the village had little money to maintain it. The aim was to achieve attention from the media by applying to be a training camp, but the village really did not expect to host world-famous footballers. Just being approved as a World Cup training camp venue was sufficient for most of the residents (Sakamoto, 2002: 15).

The Cameroon team, to the villagers' surprise, nominated Nakatsuemura as its camp venue, which was the most remote of all locations. Eventually, with great excitment, half of the villagers worked as volunteers to welcome the team. They even tried to learn French and hand made hats in the colours of the Cameroon flag. The camp was a great success and the villagers enjoyed communicating with the Cameroon footballers, although their arrival had been delayed by several days due to financial and other problems. The team was treated warmly as if the village was its second home. As a result, Nakatsuemura achieved a high reputation all over Japan. The village also developed a strong interest in football and it now has its first-ever football team. The name of the hotel where the Cameroon team stayed was changed to 'Lion Hotel', commemorating the Cameroon 'Lion' footballers. The hill near the training ground was re-named 'The Cameroon Hill'.

Similar cultural exchanges were reported in some of the other training camps and involved not only the promotion of football or foreign cultures. Human exchanges in these venues were gifts to the local people. They gained confidence and became aware of regional revivals.

## Nationalism

The link between football and nationalism has been studied in many countries, especially in Europe. Nationalism is sometimes coupled with hooliganism. There have always been tensions between English and Turkish football fans when a match is held. For the Japanese football supporters, who are newcomers to world football, however, it seemed to be too extreme to relate football to nationalism. In Japan, behaving as a nationalist is a kind of taboo after the bitter experience of the Second World War. Schoolteachers have been prone to object to singing the national anthem or hoisting the Japanese flags at school ceremonies, because they are a reminder of pre-war militarism. While the government tries to oblige them to sing the anthem or hoist the national flag at schools, there is often a difference of opinion between school principals and teachers on this issue. School principals would like to follow the government guideline, while teachers and the majority of parents are afraid of nationalistic influences on their children.

In such circumstances, it was a surprise that young Japanese spectators in football stadiums painted the Japanese *hinomaru*, symbolizing the rising sun, on their cheeks, sang the symbolic national anthem *Kimigayo* (believed to be dedicated to the emperors), and waved the national flag during the 2002 World Cup. The *Hinomaru* flags waved in a stadium were actually given to spectators by the Shinto. This incident seems to be symbolic or partly controversial, as Shinto was the official state religion until the end of the Second World War and one of the Shinto shrines, *Yasukuni*, deifies the war dead. The young supporters, probably not familiar with the past history of Japan, openly cheered the Japanese team, shouting, 'I love Japan' or 'Nippon! (Japan)' and expressed their strong support, which was viewed as openly nationalistic in Japan. Rika Kayama (2002), a psychiatrist, suggested that this phenomenon should be named 'petit-nationalism'. The younger generation is unaware of being nationalist. In this sense, it may be harmless, but it underlined the fact that real nationalism could be evoked. This petit-nationalism discourse caused a sensation in Japan in 2003.

Kayama (2002) analysed the root of this petit-nationalism in the dissociation process. Dissociation, a term drawn from psychiatry, implies to separate people or things in one's thought or feelings. She argued that the young people tended to dissociate their stress or anxiety and repress themselves. In the same way, they dissociate historical events (war) from the present day. They are innocent but irresponsible. But they also need to deal with their accumulated repression. The current young generation in Japan has largely been the victim of the economic structure of the country. The overall average rate of unemployment in 2002, according to the Statistical Bureau, was 5.4 per cent, while the average for the 15–24 age bracket hit 9.9 per cent (the rate for males 15–24 was 11.1 per cent, the highest among all age groups). Even college graduates find it tough to obtain decent jobs. Japan has projected the myth that it is an egalitarian society without social/class divisions. But the young generation these days suffers from being treated as second-class citizens. The young have become alienated from society and less motivated.

The young generation understands that traditional society must change but has no power to change it. Their frustrations are repressed. They could work off their repression and excess energy by actively taking part in festivals or events. Or they could live like hermits. Supporting football may be another answer. In real life they may be reluctant to support the War against Iraq or sing the national anthem at school ceremonies. Unconsciously, however, they could pretend to be nationalists in football stadiums. According to Kayama, their schizophrenic attitudes make it possible to survive in a society full of contradictions.

The World Cup was not the only occasion where petit-nationalism was observed. Japanese culture has boomed in Japan in recent years. Japanese classical literature has enjoyed a revival and even the younger generations find Japanese culture attractive. On the other hand, they show less and less interest in foreign countries, unlike the post-war generations who were keen to absorb foreign culture. They believe in the uniqueness of Japan, with its unique language and geographic isolation. They are convinced that Japanese people are special and no foreigners can understand Japan – thus leading to their nationalistic behaviour. Steven C. Clemens, Executive Vice President of the New American Foundation, also argued:

> Many observers today ... argue that Japan's trademark pacifism is being supplanted by a new robust nationalism, and that Washington and the world need to adjust to both the opportunities and problems of this trend ... . It is true that Japan's nationalism is becoming more evident and obvious to the world. What is not clear, however, is if Japan's nationalism is a new phenomenon, or if the rest of the world is only now awakening to a Japanese nationalism that has been brewing for decades, if not longer
>
> (*Daily Yomiuri*, December 9, 2003)

Kayama's interpretation may be exaggerated, but the phenomenon may be a warning to the Japanese. The political situation in Japan is swinging to the right. The Prime Minister Junichirho Koizumu is a controversial figure in the war disputes. The Tokyo Governor Shintaro Ishihara is one of the most extreme nationalists. Right-wing politicians could take advantage of the petit-nationalism syndrome and lead the country back to extreme nationalism.

## Foreign coaches for the Japanese team

It is not unusual for the success of national teams to be entrusted to foreign hands. In Japan an American coach was invited to manage a professional baseball team with his advanced coaching technology and management skills. Even before the J-League started, semi-professional football teams, such as club teams in universities or companies, were seeking for football knowledge from 'advanced' countries, i.e. European or Latin American countries. The time, however, was not ripe for the national team to do the same until the 1980s: as the team was not competitive internationally. While Japan was trying to lobby for hosting the World Cup in 2002, the JFA decided to place its fate in the hands of a foreign coach.

Dutchman Hans Ooft, the first-ever foreign coach for the Japanese national team, had once given a coaching session when Japanese high school football players had visited Holland. One of the company club teams in Japan, Yamaha, learned that his coaching skill was excellent and asked Ooft to take care of the team. Yamaha won the championship in the league that year and Ooft earned a reputation. Then he coached another company club, Matsuda, for five years between 1984 and 1989. In 1987, the team became the runner-up for the *Tennohai* (Emperor's trophy) Championship, one of the country's biggest football events. In 1991, Saburo Kawabuchi, the then chairman for the JFA, appointed Hans Ooft as national team coach. Kawabuchi commented that Ooft would break down the wall Japanese coaches face. Responding to this expectation, Ooft's team continued winning matches, but narrowly failed to win the Asian qualifying round to go to the World Cup in 1994. Ooft's tactics were autocratic, which was seen as a feature of the European coaching style. It was often reported that the then main players of the team, Kazuyoshi Miura and Brazilian-turned-Japanese Rui Ramos, confronted him. Miura had played in Brazil when he was young and Ramos had Brazilian roots. Hence, the confrontation may be attributed to their preference for the Brazilian coaching style which emphasized individual football skills rather than building good team play.

Ooft did not feel out of place when he became the national coach. He knew the Japanese heterogeneous cultural heritage, as he had already coached some club teams in Japan. But he did criticize the special football environment in Japan. How did he assess problems hindering development of football? According to him, the fact that both coaches and footballers had belonged mainly to company club teams until the J-League started weakened its structure. They were paid whether they won or not. Coaches also tended to hesitate to maintain their own strategies or speak out, being afraid that the media might attack them and their sponsoring companies. These weaknesses inhibited the growth of football in Japan and what Japanese footballers needed was strong management. Sebastian Moffett who wrote about the Japanese football environment in his book *Japanese Rule* also pointed out:

> Though the advent of the J-League turned football into a symbol of a more liberal Japan, it had previously been taught with the same grim ethos as every other sport there. Sport in Japan was not about playing games or having fun, but was a tool of education. It taught children about obedience and hierarchy in an organization, as well as how to withstand the pain of long training sessions. This made sport the ideal preparation for life working in a Japanese company, which highly valued the ability to work well in a group, accept strict hierarchy and tolerate punishing work hours. More than brains and learning, recruiters always looked for graduating students who had been active in college sports clubs.
>
> (Moffett, 2002: 92)

Ooft stayed in Japan after his resignation as the national team coach in 1993 and took up coaching positions in several J-League teams until 2003. The previous coach, Brazilian Paulo Roberto Falcan, took over the position of coach to the Japanese national team, but he did not last long. Unlike Ooft, he had never coached in Japan before and communication with Japanese footballers was a huge problem. The team did not improve its competitiveness either and this famous Brazilian coach soon left. Two Japanese coaches, Shu Kamo and Takeshi Okada, followed Falcan and they made remarkable progress. Under the direction of Okada, for the first time the Japanese team qualified for the World Cup in France in 1998. The team, however, lost all its matches in the first round, which led to Okada's resignation.

Frenchman Philippe Troussier was a controversial appointment as coach to the Japanese team. He was appointed by the JFA to prepare for the 2002 World Cup. He had gained his reputation as a successful coach in South Africa but was known as a player and had no experience of Japan. The JFA may have intended to 'break down the wall' with the help of a foreign coach again, as Hans Ooft had been expected to do. Foreign coaches, by then, had always been compared to Japanese coaches. It was a confrontation between Japanese culture and foreign culture, and they seemed to be poles apart. Troussier conformed to this picture of confrontation . He typically regarded the Japanese culture and Japanese people as being heterogeneous and irreconcilable with those of the West. Japan, as a land of the Orient, was incompatible for this man from the Occident. Most of his comments tended to be alienating based on cultural differences. For example, he said that facial expressions of Japanese footballers were different from those of European or African footballers, which led to a lack of communications for team play. He was also appalled that Japanese footballers showed no emotions even when they won a match. Nobody sang a song or cheered in the locker room. The Japanese footballers may be professional in terms of conforming to training programmes and strategies, but Troussier, as a European, felt something was missing.

Feeling culturally isolated, Troussier concluded that he was being treated unfairly in Japan just because he was a foreigner. The faceless, hence inhuman, image of Japanese society, lacking communication skills, was enhanced by his media experience. Troussier showed a strong dislike of the Japanese media. Journalists, especially those writing for tabloid-like sports newspapers, chased him everywhere. For Troussier, it was like being tailed by a shadowy detective. He did not feel any human-to-human relationship. Asked whether the media pressure in Japan hindered him in his work, he answered that the public in Japan had a significant lack of footballing culture because the sport was reduced to four megastars and the daily broadcast of three or four seconds of promotional images. He also added that Japan was a special kind of culture where football was perceived in a wholly different way (FIFA World Cup com., May 27, 2002).

He later expressed an understanding of the need to be moderate in Japanese society. This, however, was only a barrier to winning football matches, according to him. European individualism versus Japanese conformity, was always an issue in the Japan–West conflict. Troussier's opinion was that it seemed to be impossible to develop individualism in Japan. He insisted that such an environment was not ideal for playing football. He said that managing the Japanese team was more than technique or tactics of football, because he had to deal with the tendency of Japanese people to stick with their knowledge and be inflexible. He found a wall around Japanese society. The Japanese people believe that they should conform to norms and rules set out by society without any doubts. 'If the traffic light is red, nobody dares to cross the road in Japan even if there are no cars at all', said Troussier. Evidence of inflexibility, he thought.

Troussier found negative aspects in Japanese footballers and criticized what he saw from his Western viewpoint as their 'immature' attitudes. For this he was attacked even more by the Japanese media. Journalists wrote as if Troussier denied not only the ability of Japanese footballers but also the whole Japanese culture. It may have been true that some Japanese footballers were not getting along well with Troussier and left him out in the cold. Troussier, being more aggressive to the media, became an enemy and the media continued to represent a false image of him. The initial contract with Troussier was due to expire in June 2000. The Japanese youth football team (under 21s), which was also coached by Troussier, started to prove their competitiveness, but the national team did not seem to be successful. The JFA hinted at Troussier's dismissal. Amazingly, it was some of the young Japanese supporters who stood by Troussier, in spite of his overall negative attitudes towards Japan. They even blamed the JFA for its bureaucracy and irresponsibility (Hayashi and Kuzuoka, 2002: 156). Troussier himself was surprised at the supporters' reaction and discovered that he was regarded as a guide for the young Japanese generation which could not find its own way in a closed society (Cointot, 2001: 248).

When Troussier was appointed as a national coach in 1998, Japan was suffering from the recession after the collapse of the 'bubble' economy. Japanese standards, such as life-long employment or the seniority-based system in companies, which had contributed to the stability of the Japanese economy after the Second World War, became invalid. Older generations lost their security, while the younger generation felt a gap. The younger generations were searching for a new global standard, which may explain why they agreed with Troussier's anti-Japanese views. Troussier's conflict with the authorities, i.e. the JFA, reflected the younger generations' conflict with the older generations. Troussier eventually remained as the national coach until the 2002 World Cup. Under his direction, Japan won its first-ever match in the World Cup and qualified for the last sixteeen matches. Troussier's ability was highly admired during the World Cup, even by the media.

Troussier said that he intentionally generated a conflict between himself and his team players so that they could develop a fighting spirit. In this way, he did not compromise with the Japanese culture and fully maintained his Frenchness. He had a dedicated interpreter or personal assistant, a Frenchman, who accompanied him everywhere and translated all of his words. He did not feel the necessity to learn the language to communicate directly with his team. In fact, he had a hard time in Japan, coming into conflict with the football authority and the media. The Japanese football players, too, had the bitterest experiences of him. Troussier actually encouraged the younger players to neglect the traditional seniority-based system and be equal in the team. But, in a way, they were thrown into the Orientalism discourse too suddenly. Troussier provided them an overview of Western attitudes towards the East, and the Japanese players who had been actually been brought up in the Western environment, were at a loss. How are we different? And how should we behave? They learned not only football skills, but also cultural gaps from this Frenchman. Troussier's relationship with Japanese footballers mirrors cultural problems Japan has been facing: the old generation versus the new generation, or the traditional values versus Western values.

Brazilian star Zico replaced Troussier after the World Cup in 2002. Zico had played first and then became general manager for the J League team Kashima Antlers in 1991. He was very much liked by Japanese football fans and his communication skills with the players seems to be fairly good (he even speaks Japanese). There has been some speculation, however, whether he can manage the Japanese team as strictly as Troussier did. The Japanese media seems to be too graceful to Zico, one of the greatest players in the world, and he may be too spoiled. The result has yet to be seen. Both Ooft and Troussier, who left behind reputations as successful foreign coaches, were critical of the Japanese football environment. They evoked cultural conflicts, between the East and the West, which also drew media attention. Troussier, especially, showed his strong discontent and the Japanese media condemned him for his eccentricity, though the young generation partly supported Troussier's argument. After the 2002 World Cup, the media praised Troussier's ability in breaking down cultural obstacles and introducing a new regime. He was often compared to another successful foreigner in Japan, Carlos Ghosn, the President of Nissan Motor Company, who was perceived as haviang worked a miracle in staging a recovery for the company. The Japanese people may have wanted barriers to be broken down, but not from inside. It had always been pressure from abroad which could change Japanese society, like *Kurofune* or the Black Ships of the American squadron, which urged the country to change its isolation policy and open up to foreign trade as well as diplomatic relations in the late nineteenth century.

## Female football fans in Japan

The most noteworthy feature for the foreign media during the 2002 World Cup was the remarkable attendance of Japanese female spectators as well as the strong support for foreign teams. Young Japanese supporters enthusiastically cheering non-Japanese teams was unfamiliar to the international press. One of the favourites in Japan, to its own surprise, was the English team. Supporters wore English uniforms and painted St George crosses on their faces. Such an enthusiastic strong support for overseas countries seems to be unique to Japan. 'Usually with England the locals tend to be hostile or fearful but here there is a genuine warmth towards us', said Gavin Burnage of the Football Supporters' Association. 'People have gone out of their way to show us around, the police have given us presents and we have been invited to come back and stay' (The *Guardian*, June 21, 2002).

Female supporters were also conspicuous. The Leicester Group in the UK has been prominent for its research into football hooliganism and discerned that hooliganism is rooted in *machismo*. This may be applicable to most European countries. Football is deemed to be an enemy by the majority of women, to say nothing of feminists. In Japan, however, football and *machismo* are not all part of the same ethos. On the contrary, female supporters were dominant when star footballers such as David Beckham played in matches. Footballers were treated as pop idols. David Beckham captivated a large number of Japanese supporters. Youngsters imitated his Mohawk hairstyle. Hundreds of English official team uniforms immediately became out of stock in one shop (World Sports Plaza Shibuya East). Approximately 20,000 copies of Beckham's autography, which was translated into Japanese, were sold in Japan, and it was listed as a bestseller. Female fans in all generations, including in their forties and fifties, followed him around. The British newspapers wrote up this 'strange' phenomenon in the land of the rising sun.

What was behind these phenomena? Three interviews with enthusiastic female supporters conducted at the end of 2002/early 2003 illustrate what was involved. Y, a full-time employee, is in her late thirties and single.[2] She has been into football for more than ten years, even before the J-League boomed in Japan. We have included part of our conversation with her below. This is presented as a form of extended narrative in order to capture the complexity of their support for foreign teams and players:

Q: When did you first encounter football?
A: When the World Cup was held in Italy in 1990, I watched the games every day – they were actually broadcast at midnight. I found them exciting. I became fascinated by football outside of Japan. But after watching some real J-League games in stadiums, I got to know the thrill of seeing the whole game. Besides some Japanese club teams, I followed non-Japanese national teams such as England or Italy. At the beginning, I backed a particular footballer, but then gradually developed an interest in football as a sport.
Q: Do you watch the match by yourself?
A: Basically I go to matches by myself, but sometimes with friends, whom I got acquainted with on the Internet. They are purely 'football'-dedicated companions. Recently I went to the match, Japan versus Argentina. I saw many female groups in the stadium. They were not interested in the football match. They just yelled in shrill voices, only supporting particular footballers. It was devastating. During the World Cup, I also went to the match where the English team played. Female spectators knew nothing about the team except David Beckham. Why on earth did they come to watch the match? These 'out-of-the blue' fans are nothing but a nuisance. Football is not a pop star concert.
Q: You are also interested in the J-League matches, but why do you think many female supporters follow non-Japanese footballers only?

A: Well, honestly speaking, they (mainly the Westerners) are good looking. If you do not understand what they say, handsome footballers would keep their positive images, too. Also, these supporters would like to boast 'I am different from the others, because I support the English team, not the Japanese'.

H, a contract employee, is in her late twenties and single.[3] She is a fanatical fan of the Irish team. Before getting involved in football, she stayed in Galway, Ireland, for a few months to study English. This provided the motivation to follow the Irish.

Q: Can you explain how you supported the Irish team during the World Cup?
A: I was working on a contract basis because it is easy to quit the job. So I left my job before the World Cup kicked off. My trip started with Izumo where the Irish team had their training camp. My friend and I drove a car all the way from Tokyo to Izumo for many hours and we were in time to welcome the team at the local airport. On the second day, we visited the training stadium and asked for the autograph of the available players. I was lucky enough to be given the present of a spare uniform by one player. We also met a group of Irish people who live in Japan. They taught us some supporters' songs. I watched the first Irish match against Cameroon in the stadium from the Cameroon side. I could not share the feeling with other Irish supporters, but on the way back home I enjoyed conversations with them on the train. Then the Irish team moved to the hotel in Chiba (near Tokyo) for their next match, so did I. I did not have a ticket for the match against Germany. It was a dramatic one ending up in a draw. I watched the match on telly and joined the Chiba crowd afterwards. Can you believe I was mingling with the team and supporters in the party held at the hotel? My friend and I actually had a series of tickets for the Portugal group. We flew to Seoul and stayed in a weekly rental apartment (it is much cheaper!) for nineteen days. I could manage to get a ticket for the last Irish match against Spain. I really enjoyed it, as I was together with the Irish groups. I was not impressed by South Korean supporters' aggressive behaviour, keeping on booing through the matches. I was cheering Spain, then Germany. I did not want the South Korean team to come over to Japan for the final.
Q: When did you get interested in football?
A: I watched the Champions League matches on TV. As Ireland has been my favorite country, I was thrilled to know that Roy Keane, the team captain of Manchester United, was Irish. Then I had a chance to see the programme called 'The Serie A Digest', covering the renowned Italian League. I fancied some of the footballers. Good-looking men were the main attraction at the beginning. After I got to understand more about the game, I became interested in competitive footballers.
Q: Why did you not support the Japanese team?
A: I do not like doing what other people do. I want to be independent.

M, currently studying at a technical college, kept company with H during the World Cup.[4] She is in her mid-twenties and also single. She had actually been supporting the Italian team since her teens. It is she who introduced H to football. This time she shared the enthusiasm for the Irish team with her long-term friend. She resigned her job before the World Cup, too.

Q:   When did you start getting interested in football?
A:   I fell in love with Roberto Baggio who was then playing with AC Milan. I read everything about him and watched the televised Toyota Cup match, when he came to Japan. Then I saw the Championship final on TV. It was Bayern FC versus Manchester United. Manchester United won and came to Japan. This time I bought a ticket. It cost ¥25,000 (£130)[1], far more expensive than the official price, as I got it in an auction shop. I started subscribing to pay TV in order to watch all Manchester matches. But I also have a liking for the Real Madrid, as the members were all good looking. Then I saw 'Serie A Digest' on TV. I really loved the Italian footballers. In 2000, I travelled around Italy in the summer. It was unfortunately off-season. I gathered information on the Internet and found that an unofficial match was held at the AC Milan chairman's mansion and open to public. Of course, I went to watch it. Then Real Madrid came to Japan. This time I bought a ticket on an Internet auction, costing ¥20,000 (£105)[1], which was actually five times more expensive than the official price. I even stayed in the same hotel as the team and I went to see their training sessions.
Q:   Why do you not support the Japanese team at all?
A:   I am not nationalistic. Even for the Olympic Games, I usually do not support any Japanese athletes. If Japan and Italy have a football match, I go for Italy. I always watch their games, so their faces seem to be more familiar than any Japanese footballers. I find the J-League matches rather poor quality. The supporters are also old-fashioned, just like noisy baseball fans. I do not like middle-aged male supporters who behave badly in the stadium.

Interestingly, all three of the interviewees developed their interest in football through an indirect medium: television. They had actually never seen live matches, professional or non-professional, until they went to a big international game in the stadium. The classic television programme is called *Mitsubishi Diamond Soccer* and showed European football matches from the early 1970s. Then NHK, or the Japan Broadcasting Corporation, the only state-own television station in Japan, broadcast the World Cup matches for the first time in the late 1970s. Other national stations, terrestrial and satellite, started covering the Italian, Spanish or English leagues in the 1990s. Football programmes covering foreign games are now thriving. The media coverage has had a big impact on potential football supporters in Japan.

    The first motivation for the interviewees becoming attracted to football was also nearly identical: good-looking footballers, in this case all were Caucasians from Europe. But they all said that they later developed their interest in football itself and started judging players not by their appearance, but by their skill. Two of them, M and H who are in their twenties, quit their jobs so that they could concentrate on watching the World Cup matches. This was not extreme because they wanted to have a few free days. For many company employees in Japan, it is difficult to take more than a week off. A paid holiday is becoming a mere name. Finding another job after quitting may be possible in their twenties, but awfully difficult in their thirties and later, particularly for women. M re-entered a college to study, while H remains a contract employee. Contract employment is insecure under Japanese Labour Law, which mainly protects full-time workers only. In other words, if they want to have free time and do not seriously need to earn a living (many young women live with their parents), working on a contract basis is ideal.

They all started watching the matches before 1993. After the J-League was launched, however, they continued following the leagues overseas (in Europe). The quality of football may be one of the factors behind this decision. The media was becoming more and more borderless due to globalization and technical advances. Nowadays, TV programmes all over the world can be watched through pay satellite channels. Like these three interviewees, the audience can acquire a discerning eye not by watching matches live, but through TV. Because the J-League was still in the embryo stage, the quality gap with the European leagues was apparent. The only way to make the lower quality J-League attractive could be by grass-root level exchanges with other local clubs. They also hesitate to go to the J-League matches because of the typical male supporters. Male, especially middle-aged male supporters, were noisy and sometimes intoxicated. They also forced everyone to sing or cheer together – which is the common scene in baseball matches. Baseball is deemed to be the national sport of Japan and many men follow certain teams. In other words, baseball is categorized as a symbol of the 'old' generation, while football is the spirit of the 'new' generation. The old generation represents the conservative male dominated society that has oppressed women in Japan. They have been particularly disliked by the young female group such as these interviewees. The formula for male audience = macho (old generation) underpinned the interviewees dislike of the J-League. In Europe, on the other hand, the formula transforms to 'footballers and hooligans = macho', which also keeps female audiences away from football matches.

Yet, the J-League stadiums have been filled with a larger number of women and children compared to any European leagues. It was reported that the audience in Japan consisted of 60 per cent male and 40 per cent female, at the same time 50 per cent in their teens/twenties and less than 30 per cent in their thirties (Takahashi, 2002: 194–195). Although some women, such as these interviewees, hesitate to go to domestic matches, the J-League has succeeded in attracting many female supporters. Another remarkable similarity between the interviewees is the fact that they are critical about the impromptu female supporters such as the fans of David Beckham. They clearly distinguished themselves from this group, although for most of the spectators or press, both may look identical. The overall impression that everyone was frantic about David Beckham during the World Cup, as repeatedly reported in TV programmes and newspapers, may be a biased image.

The interviewees can be categorized as a new group of football supporters. They are neither nationalistic (rather anti-nationalistic) nor impromptu capricious fans of a certain footballer. They are independent and active women, far different from a traditional stereotype of Japanese 'obedient and dependent' women, as they dare to go to matches by themselves, gather information using high technologies such as the Internet, get tickets from various sources, and travel abroad to watch matches. They have comprehensive knowledge of games and have liked football for a long time. This group could be valuable supporters for the J-League and the Japanese national team, if their matches attract them.

## Conclusion

The FIFA 2002 World Cup proved a great success. The Japanese organizers recorded a profit of nearly £30 million.[1] Japan and South Korea were widely acclaimed for their achievement. On a more profound level, however, Japanese domestic issues, large and small, were exposed. These included regional problems, nationalism, difficulties in cross-culture communications, generation gaps, gender issues, and social value issues. In addition, the World Cup was held when Japan was going through the worst recession since the Second World War. The unemployment rate continued to rise and the people lost confidence. The next day after the Turkish team had beaten the Japanese in the quarter-final, three of the largest national newspapers were loud in praise: 'Well done and thank you' (*Asahi Shimbun*, June 19, 2002), 'We appreciate and applaud them' (*Mainichi Shimbun*, June 19, 2002), 'The Japanese team gave us power' (*Yomiuri Shimbun* June 19, 2002). The metaphor intended to be drawn from these articles was that the achievement of the Japanese team would symbolize future economic recovery. The *Yomiuri Shimbun* article concluded: 'The long-term strategy, which was implemented in the Japanese team, was the key to the success. This was a message to the Japanese people currently living in stagnation. The message is that we can do it. If we continue building up a competent system in the world, the economy will recover. We had the energy of these young footballers.'

The target readers of this article seemed to be middle-aged males, or the 'old' generation, who used to play a key role in realizing the economic miracle of Japan. They were proud of their achievement, but deplored the current economic situation. But how does the younger generation feel about the implication that football is being used as a metaphor for Japan's economic recovery? It seems that youngsters just watch and enjoy football as a pure sport and nothing will change through it. They do not know how Japan was when the economy was at its peak. Do they need to be given 'power' to deal with the recession by means of football? The answer seems to be, no. The generation gap may be deeper than it was thought to be. The Japanese press is also prone to emphasize too much the economic factors of the World Cup. But the World Cup brought something more than money. Though problems are present, we envisage opportunities for grass-root international exchanges, a wider variety of spectators including females, potential interests in playing football, and further improvements of stadium and club houses. In this way, Japan will confront the second stage of its development in the football world.

## Notes

1 Exchange rate as of December 21, 2003.
2 Interviewed in November 2002.
3 Interviewed in December 2002.
4 Interviewed in January 2003.

## References

Cointot, J. P. (2001) *Troussier Le Marginal*, trans. Sato Udagawa and Yoko Yoshimura (2001) Itanji Troussier, Tokyo: Kadokawa Shoten.

Hiratsuka, A. (2002) *Karappo no Sutajiamu karano Chousen* (A Challenge from Empty Studia), Tokyo: Shougakukan.

Hayashi, S. and Kuzuoka, T. (2002) *Soccer wo Chiteki ni Tanoshimu* (Intellectually Enjoying Football), Tokyo: Kobun-sha.

Kayama, R. (2002) *Puchi-nationalism Shokogun* (The Petit-nationalism syndrome), Tokyo: Chuou Koron Shinsha.

Moffett, S. (2002) *Japanese Rules: Why the Japanese Needed Football and How They Got It*, London: Yellow Jersey Press.

Sakamoto, Y. (2002) *Cameroon ga Yattekita; Nakatsue-mura Sonchou Funsennki* (Cameroon Has Arrived: The Diary of the Mayor of Nakatsue Village), Tokyo: Sendenkaigi.

Takahashi, Y. (2002) 'Soccer spectators and fans in Japan', in E. Dunning, P. Murphy, I. Waddington and A. E. Astrinakis (eds) *Fighting Fans: Football Hooliganism as a World Phenomenon*, Dublin: University College Dublin Press.

# Chapter 9

# Physical cognition in sport
## Wisdom buried in modernization

*Hideki Nishimura*

## Introduction

The wisdom of modern science segregates subject and object and grasps the latter by structuralization through the means of 'logos' – universal, unitary and objective language. Wisdom in sport, on the other hand, results from an active–passive interaction between subject and object. And it grasps the totality of the object without regarding the relations between various parts. These points indicate, so to speak, a mode of physical cognition. This chapter, positing that wisdom in sport is part of a wisdom that has been buried in the process of modernization, explains the characteristics of this kind of wisdom and enquires into its importance.

## Wisdom in science and wisdom in sport

The wisdom of science segregates subject and object perfectly in order to be universal, unitary and objective. It therefore makes possible the use of logical and deductive evidence. This frees mankind from irrational restraints and makes life more comfortable, but by changing the sensibility of mankind it also obliterates the vivid and intimate relationship between mankind and the environment. Nakamura (1979: 53) asserts that 'in modern civilization there emerged a distance between man and nature, a distance giving an advantage to eyesight and resulting in the objectification of nature'. He further says that this objectification of nature by eyesight had been advanced remarkably wherever science and technology were developed conspicuously, but that 'while all that was watched and known was objectified and abstracted, the watcher and knower had an outlook that objectified and governed all that was watched and known'.

The world has been objectified and separated from the subject. Science can no longer have any aim but the meaningless progress of inhuman expert technique, and it quantifies even the sensibility of mankind. A physics that respects utility can quantify colour and sound as movements of material, but what it misses then is the sensibility of mankind that has no relation to molecules and particles. Michel Henry (1987) calls the scientific self-righteousness that excludes such sensibility 'barbarism'. Thus the environment that had been in vivid, intimate relation to mankind was objectified, quantified, divided and made an object of human aggression. In attacking, splitting, changing, pulverizing things and animals (and, periodically, also men), man extends his dominion over the world and advances to ever richer stages of civilization (Marcuse, 1956: 52). Human aggression is thus elevated. As Marcuse (1956: 87) observes: 'And the fact that the destruction of life (human and animal) has progressed with the progress of civilization, that cruelty and hatred and the scientific extermination of men have increased in relation to the real possibility of the elimination of oppression – this feature of late industrial civilization would have instinctual roots which perpetuate destructiveness beyond all rationality'.

If this aggression towards the environment is suppressed, the superego tends to become more aggressive to the ego. When the superego controls its aggression towards the outside world, it becomes increasingly strict and gives excessively moralistic orders to the ego. Persecuted, the melancholic ego falls into anxiety over death (Freud, 1940). This objectification of the world is the source of environmental pollution and destruction, as well as disease of mind – mental illness. The rise of the wisdom of modern science has buried the wisdom resulting from the interaction between subject and object. Nakamura (1993a) calls these two kinds of wisdom the 'wisdom of northern Europe' and the 'wisdom of southern Europe'. The wisdom of northern Europe is primarily a product of the Netherlands, Germany, France and England. It is the modern wisdom comprising the trinity of Protestantism, capitalism and natural science, and it has revolutionized human life by governing things and the environment rationally. But to be universal and accurate, it has had to exclude feeling and taste and be serious, stern, and ascetic.

The wisdom of southern Europe, in contrast, is essentially the tradition of mind in Naples and has been excluded by the wisdom of northern Europe. It is a cosmological grasp of the world: a way of thinking in symbolism that sees signs not as unitary but as polymerous, a way of thinking that attaches importance to performance as interaction of the subject and object. It grasps the object as an 'image' synthetically. This image can throw light upon the abundant meanings of things, can respond to the multilayered reality of human life and can produce a wisdom of innovation and creativity. Furthermore, in this image is a physical wisdom that can be grasped by 'somatic sensation' (Nakamura, 1979: 109) – that is, by the senses of touch, heat, pain and kinesthesia (i.e. the inner perception of a spinal nervous system).

Nakamura (1993b) calls the wisdom of southern Europe 'theatrical wisdom' because it indicates an organic and dynamic human world, and calls it the 'wisdom of pathos' because it is associated with the reactions of the object (i.e., passivity). According to Nakamura, the sciences having such wisdom are psychiatry, cultural anthropology, comparative behavioural science and symbology. Based on clinical or field work, exponents use the dynamic interaction between the body and the world to show us the hidden depths of reality which commonly we easily perceive.

The wisdom of modern science systematizes all phenomena by using a strong logic, stripping them of their individuality. As a result, they are not unique and the abundance of reality is forgotten. We must, instead, find as many logics as there are phenomena. We need a wisdom that does not lose the concreteness of sense and yet is rational. To attain that kind of wisdom we must enter into various realities and must experience their worlds. Nakazawa (1989) says that 'To reform, we must ourselves become anomalous subjects, enter a heterogeneous space of power and there continue our unending effort to learn how we should live'. It is in this context that the sciences mentioned above are based on the wisdom of pathos.

Piaget (1945) found that a potential cognition operating through 'somatic sensation', which is an inner perception the body possesses, is already evident in babies. In this 'sense-motion intelligence' that begins the development of intelligence, the constitution of reality is 'entirely dependent on perception and motion'. That is, the somatic sensation (physical sensation) gained by moving the hands and feet to touch the external world is gathered and structuralized as a cognitive schema by which the external world is grasped and ordered. This regenerative and functional assimilation of a schema is 'functional play' (play of practice), and it brings a baby functional pleasure. Playing with clay and with toys such as building blocks is important in this context because it results in the accumulation of intelligence based on the development of somatic sensation.

This cognition by somatic sensation is not limited to babyhood. It is thought that cognition is fundamentally associated with physical practice. Ikuta (1990) notes that Junzo Karaki said that reading with the intention to understand a systematic set of facts used to be accompanied by physical activity. It was, for example, recommended in *sudoku* (a method of reading to follow the voice of a master), that the reader put return marks and katakana opposite the big ideographs on a wood-block print of the Nice Chinese Classics, and was a method of reading with a fan in one's hand. Ikuta also says that real human wisdom is always the result of physical practice, regardless of whether the objective is the understanding or the physical exercise. Wisdom in sport seems to be based on this kind of cognitive operation, on the potential commitment of the body to the external world. Moreover, in the point that the whole body is committed to the world and the situation is understood immediately, wisdom in sport exemplifies the characteristics of the wisdom of southern Europe.

## The sensation of water when swimming

To swim well and fast, one needs to grasp a sense of the water. As Nakai (1975) said:

> We cannot understand the crawl stroke by simply looking at hundreds of photographs of the form of swimmers using this stroke. In the drill extending over a long period we must instead find ourselves swimming in feeling

(mood), as when we entrust ourselves to the water and float on it easily. Continuing to swim in this way – comfortably and effortlessly – we can understand the form of the crawl. When we can capture such a feeling as entrusting ourselves to the water limply or such a comfortable and delightful feeling that we cannot express it, it is a beautiful feeling. Or more than this, a sense of beauty. Our body has groped and found an inevitable rule, an unmistakably clear mode, form, model.

This 'feeling such as entrusting ourselves to the water' – a sense of beauty – is the sign of a swimmer in harmony with the water. It is not the feeling of a swimmer who controls the water by grasping it as an object and working on it. The swimmer must work on the water in accordance with the condition of the water, in accordance with the response the swimmer derives from the water by touching it.

When one's body is in water, the force of gravity acts on the water by the body sinking. On the other hand, buoyancy acts on the body to make it float. The position of the centroid – that is the centre of gravity – differs between adults and children, men and women, and the fat and slender. That is, it differs by virtue of the different figures and compositions of various bodies – the various proportions of bone, fat and muscle. Similarly, the position of the centre of buoyancy varies between individuals because of their unique characteristics. While the centre of gravity is generally in the lower half of one's body because that is the half that has larger muscles, the centre of buoyancy is in the upper half of one's body because that is the half containing lungs filled with air. A beginner swimmer's legs therefore sink, and the beginner swims slowly and inefficiently. When we can swim comfortably by using strokes, to swim easily and fast, the centre of buoyancy must be shifted backward and placed near the centre of gravity so that the lower half of the body receives more buoyancy. For that purpose, one must work on the water by making up one's own original posture appropriate to forward movement. Each swimmer will assume this posture by working on the water in accordance with the buoyancy with which the water responds.

Moreover, when a person moves his body to swim, reaction and (dynamic) lift together produce thrust. Until the latter half of the 1960s, the theory of propulsion by reaction was advocated. According to this theory, swimmers move forward in reaction to their pushing water backwards. But in the early 1970s it was shown that, since many of the strokes of the world's best swimmers include motions in transverse and longitudinal directions, lift must be a major part of thrust. Lift is a force that floats a moving body, and the purpose of motions in transverse and longitudinal directions is to turn a flow of water downward in order to receive that force. This is similar to the way that the wings of an airplane use the wind on take-off. But, in certain circumstances, the motion that produces a swimmer's lift brings forth a resistance that prevents thrust. Avoiding this defiance is important for reasons similar to those that make important the increasing of both resistance and lift.

Thus, a swimmer moves his body in accordance with all aspects of the water in which he swims, apprehending them with his body through its interactions with the water. However, the several elements making up the aspects of water – reaction, lift, counter-force, etc. – are not grasped as individually distinct. They are grasped as an undifferentiated whole, and the motion of body is thus determined on the basis of such an inclusive sense as the swimmer's perception that 'this degree is good'.

## Physical perception of the external world

The sensation that grasps the condition of the water interactively and wholly is nothing more than physical sensation. This sensation is the inner perception of the spinal nervous system. The somatic sensation we use in sport is a central one that includes skin sensation represented by touch sensation and kinesthesia represented by muscular sensation. This somatic sensation as an inner perception is the consciousness with which we feel the condition of our body from the inside. This consciousness on the inside of our bodies is continuous with our perception of the external world. That is, there is a relation by which somatic sensation as an inner perception comes into existence through our perception of the external world. For example, we perceive part of the external world (e.g. the ground) by standing on it, and at the same time we also feel our feet from the inside. Swimmers perceive part of the external world by working on the water they swim in, and at the same time they also feel their bodies from the inside by the buoyancy, reaction and lift they receive in response to their work.

Wisdom by somatic sensation is a wisdom that is obtained by interaction between the world and the body. It is wisdom that grasps the totality of the external world in terms of inner perception by interacting with the external world. Because the inner perception of the body is individually subjective and is not distinctive, the external world that is grasped by it is characterized by a totality of aspects whose interrelations cannot be explained by 'logos'. Let us now consider some concrete examples.

To improve the technique with which we execute a shot in basketball, we must grasp the sensation of what is called touch. It is the feeling we have when we throw the ball with our hands with such strength and in such a such direction. In this case, conditions of the external world like the distance to the basket, the direction of the basket and the weight of the ball are replaced by the sensation of touch. That is, by judging the conditions of the external world totally and subjectively, we replace them with the feeling we have when we throw the ball. And, by repeatedly learning from the success or failure of our shots, we learn the proper sensation of touch. This sensation of touch is the perception of the external world gained from the result of learning whether or not a thrown ball goes through the hoop. At the same time, it is the inner sensation that the reaction produced by throwing a ball brings to our hands.

Thus, we build up an active–passive relational structure in which the sensation of the external world and the inner perception intersect each other. This structure occupies a space between the subject and the object (the external world). That is, the sensation of touch is a sensation of the external world but is also an inner perception. Building up this active–passive structure, our inner perception grasps a total aspect of the external world properly and improves our shot technique.

## Body extent and the external world

Such an interaction between a subject and the external world is not limited to cases in which the subject comes into contact with the external world, as in the above mentioned examples of swimming and basketball. Something similar can occur when the subject is distant from the external world. The interaction in this case is performed through an extension of the body. Ichikawa (1975: 17–18) says that the 'body as subject' (the body that lives from the inside and grasps itself directly) does not have any external limit and extends beyond the skin. The body of the skilled surgeon extends to the pointed end of the probe he wields, and he perceives the external world with that pointed end. Similarly, the body of a driver extends to the size of the car he is driving, and the extent of that car is internalized into his body space.

Thus, the body perceives the external world by extending, and what we have in this case is the 'active-conversational grasp of the object by which the subject not only receives a stimulus from the object but also questions the object and receives an answer' (Ichikawa, 1975: 17–18). That is, the subject grasps the object by means of the interaction between the subject and the object. This is possible because, as stated before, the inner perception can link us to our perception of the external world. As Ichikawa (1975: 35–36) says, 'the body in opposition to otherness is a form of grasping one's own body by means of otherness'. When we pass our hand over the edge of a desk, we are aware of the sharp corner and of a rough feeling on the edge of the desk. At the same time, we feel our own hands by touching the desk. The perception of the external world is at the same time the perception of the inner world. To touch is to be touched at the same time. Activity easily changes into passivity, and passivity changes into activity. Hiromatsu (1989) expresses such an aspect of experience when he refers to 'an aspect joined together of subjective object = objective subject'.

When the body extends, this joined together aspect is made up in the place to which the body extends. Ichikawa (1975: 37) gives the following examples. 'When I see a piece of scenery, suddenly I become aware that I am grasped by the perspective from the opposite side and arranged in the perspective (that is, I am watched by the scenery). My body switches from the body as subject to the body in opposition to otherness in the depth. I do not grasp the scenery but am grasped by the scenery, and I who watch trees soon find myself being watched by trees'. The body as subject extends to a focus of the scenery grasped by the perspective, and there it experiences the joined together aspect of the subject–object. The body extends to perceive the external world scenery (the perception of the external perception) at the same time as the body is itself perceived by the scenery (the inner perception).

Osawa (1990: 26–27) explains such a condition as an isonomic motion of a 'centripetal operation' and a 'centrifugal operation' in 'the body of process stage'. The centripetal operation is the 'function of self-centralization that grasps phenomena on the basis of an aspect – a horizontal structure – arranging it in the neighbourhood of (one point on) the body on this seat', while the centrifugal operation is 'an operation that converts this point (operation point) on the body being central in the neighbourhood to another place'. A perspective comes and goes between the perspective that places the operation point on the subject and the one that places it on the object; thereby the object can be grasped.

The body thus extending shows that the inner perception is potentially concerned with the condition of the spacial external world. The 'body schema' in a layer of the 'habitual body' that Merleau-Ponty (1945) assumed is thought to be a system of readiness that makes this possible. He says that, before cognition, this system projects into the external world a bunch of potential operations that serve as an existential 'intentional arc'. We can suppose that a potential structure of active–passive relation is made up in the space between our inner perception and the external world. Yuasa (1986: 213) says: 'Speaking in Ponty's style, we would say that the inner perception of the body is incarnated in the physical space'. The expression 'incarnation' means a making up of this potential structure of relation. So it is in this relation that the external world can be grasped by our inner perception.

Such a potential grasp can be said to direct our bodies on a potential action in advance of perception, to have our bodies provide for a perception, and to stretch around our bodies a space in which we can respond to a perception at any time. The appearance of a world joined together where the subject who sees and an object that is seen are not yet distinct is what Sakamoto (1986: 107) calls 'primitive experience'. It is an attitude in which at any time we can pass into a condition of distinct consciousness while the body and mind are undifferentiated. Sakamoto shows, for example, the following condition: 'A white object that wriggles in a nook of my view is a dog in a neighbouring house that tries to attack me, but I do not recognize that the white object is a dog. Sometimes I nevertheless pull myself up the way I did when I was attacked.' This 'primitive experience' is based on making a space already outlined.

## The offence and defence centring on *maai*

In kendo the extent of the body is a space where at the time of an opponent's invasion we can instantaneously and automatically take the offensive by grasping the invasion by means of an inner perception of the body. It is *maai*. In the process in which my opponent and I each extend our bodies, I can take the offensive when my body is not being grasped by an extension of my opponent's body but an extension of my body grasps my opponent's body. At that time I perceive my opponent's latent behaviour, and I take him within the range of my offence. If I fall into an adverse position, I am within the range of my opponent's offence. Therefore, by means of both shortening and extending my space little by little, I learn the locations of our offence *maii*.

To bring opponents into this *maai* as an extension of body, I develop a potential called 'pushing each other's sword guard'. Both my opponent and I search each other's spaces, each trying to bring the other into his own range of offence without being grasped by the other's *maai*. But when I move in so as to take my opponent into my range of offence, I am often taken into my opponent's *maai* of offence. For example, if my opponent retreats when I take a step forward, I take another step forward. If instead my opponent steps forward, I either respond by taking a step backward or find some other way out of the difficulty by taking a step forward. Even if I find myself within my opponent's *maai*, I have not necessarily been defeated. If I can evade my opponent's attack, I can bring my opponent into my *maai* by yielding an inch. Repeating such actions, I learn the location of my opponent's *maai*.

'Pushing each other's sword guard' is usually done by charging at our opponent's weakness. That is, we want to invade by moving in a direction to which the opponent will find it hard to extend his body; i.e. one in which it will be hard for him to take a defensive posture. This is a direction in which physical exercises do not improve movement. It is the side that is less skilful, i.e. the left side in right-handers. It is therefore generally thought that in 'pushing each other's sword guard' we would oppose such a weakness and invade at that point, or by pretending to do so and turning the opponent's attention there, we would induce him to make an unguarded movement in another direction. As the extent of the body is one of the body's inner perceptions to the external world and this inner perception belongs to the consciousness persistently, a propensity of the consciousness for any one weakness reduces the extent of the body in other directions.

Takuan was a priest and a Zen master in the Edo period, who taught both the third shogun Iemitsu-Tokugawa and Munenori-Yagyu, the author of *Shinkage*-style, the book of hereditary tactics. He explained the art of fencing from a mental attitude in Zen and called the condition of mind in amateurs and unskilled men *Mumei-juchi-bonno* (the dark state where man lives with perplexity). In contrast, he called the condition of mind in masters and experts *Shyofutsu-fudochi* (the immovable state that is called *zanmai* or *mushin*). *Mumei-juchi-bonno* is the condition of mind that attends to only one thing. Takuan said: 'If the swordsman places his mind on a sword, his mind is absorbed by the sword; if he places his mind on keeping a good time, his mind is absorbed by keeping a good time; if he places his mind on the sword which he strikes, his mind is absorbed by the sword with which he strikes. In these cases, his mind is stagnant and he thereby becomes a cast-off skin' (revision by Yoshimaru, 1915: 210).

That is, when the mind is attending to only one thing, the real trick (art) cannot be displayed. Takuan also said: 'The mind that moves with perfect freedom forward, left, right, and in every direction is what we call *Fudochi*' (immovable wisdom) (Yoshimaru, 1915: 210). The state of mind that moves with perfect freedom and is not stagnant anywhere is the mind of the expert. Because the expert has a still mind (i.e. *Fudochi*) that is not frightened, he does not attend to only one thing and he is unrestricted. This means that it is important to grasp the totality of the latent external world by means of the extent of the body. When each condition is inspected one by one, a trick, like total integration, is impossible. The wisdom of a trick is what integrates each partial condition, while they are still in undifferentiated relations we cannot speak of them in a definitive way.

## Common comprehension in team play

According to G. H. Mead, to acquire a consummate self, we must obtain an attitude of 'generalized others'. Generalized others are sets of the roles systematized in a community, organization, and – in a wider sense – the total society. They are roles we must understand. In the process of self-development in childhood, role acquisition is accomplished through the playing of games. Taking a baseball team as an example of a social group, Mead (1934) referred to the adoption of an attitude that is systematized by the others on the team. Here, he gave a simple and clear example showing that the reaction of catching the ball becomes possible by the adoption of the attitude of the other who throws the ball. But a baseball player must also adopt a more complex organizational attitude.

Kanagawa (1989) gives the following example: when a batted ball rolls in the direction of first base, not only must the first baseman hold a position enabling him to catch the ball, but the pitcher must run to first base so he can cover it and the right fielder must advance in the direction of first base so he can be in a position to react if the first baseman makes a bad throw. On such an occasion, the judgement of the role-performance of these three players is rather simple: what the three players expect of each other is grasped as the role of each player in that player's previous position. However, when there are choices as to the roles of each player in a specified scene (i.e., choices as to the adoption of which other's attitude), how is it guaranteed that each player's judgement is consistent with a continuance based on a common cognition? That is, how do players know what they expect of each other, and how can they succeed in a co-operative play requiring exact agreement? Furthermore, in sport this judgement must be made in an instant and cannot be postponed. We should closely examine the mechanism of this instantaneous role acquisition in sport.

Serres (1991:530) refers to an immediate judgement that is based on the experience engraved in the brain, nerves and muscles. Taking the case of rugby football and basketball, which he had played himself, what he wrote is worthy of quoting at some length:

Usually when the ball is passed – quickly so as not to be intercepted – it is exchanged from one hand to the other hand skilfully. And in most cases, a call, a word, a cry, a short interjection, a sound, a signal with the hand, and a cautious sharp look are exchanged, even if they are not previously established signals. Thus the ball runs on a circuit diagram these signals draw, in company with the signals or after the signals or at the same time as them. Suddenly the ball replaces these signals, all the other signals fall away … . We don't stare at each other any more, don't see each figure, don't hear each voice, don't exchange conversation with each other, don't call out to each other; we close our eyes, stop talking, lose every word, and become a monad. Yes, we know each other, regard each other, love each other, guess each future quickly, and we don't make mistakes, the totality of the team doesn't make mistakes any more. At last, the team begins to play the game. When I move to the right quickly, so and so teammates know that I will move there, while I know that the teammates know it and that the ball ought to wait for me. As the ball runs very fast, it weaves a relationship of certainty between us. And as this woven safety net has no defects, the ball can circulate more quickly. Then the ball runs more and more quickly and therefore can weave relations more quickly.

Teammates first play co-operatively by recognizing each other's roles by means of signals, but the communication accomplished by voice, gesture, and the expression of the eyes soon falls away and finally there is a perfect understanding that does not require conscious judgement of intentions. 'I' melts into the movement of the team as 'a fluid complex' (Sheets-Johnstone, 1981: 405) that involves both I and the others. Similarly, the assembly of individual teammates melts into the movement of the whole team. Then the movement of one player is a team movement that involves the other players, and the movement of other players is a team movement that involves each player. Therefore, all of the teammates can autonomously and instantaneously determine which role each of them needs to play in any given situation. Sheets-Johnstone calls such wisdom 'an implicit bodily logos' (405).

When all six members of a volleyball team have experience at all positions, the setter tosses the ball in various ways – for a quick attack, for delayed spiking, and for many other moving attacks – by making instantaneous judgements of each situation. At the same time, the right and left forwards make the same judgement as the setter's and move into appropriate positions at the same time as the setter is tossing the ball … all while three back players take defensive positions optimal for the occasion when such an attack is blocked by the opponents. The common possession of 'an automatic memory machine' by which teammates can immediately adapt to all situations is determined more clearly in volleyball than other sports because all six members rotate through all the positions. The tactic that needs the quickest judgement in basketball is the swift attack. Immediately after stealing a ball held by an opponent, intercepting a ball thrown by an opponent or taking a rebound ball, and almost immediately after a successful field shot or free throw by an opponent, the opponent's end of the court is invaded by using quick pass work. In the following, we shall suppose a swift attack directly after taking a rebound ball as shown in Figure 9.1.

When player A takes a rebound ball, he/she and his/her teammates unconsciously project the domain in which action is possible as soon as they grasp all aspects of the situation: the score, the lineups of teammates and opposing players, and the positions of each of them. But, at that time, it is impossible to assert that a sequence of common diagrams of action flashes through the minds of teammates as it does when a setter tosses up the ball in volleyball. The extent to which the diagram of actions is made a draft and forecasted depends on the circumstances. Sometimes the teammates will look two moves ahead, and other times they will look three or more moves ahead. On the other hand, the diagram of actions flashing through the mind differs from player to player. Strictly speaking, total aspects are perceived at momentary intervals, and a common diagram of actions is forecasted several moves ahead.

E runs parallel to the right sideline, taking in advance that A will pass the ball toward that sideline. At the same time, A passes the ball towards the right sideline, taking in advance that E will run parallel to that sideline. E becomes the player who receives the pass from A not because either of them decides it but because they position each other's action in their own schema of action. C runs, taking in advance that the ball will be returned to the centre by E as soon as E runs parallel to the right sideline and A passes the ball in that direction. On the other hand, E understands that C will run towards the centre, C understands that D will run parallel to the left sideline, and D understands that the ball will be passed to the left sideline from the centre by C. Furthermore, as soon as C passes the ball to D, C runs forward expecting the return pass from D, who expects C to run forward. And D runs towards the goal, expecting the return pass from C as soon as C gets the pass from D. E, who received the first pass directly after the rebound ball that started this swift attack, knows that he/she should run towards the goal because, even though he/she cannot be certain of the detailed motions of each of his teammates, he/she can nonetheless anticipate the overall stream of movement that the actions of his/her teammates will produce. Thus the anticipation based on the instantaneous perception of the total aspect is repeated and sometimes amended. Thereby, the relations among the players are actually interwoven, as a result, the total circle of team play is accomplished.

In the instantaneous judgement of the state of the external world, several parts (the movement of players and the ball) are interwoven and the totality of their relations and arrangement are grasped. Such a grasp of the totality is thus common to all teammates. This instantaneous 'alignment' of all teammates is not produced consciously. Ichikawa (1975: 188–89) calls the alignment that is based on the sensation-movement sympathy in a pre-conscious dimension 'sympathetic alignment', and he says that in it there are 'the same type of alignment that identifies with the action of teammates in the sensation-movement' and 'role alignment that grasps and understands the role and action of others sympathetically by means of an identical relation to the present state'. For example, a man who is enthusiastic about watching boxing identifies with the movement of his favourite boxer by setting his jaw, thrusting out his hands, and swinging his body on either side (the same type of alignment). As he grows excited, he begins to move by anticipating his favourite boxer's movements, by tracing the movements of the opponent boxer and by aligning complementarily in the guise of response to the opponent's actions (role alignment).

Role alignment is fundamental to dance, group sport, drama, ensemble performances and various kinds of group labour and co-operative intellectual work. It is also a fundamental physiological–psychological process that makes close teamwork possible. 'I not only understand a site of actions of others, but I also live the site as my own site. The teamwork that looks like a work of God and what is called mysterious ensemble indicates a mutual permeation or mutual fusion of such sites of actions' (Ichikawa, 1975: 187). This 'mutual permeation' indicates that one's own inner perception and the inner perceptions of others come out from the skin that is the boundary surface of our bodies, and that they make up an active–passive relational structure that contains each body. The inner perception of one's own body – feeling one's own body from within – is brought to perceive others at the same time, conversely perceiving others is brought to one's own body from within.

Therefore, the self and the others can 'realize and internalize even the mutual sensation, emotion and the state of mind (as it were) physically' (Ichikawa, 1975: 189) by means of each other's inner perception. Because one's self potentially

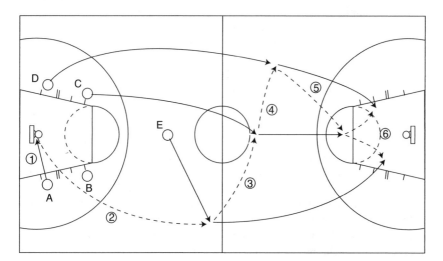

*Figure 9.1* An outline of a swift attack in basketball. 1. A takes a rebound ball. 2. A passes the ball to E. 3. E passes the ball to C. 4. C passes the ball to D. 5. D returns the ball to C. 6. C passes the ball to D or E. 7. D or E shoots the ball.

grasps, by way of one's own action, what one's teammates will do next, one can instantaneously envision the ranges of one's teammates' actions. At the same time, his teammates can anticipate what one will do next and can select their own action in conformity with it. The reason that play, games and sports are used to intensify friendships is that they bring about a mutual permeation of perception, or mutual understanding, by means of the alignment in the diagram of actions.

## The operation of latent cognition

Cognition by means of inner perception is typically seen in *Geido* (Japanese arts). A pupil acquires an art by tracing a master's art accurately and thoroughly. 'Tracing' here indicates not only to follow the course of the master making an object but also to sketch the object by means of somatic sensation (physical sensation). The object is perceived as an 'image' by means of somatic sensation as inner perception. The most effective method of the perception by such tracing is by imitation. A pupil comes to understand a master's art by identifying with the master in imitation.

Amagasaki (1990) says that while Western study is based on the scientific method that resolves the object we must learn into elements and compiles the elements systematically, the practice of Japanese art is typically based on a very ambiguous method that uses imitation as much as possible. When we want to learn a foreign language, for example, or ballet or the piano, the method of study has a precise system and constructs a curriculum from which we can learn each element one after another. It puts materials in order from easy to difficult matter, or from a simple element to the composition of elements. For example, the method of study is systematized from the alphabet to a word, from an easy word to a difficult word, from a simple sentence to a complex sentence and then to a long composition. In *Nihon Buyo* (Japanese dance), in contrast, even a beginner who has not even a rudimentary knowledge of Japanese dance begins by imitating a master's motion in time to a tape of Japanese music.

The study method comprising such a total following of forms is also valid for sport, especially in Japan. In *Nihon Budo* (Japanese military arts), a total 'posture' or 'form' is strictly emphasized . This pattern of thought seems also to have penetrated sports introduced from the West, such as baseball and tennis. With regard to the batting style in baseball, for example, American major league players use many individual forms (such as the crouching style and others), while all Japanese major league players seem to use a similar style, being influenced by the tradition of a study method strictly emphasizing form.

The cognition-by-inner-perception seen in the practice of Japanese arts is valid not only in the process of mastering arts but also in the displaying of art. According to Nishigata (1980), a characteristic of Japanese dance is that its rhythm is based on simple double time and that the same rhythm composed of *ma* (interval) – *omote* (face) and *ura* (back) – flows by repeating *omote* and *ura* continually. This rhythm of *ma* – *omote* and *ura* – is based on the human breath (breathe in and breathe out) and pulse. One breath cycle is one interval *hitoma*. Half of this is called a half interval *hanma* and is suited to *omote ma* or *ura ma*. This one beat of *omote* or *ura* continues in a regular cycle as smoothly as the heart beats or the pulse pounds, and such a rhythm is the *tsune ma* (regular interval) on which Japanese dance is based. But it is interesting to change this simple double time – *omote* and *ura* – by means of making free use of *nuki ma* or *kakure ma* or *nijimi ma* which takes off this *tsune ma* consciously. Simple double time, *omote* and *ura*, is not suited to the two quarter notes in Western music because it changes in one opus. That is, it occasionally becomes fast or slow. This fast or slow speed is called *nori*, and *ma* where the tempo is fast is called *haya ma*. Japanese say in regard to this that *nori* is quick. When a dancer asks a musician to raise the *nori* here, the tempo becomes quicker. And, when a dancer asks a musician to lower the *nori*, the tempo becomes slower.

The rhythm of Japanese dance is so free that it can be co-ordinated by the tone between the dancer and musical performer. Therefore, they both need to know the sensation of one *ma* (interval). The rhythm of Japanese dance is based not on a universal criterion, such as the musical note in Western music, but on a 'sympathetic alignment' that is produced by the dancer and performer case by case. They can both perceive and internalize even mutual sensation, emotion and the state of mind, as it were physically by means of the mutual permeation of each other's inner perception. Such a relation of sympathetic alignment is typically seen in the relation between a *shamisen* player and a puppet master and the narration by the *tayu* (entertainer) in *Bunraku* – *ningyo joruri* (puppet play), in the relations between actors or between an actor and the *geza* (right-hand side of the stage) music player in *Kabuki* play, and in the relation between the host and the visitor in *Sado* (the art of ceremonial tea-making). It is said to be the essence that permeates Japanese arts.

This understanding by inner perception (i.e., physical cognition) is experienced not only in sport and in the arts that are accompanied by physical practice. As noted in the Introduction, it seems to be the foundation of all cognition. Schneider disease is an agnosia produced by damage to the visual area of the occipital lobe of the cortex. Someone afflicted with this agnosia has a visual cognitive disorder that can be compensated by physical practice. For example, when he sees a triangle drawn by a dotted line he cannot recognize that it is a triangle, but when he traces the dotted line with the tip of a finger he recognizes that it is a triangle. As noted earlier in this chapter, Merleau-Ponty suggested that in advance of cognition a series of potential operations making up an existential 'intentional arc' is projected from 'the habitual body-subsisting body' to the external world. Here, we can suppose the tracing over the external world by somatic sensation as inner perception.

In cognition science, Condon (Sasaki, 1987) has discovered in a film driven at a very low speed that the rhythm of the micromotions of the bodies of two people conversing 'align' as if one person is the mirror-image of the other. He has called this 'mutual synchrony'. Hall (1983), also referred to the alignment in rhythm that appears at the level of the physical behaviour of human beings – for example, basketball players and an ensemble of jazz musicians. Sport clearly indicates the physical character of such an operation of potential cognition. Although the cognitive operation in the practice of Japanese arts is not experienced in strong and dynamic motions like those in sports, it must be one that requires a refinement of the body's inner perception at a very subtle level.

## Conclusion

Wisdom in modern science has completely segregated the subject and the object and has grasped the latter on the ground of structuralization by means of 'logos' – universal, unitary and objective language. It has liberated mankind from irrational restraints and made life comfortable by governing objects and environments rationally. On the other hand, the vivid intimate relation between mankind and the environment has been lost, resulting in environmental pollution and mental illness. There is another wisdom, however, that has been buried in the development of this modern wisdom. It attached importance to the physical interaction between subject and object, and it grasped the object as 'image' synthetically. We still find a glimpse of such wisdom in sport.

The sensation that grasps the condition of an object interactively and wholly is nothing more than physical sensation. This sensation is an 'inner perception' of the spinal nervous system. Central to it in the case of sport is a somatic sensation comprising the skin sensation represented by touch sensation and the kinesthesia represented by muscular sensation. The subject grasps the totality of the external world in terms of inner perception by interacting with the world through this 'somatic sensation'. This understanding by inner perception (i.e., physical cognition) is not experienced only in sport and in arts that are accompanied by physical practice. A potential commitment to the external world by physical sensation is fundamental to all cognition. When someone with Schneider's disease is shown a drawing of a triangle, they cannot recognize it as a triangle until it is traced with a fingertip — that is, until the visual stimulation is accompanied by physical practice. With regard to such a thread of connection, Merleau-Ponty has speculated that in advance of cognition a series of potential operations, an existential intentional arc is projected from the body to the external world. Here we can suppose the tracing over the external world by somatic sensation is a form of inner perception corresponding to this intentional arc. Such a character of wisdom has been buried and hidden in the process of modernization.

# References

Amagasaki, A. (1990) *Kotoba to Shintai* (Language and Body), Tokyo: Keiso-Shobo, pp. 181–184.

Freud, S. (1940) 'Das Ich und das Es', in *Sigmund Freud, Gesammelte Werke Bd. XIII*, London: Imago Publishing Co., Ltd, trans. T. Imura *et al.* (1970) *Freud Chosaku-Shu Dai Roku-Kan.* Tokyo: Jinbun-Shoin, p. 296.

Hall, E. T. (1983) *The Dance of Life: The Other Dimension of Time*, New York: Anchor Press, trans. A. Unami (1983) *Bunka to shiteno Jikan.* Tokyo: TBS-Britannica, pp. 205–208.

Henry, M. (1987) *La Barbarie*, Paris: Grasset & Fasquelle, trans. Mochizuki, T. (1990) *Yaban – Kagaku Shugi no Dokusai to Bunka no Kiki*, Tokyo: Hosei Daigaku-Shuppansha, pp. 7–39.

Hiromatsu, W. (1989) *Shinshin Mondai* (The Problems of the Body and the Mind), Tokyo: Seido-sha, p. 183.

Ichikawa, H. (1975) *Shintai Toshite no Shintai* (The Body as the Mind), Tokyo: Keiso-Shobo.

Ikuta, K. (1990) *Waza kara Shiru* (Learn from Performances), Tokyo: Tokyo-Daigaku-Shuppansha, p. 134.

Kanagawa, C. (1989) 'Yoji no Jiga Hattatsu – Mead no Jiga – Ron no Shiza kara (The Development of Self in a Little Child – from a View of Mead's Theory of Self)', in E. Kajita (ed.) (1989) *Jiko-Ishiki no Hattatsu Shinrigaku* (Developmental Psychology of Self-Consciousness), Tokyo: Kaneko-Shobo, p. 199.

Marcuse, H. (1956) *Eros and Civilization: A Philosophical Inquiry into Freud*, London: Routledge and Kegan Paul.

Mead, J. H. (1934) *Mind, Self, and Society from the Standpoint of a Social Behaviorist*, edited and with an introduction by Charles W. Morris, the University of Chicago Press, p. 159.

Merleau-Ponty, M. (1945) *La Phénoménologie de la Perception*, Paris: Gallimard, trans. Y. Takeuchi and S. Ogi (1996) *Chikaku no Genshogaku 1.* Tokyo: Misuzu-Shobo, pp. 172–246.

Nakai, S. (1975) *Bigaku Nyumon* (A Primer of Esthetics), Tokyo: Asahi-Shinbun-Sha, p. 13

Nakamura, Y. (1979) *Kyotsu Kankaku Ron-Chi no Kumikae no tame ni* (Theory of Common Sense for the Rearrangement of Wisdom)', Tokyo: Iwanami-Shoten.

Nakamura, Y. (1993a) 'Runesansu to Ningen no Me no Tanjo (The Renaissance and the Birth of the Eyes of Humankind)', in T. Sato *et al.* (1993) *Enkinho no Seishinshi- Ningen no Me wa Kukan o do Traete Kitaka* (History of Perspective: How the Eyes of Humankind Have Grasped Space), Tokyo: Hibonsha.

Nakamura, Y. (1993b) 'Pathos ron' (The theory of pathos), in *Nakamura Yujiro Chosaku-Shu* (A Collection of Writings by Nakamura Yujiro), Tokyo: Iwanami-Shoten, pp. 123–129.

Nakazawa, S. (1989) *Akutoteki Shiko* (The Thought of Scoundrels), Tokyo: Hibon-Sha, p. 243.

Nishigata, S. (1980) *Nihon Buyo no Kenkyu* (The Study of Japanese Dance), Tokyo: Nanso-Sha, pp. 102–113.

Osawa, M. (1990) Shibtai no Hikaku Shakaigaku (Comparative Sociology of the Body), Tokyo: Keiso-Shobo, pp. 26–27.

Piaget, J. (1945) *La Formation du Symbole Chez L'Enfant*, Delachaux et Niestlé, Neuchâte et Paris, trans. S. Ootomo (1977) *Asobi no Shinrigaku*, Tokyo: Reimei-Shobo, pp. 51–54.

Sakamoto, H. (1986) *Kokoro to Shintai – Genichigen-Ron no Kozu* (Mind and Body – the Composition of Monoism), Tokyo: Iwanami-Shoten, p. 107.

Sasaki, M. (1987) *Karada: Ninshiki no Genten* (Body: The Origin of Cognition), Tokyo: Tokyo-Daigaku-Suppankai, pp. 151–154.

Serres, M. (1991) *Les Cinq Sens – Philosophie des Corps Mêlés* (1st edition), Grasset and Fasquelle, trans. C. Yoneyama (1992) *Gokan – Kongotai no Tetsugaku*, Tokyo: Hosei-Daigaku-Shuppan-Kyoku, p. 530.

Sheets-Johnstone, M. (1981) 'Thinking in movement', *Journal of Aesthetics and Art Criticism*, 39(4): 399–408.

Takuan (Edo period) 'Hudochi Shinmyoroku', in K. Yoshimaru (ed.) (1915) *Bujutsu Sosho* (A Series on Military Arts), Tokyo-Kanko-kai.

Yuasa, Y. (1986) *Shitai – Toyoteki ShinShin Ron* (Body – the Theory of Body and Mind in the Orient), Tokyo: Sobun-Sha, p. 213.

# Chapter 10

# The changing field of Japanese sport

*Takayuki Yamashita*

## Introduction

In this chapter my aim is to highlight the key changes that have occurred in Japanese sport under the influence of current globalization processes. Particular attention will be paid to the decision-making processes of Japanese capitalists and how these decisions have affected the development of sport in Japan. A British sociologist, Joseph Maguire (1999), argues that sport is undergoing major changes under globalization. With regard to nation states, within which many influencing factors are apparent, a better understanding of recent fundamental changes can thus be gained if reference is made to these globalization processes. Moreover, if we limit our observation to the nation state level, this impact appears as an unresolved complex and interwoven configuration. Maguire (1999) uses the term 'The global sports figuration' to emphasize the increasing pressures now being put on sport on a global scale, rather than using a term which places the emphasis on the more traditional model of the nation state.

These pressures are exerted when temporary alliances occur between governing bodies in order to keep pace with the globalization process. Most recent changes in sport, as a cultural apparatus, have reflected the conflicts arising between powerful allegiances. However, we must pay attention to the conditions of the so-called core nation states, not only for the purpose of their adjustment to the globalization process, but also to understand the power structure into which they integrate other local powers in order to maintain their hegemonic position. The activities of the Japanese power elite in the mid-1980s is an example of this kind of strategy. As the result of this, the Japanese field of sport has been restructured. Therefore, we must look beyond simple exteriors to grasp the inner dynamics of this complex phenomenon and its impact on sport.

## The nature of change in the mid-1980s

Globalization requires that individual nations adopt neo-liberal economic policies in order to develop a world market which transcends national boundaries. Here, there is a need to reconstruct a market which is more open to capital flows.

These changes in capital flows require government deregulation initiatives coupled with the introduction of privatization policies. These, in turn, result in government decentralization and, as a further result, decreased spending on social policy. For such policies to be implemented, the nation state must be domestically stable. In other words, a strong nation state is required. It sounds paradoxical. However, these processes are essentially the methods now being exploited to create a new political and economic regime, both locally and globally, thereby attempting to avoid the conflict and disorder which would otherwise arise. As Gray (1998) argues, today's globalization can mean many things but is mainly characterized by a developing free world market that is engineered by the core nation states themselves linking with global capitalism. He further argues:

> One of Thatcherism's many ironies was its relationship with the nation-state ... The nation-state was held to be supremely important. National culture was claimed to be vital to social order. Yet neo-liberal economic policies prised open the British economy to world markets as never before. A rhetoric of inexorable economic globalization was combined with assertion of the unique authority and indispensable utility of a common national culture.
>
> (Gray, 1998: 35, cf. Gamble 1988)

Considered in this light, a strong sense of national order must be 'reconstructed'. As Mosse noted with regard to the role of this cultural apparatus: 'it was necessary now to use old traditions and to adapt them to a new purpose. Festival, gestures, and forms had to be newly created which, in turn, would themselves become traditional' (1991). We can find historical precedents with Thatcherism and Reaganomics. Both governments tried to adopt neo-liberal economic policies while at the same time advocating the idea of 'a Strong America' or 'a Strong Britain' by recalling and re-inventing 'an imagined community' (Anderson, 1991). In Britain, their nostalgia invoked a return to the romantic notion of 'Little England'. At the same time, the phenomenon of football hooliganism became a daily occurrence in the British media (cf. Taylor, 1982; Clarke, 1978).

Globalization proceeds with such dialectical and correlating policies. These policies may, at first glance, seem at odds with each other. In fact, the conditions do not only create a trans-national consciousness, but also promote a sense of 'nationalism'. Nevertheless, it must also be borne in mind that attempts to revive nationalism have been executed by the general public and traditional capitalists, as a corollary of vested interests as well. Reviving nationalism, however, will not necessarily guarantee that a sense of identity or belonging will be generated in that nation. As Gray has observed: 're-engineering the free market is hardly a conservative political project. Its effect is to sever cultural and institutional continuities, not to renew them. The Right's project in present circumstances cannot be the conservation of cultural tradition' (1998: 36). Here we can see that one of the ironies of globalization is that the basis of its success is the creation of a powerful and commercially viable illusion of nationalism. But in order to fully realize this potential success, the opposite must be true. The nation will exist in a condition of perpetual transition and this effect is the core element of the globalization process (Balibar and Wallerstein, 1991).

Japan is no exception, as a similar strategy was proposed in the mid-1980s. Arguably, the origin of this policy change was the report filed by the Second Ad Hoc Commission on Administrative and Fiscal Reform, established by the prime minister in 1981 (Yamashita and Seino, 1995). Following this proposal, a consensus spread into the political and industrial domains. In short, this plan was aimed at reforming Japanese society on several levels, not only the financial and administrative but also social welfare, education, culture and other social institutions. The policy change gained further support via the Plaza Accord[1] on exchange rates in 1986. A political scientist, Watanabe Osamu (1999), argued for a clean break in the dynamics of Japanese capitalism following the 1985 Plaza Accords, when a sharp rise in the value of the Japanese Yen induced companies to aggressively shift their production overseas. As a result of this, the domestic production of Japanese industries fell into a crisis. Japanese foreign direct investment grew rapidly and, at the beginning of the 1990s, it ranked third in the world (cf. Dicken, 2003: 54–57). This dramatic change emerged from a neo-liberal economic policy that also accelerated the opening of Japanese markets to other countries. The shift from domestic to overseas production represented a transition from a domestic-centred capitalism to a global capitalism. Encouraged by this, Japanese capitalists rapidly expanded their globalizing processes. Such social conditions gave rise to the changes in Japanese sport as well.

## The nature of changes in sport

Firstly, a privatization policy was implemented with regard to sport and the industrialization of sport developed rapidly. Secondly, fundamental changes in the attitudes of society have been linked to sport culture. As a result of this, the characteristics of Japanese sport, as a cultural apparatus, began to change. Before turning to a closer examination of this change, it may be worth referring to the work of Defrance and Pociello (1993). They raised several important issues concerning changes arising in the field of sport in France between 1960 and 1990. Their work has provided us with a useful structural overview via which changes in Japanese sport can be analysed. I shall outline their arguments below.

They assert that the field of sport in France experienced a reversal of the situation that prevailed between the 1960s and the 1980s. From the mid-1970s onwards, the field of sport in France has been governed by the alliance of two main bodies, the schooling system and sport federations. These two allies have developed strong links with the state. The ideologies brought forward by these alliances, namely the federal and the educational ideologies, have given French sport a sense of 'legitimacy'. Sport was thus viewed in a more managerial manner, with its own ethos. Values in sport became akin to those embodied in the indus-

Les Polarisations Institutionnelles Des Champs Sportifs Nationaux Positionnement et Enjeux des "Acteurs"

**Jacques Defrance, Christian Pociello, 1994**

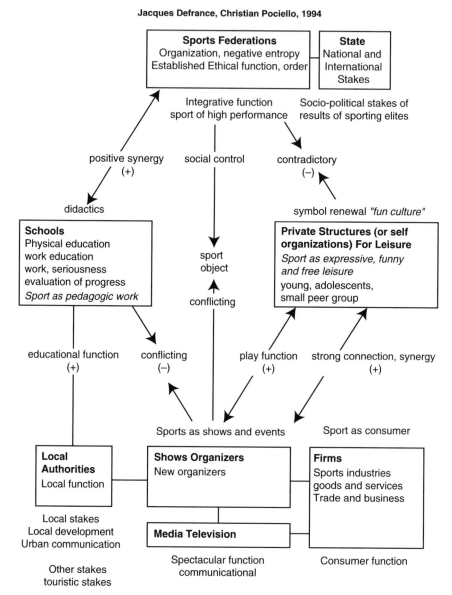

*Figure 10.1* Structure and functions of the field of sport in France (1960–1990) (Defrance and Pociello, 1993: 13)

trial society, namely a strong work ethic, the importance of achievement, sense of effort, and evaluation of progress and merits. However, as a result of further social changes, the dominance of the controlling bodies has faded and these 'legitimized' views of sport have begun to hold sway. For this reason, the predominance of the central institutions and of the educational pole faded, whereas the play function and the entertainment function of sports grew stronger. The political and administrative montage put together by the state gradually came apart. The recession in 1973–75 played a significant role in this downfall. Furthermore, private networks, including those that volunteer their time for organizing leisure and sport were gradually gathering force. Sport was becoming less discipline for discipline's sake and instead was becoming more expressive, enjoyable and recreational. Consequently, the very activities that updated and reinforced the play function have redefined themselves against the hierarchical, centralized and standardized institutions as well as against pedagogical seriousness. By virtue of this, a strong alliance between the commercial, media and play functions has been formed in opposition to the former alliance between the schools and sports federations (Defrance and Pociello, 1993).

The socio-cultural factors, which resulted in a French 'reversal of the situation', were not necessarily those prevalent in Japan but we can find analogous circumstances. So the question arises what are the factors that have brought about the change in the field of sport in Japan? Initially, the government determined a new industrial policy that was more progressive and aimed at reorganization of the structure of industry in order to be prepared for global competitions in the twenty-first century. While this policy claimed to establish and secure new industrial areas such as biotechnology, it focused on an objective that was very much driven by domestic demands. This was intended to compensate for the structured reorganization industry.

Leisure and sport were also incorporated into this new policy and as a result it paved the way for change in Japanese sport. Moreover, neo-liberal economic policy formed the underlying basis and, in line with this, the public sector was reduced. While support from the government began to decline, business enterprises took advantage in the mid-1980s of the opportunity to enter the field of Japanese sport. Following the US example, various Japanese companies entered extensively into immature areas of sport, such as the sports club business, during the 1980s in Japan. Figure 10.2 and Table 10.1 illustrate how rapidly the sports club market grew during the 1980s and represents the accumulated number of commercial sports clubs (sports facility complexes) in Japan. This evidence demonstrates that the number of sports complexes rose dramatically from 178 to 1,620 between 1982 and 1993 (a 9.1 times increase). The number of annually established sports clubs also rose to over 200 between 1987 and 1989. The total number of commercially based sports clubs was only 148 in 1981 in Japan and, as Figure 10.2 highlights, this figure has more than doubled since then.

Moreover, this chart indicates a market scale (Yen based) along with the increasing number of companies. This market scale increased from 230 billion Yen (approx. $2.01 billion) to 3,100 billion Yen (approx. $27.12 billion) between 1982 and 1993, which reflects a 13.4 times increase (maximum 3,360 both in 1990 and 1991). The formation of companies grew particularly rapidly, after the Second Ad Hoc Commission submitted a final report in 1983.

Under these conditions, a fundamental change in the Japanese social consciousness towards sport occurred. Consequently, the legitimacy of sport in Japan, as a discipline, once assured by the education system and the Sport Federation, in conjunction with the state, began to falter.

As the graph in Figure 10.3 shows, following the period of high economic growth in Japan, which we could observe in the early 1970s, Japanese people placed greater importance on 'spiritual richness' than 'material affluence'. Before the 1980s this trend had increased rapidly. Coinciding with this trend, on the basis of 'community sport', which was promoted by the government during the 1970s, new sporting activities and voluntary groups in residential areas gradually

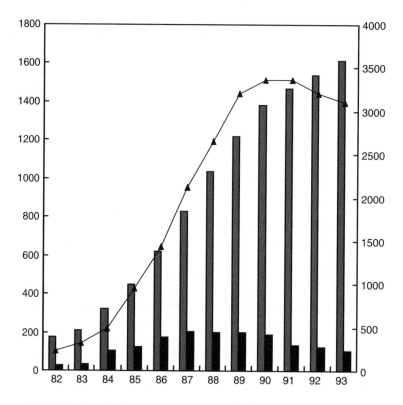

*Figure 10.2* The accumulated number of commercially based sports clubs (first bar), the number of sports clubs established each year (second) and the growth rate of market scale (line graph, measure: ¥100 million yen) (Yamashita and Yuzuru Taneda, 1997: 190)

*Table 10.1* Sport clubs and market scale

| Year | Accumulated number of sports clubs | Number of sports clubs established each year | Market scale ($ 100,000) |
|---|---|---|---|
| 1981 | 148 | – | – |
| 1982 | 178 | 32 | 2,090 |
| 1983 | 215 | 37 | 2,818 |
| 1984 | 322 | 107 | 4,455 |
| 1985 | 450 | 128 | 8,636 |
| 1986 | 625 | 175 | 13,000 |
| 1987 | 834 | 209 | 19,270 |
| 1988 | 1,038 | 205 | 24,090 |
| 1989 | 1,223 | 204 | 29,090 |
| 1990 | 1,386 | 192 | 29,090 |
| 1991 | 1,468 | 135 | 30,550 |
| 1992 | 1,540 | 126 | 30,550 |
| 1993 | 1,620 | 104 | 29,090 |

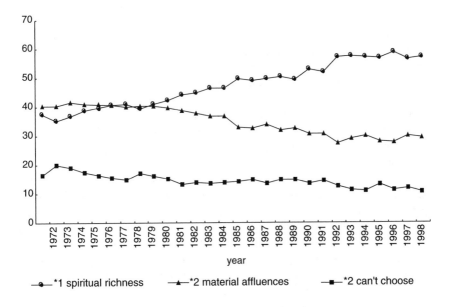

—●—*1 spiritual richness     —▲—*2 material affluences     —■—*2 can't choose

*Figure 10.3* The public opinion (Cabinet Office, Government of Japan, 'Quality-of-Life Policy' 1999, http://www5.cao.go.jp/seikatsu/senkoudo/senkoudo.html)

emerged. These voluntary groups developed new ways of managing sports and through their lifestyles redefined the meaning of sport for themselves.

Linking with these trends, emerging enterprises in the field of sport in Japan adopted a more market orientated approach to sport. These enterprises invented a new symbolic meaning for sport and attached it to their commercialized image. Their new invention, for example, can be seen in the type of new synergic sport commodities such as sport linked with beautification and with travel. Of notable importance is the fact that their target for marketing was mainly women (cf. Yamashita and Taneda 1997). Through this strategy, they emphasized feminine traits, rather than traditional masculinity in their advertisements in order to attract women to sport. They tried to change traditional conceptions of sport by using widespread advertising campaigns in the media. This had a major impact on people's image of sports.

This new alliance between companies and the reformed public has led to the acquisition of a new 'symbolic capital' for sport in Japan, which was different from the earlier notions of sport focusing mainly on educational and competitive values and masculinity. Rather, it has emphasized a fashion sense linked with commercial goods. It is to be noted that enterprises played a key role in the change in people's fundamental consciousness regarding sport. Sport was elevated to a new status in people's lives, breaking away from such traditional values as nation and race (see Yamashita, 2003).

Finally, we can also see a new complicated relationship emerging as a result of the new alliances and conflicts arising between parties involved. Of paramount importance, as mentioned above, was the new alliance between business enterprise and Japanese people. However, it is also apparent that another conflict, concerning jurisdictional disagreements, was developing between government agencies. The main conflict had arisen between the Ministry of International Trade and Industry (now the Ministry of Economy, Trade and Industry) and the Ministry of Education (now the Ministry of Education, Culture, Sports, Science and Technology). This conflict indicated that sport, as a cultural apparatus, had been changing. Until these changes Japanese sport had been posited as educational, that is, as a 'disciplinary power' (Foucault, 1979). This is also true of countries that imported sport for the purpose of nation building. However, this disciplinary attitude did not sit well with the new market orientated sport in Japan. Consequently, a conflict had arisen between the 'old' disciplinary approach to sport for social integration and the 'new' market orientated approach. This conflict can be characterized by jurisdictional debates between government agencies that reflect and represent disciplinary conditions and private enterprises.

In today's Japan the maintenance of the disciplinary role of sport has become less significant. One reason for this is the strong alliance between private enterprises and mass advertising campaigns. Another is that disciplinary power itself is gradually losing its socio-cultural base, which has also been accelerated by the recent decline in the birth rate and an increased awareness of human rights. Both contributed to the change in the characteristics of sports clubs in schools which for long formed the basis of Japanese sport. The ruling bodies have acknowledged this problem and have begun planning the renouncement of the traditional role of sport. They intend to assign a new role to sport, from its disciplinary one to a more aesthetic representational one. Two recent policy proposals are a symptom of this change. In the late 1990s the committee for reforming education supervised by the Ministry of Education proposed removing certain subjects, including sport, from school curriculums and introducing them to local communities in a structured way. This example indicates that the Japanese government does not attribute great educational importance to sport. Another symptom is that the government allocated significant resources to the building of a new Sports Institute for high performance sport in 2001. This had been a long-standing request of the Sports Federation. There is, then, a complex hegemonic struggle at work currently in Japanese sport, which reflects a change in the methods of Japanese capitalists as they adjust to global conditions. In the following section this new role of Japanese sport will be discussed more fully.

## What does sport represent and how is it represented?

In discussing the new role of sport in Japanese society I shall focus my attention on an example from the last decade. In addition, consideration is given to what sport represented and how it is represented in this recent phase of globalization. Two case studies are provided: the 1998 Nagano Winter Olympic Games and the FIFA 2002 World Cup co-hosted by Japan and Korea. In both events, different issues regarding the relationship between globalization and nationalism in the sporting context occurred. A variety of dynamics acted on each event, reflecting both the widespread cultural differences between the Olympic Games and the FIFA World Cup, and the differing social contexts of the late 1990s and the early twenty-first century. Both events were bounded by these historical and cultural contexts and came to represent them.

## Nagano: The Opening Ceremony of the 18th Winter Olympics

The 1998 opening ceremony at Nagano conveyed a strong representation of a specific 'Japaneseness'. This Japaneseness seemed rather peculiar. In contrast to the previous summer and winter Olympic Games held in Japan, Nagano simultaneously represented the traditional supra-national Olympic ideas of peace and friendship and emphasized a specific Japaneseness. How do we interpret this relationship between this Japaneseness and the Olympic ideal? As Tomlinson (1996) suggested, other games also reflected the paradoxes inevitable in a globalizing world. This is precisely the issue I wish to examine.

The opening ceremony of the Nagano Olympics incorporated two related themes, one closely connected to the concept of nation or national identity and the other invoked the idea of a world community. These two themes were clearly expressed in the official discourse of the organizing committee that wanted to 'present the Japanese culture and history to the world' and to 'realize a festival of peace and friendship' (The speech at the opening ceremony by the President of the Nagano Olympic Organizing Committee on 7 February 1998). These two concepts, the universal and the local, or world and nation, have surfaced in every Olympics, although the representation of their relationship has varied. These representational differences can be seen to reflect the differences in the world views of the organizers in each host country.

The particular world view presented in Nagano was quite complex, yet full of inconsistencies. Although the ceremony, as a text, can be open to several interpretations, as Stuart Hall argues, the message may not be pluralist. There are, of course, limits to its interpretation and the polysemic quality of a text is 'hierarchically organized into dominant or preferred meaning' (Hall, 1980: 134). The ceremony was constructed with various textual elements and of linked texts and, therefore, in order to 'read' Nagano correctly, it is critical that one clarifies this construction and unfolds the meanings of the elements and links. In my analysis, I identified approximately 24 elements in the opening ceremony and arranged them as a chronological narrative (see Table 2). Table 2 identifies those elements by their basic meanings and by their broadcast commentary. Because these textual elements fell into two distinct categories, the analysis is presented in two sections.

## Representations of 'Japaneseness'

In a television interview, the chief spokesperson of the Nagano opening ceremonies, Mr Asari Keita, emphasized that their aim was to present the value and the individuality of Japanese culture. The articulation of these aims is consistent with the way in which the first half of the ceremony was designed. Even though the ceremony began with the ringing of a Buddhist temple bell, most of the ceremony invoked memories of Shinto rituals, creating a cultural atmosphere that most Japanese people could easily envisage and identify with. In particular, there were striking resemblances between the opening ceremony and Shinto purification rituals. In Shintoism, before invoking a deity, it is necessary to perform a purification to create a 'sacred' place and time. At Nagano, a similar purification ritual took place before the Emperor made his divine appearance. The 'texts' articulated in certain elements of the ceremony are as follows:

Shared historical memories: the ringing of the Zenko-ji Temple bell, the ceremony of building the sacred pillars, the entrance of the *dosojin* (the guardian deities of travellers) and the 'snow children' (*yukinko*) are examples. These elements are all linked as local memories and convey the imagined mentality of traditional communal life in Japanese rural areas (see Anderson's (1991) imagined communities).

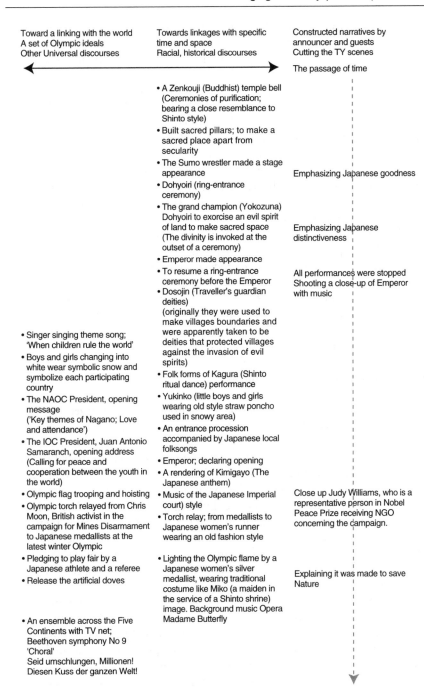

**Toward a linking with the world**
A set of Olympic ideals
Other Universal discourses

**Towards linkages with specific time and space**
Racial, historical discourses

**Constructed narratives by announcer and guests**
Cutting the TY scenes

The passage of time

- A Zenkouji (Buddhist) temple bell (Ceremonies of purification; bearing a close resemblance to Shinto style)
- Built sacred pillars; to make a sacred place apart from secularity
- The Sumo wrestler made a stage appearance
- Dohyoiri (ring-entrance ceremony)
- The grand champion (Yokozuna) Dohyoiri to exorcise an evil spirit of land to make sacred space (The divinity is invoked at the outset of a ceremony)
- Emperor made appearance
- To resume a ring-entrance ceremony before the Emperor
- Dosojin (Traveller's guardian deities) (originally they were used to make villages boundaries and were apparently taken to be deities that protected villages against the invasion of evil spirits)
- Folk forms of Kagura (Shinto ritual dance) performance
- Yukinko (little boys and girls wearing old style straw poncho used in snowy area)
- An entrance procession accompanied by Japanese local folksongs
- Emperor; declaring opening
- A rendering of Kimigayo (The Japanese anthem)
- Music of the Japanese Imperial court) style
- Torch relay; from medallists to Japanese women's runner wearing an old fashion style
- Lighting the Olympic flame by a Japanese women's silver medallist, wearing traditional costume like Miko (a maiden in the service of a Shinto shrine) image. Background music Opera Madame Butterfly

Emphasizing Japanese goodness

Emphasizing Japanese distinctiveness

All performances were stopped Shooting a close-up of Emperor with music

- Singer singing theme song; 'When children rule the world'
- Boys and girls changing into white wear symbolic snow and symbolize each participating country
- The NAOC President, opening message ('Key themes of Nagano; Love and attendance')
- The IOC President, Juan Antonio Samaranch, opening address (Calling for peace and cooperation between the youth in the world)
- Olympic flag trooping and hoisting
- Olympic torch relayed from Chris Moon, British activist in the campaign for Mines Disarmament to Japanese medallists at the latest winter Olympic
- Pledging to play fair by a Japanese athlete and a referee
- Release the artificial doves

- An ensemble across the Five Continents with TV net; Beethoven symphony No 9 'Choral' Seid umschlungen, Millionen! Diesen Kuss der ganzen Welt!

Close up Judy Williams, who is a representative person in Nobel Peace Prize receiving NGO concerning the campaign.

Explaining it was made to save Nature

*Figure 10.4* The articulation of the opening ceremony in the Nagano Olympics

The emperor's gaze: the dedication of folk forms of *kagura* (Shinto ritual dance) to the god of the shrine and the *yokozuna dohyo-iri* (a ritual ceremony for champion sumo wrestlers entering the ring and performed within the precincts of a shrine).

Elements of Shintoism: all of the purification rites evoked a Shinto style or atmosphere, enhanced by a rendering of the Japanese anthem with *gagaku* (a traditional Shinto style of music from the Japanese Imperial court), the traditional costumes worn by the torch relay runners, the lighting of the Olympic flame by a female Japanese medallist, the wearing of a traditional costume reminiscent of a *miko* (a maiden in the service of a Shinto shrine) with the music from the opera of Madame Butterfly[2] in the background all the time. It seems that the intention of the organizers was to emphasize a redefined Japanese distinctiveness rather than to highlight commonality across cultures.

These three texts conveyed the representation of 'Japaneseness' that was planned by the promotional staff. According to Benedict Anderson (1991), the modern nation state must always reproduce a common illusion which generates an imagined community and determines people's identities and a sense of belonging. Yoshino Kosaku (1997) argues that there are two ways to examine the boundaries of the nation state. One focuses on common history or origin, especially the imagined ethnic origins of a people, while the other draws upon the idea of cultural distinctiveness (such as shared racial characteristics, personality traits and special etiquette). I would argue that the boundaries of Japaneseness, evoked by the texts in the Nagano opening ceremony, were of the former historical type.

If this was the case, the 'invention' of traditions may be utilized in order to generate an artificial history (see Hobsbawm and Ranger, 1983). However, it is important to recognize that history itself is an artificial construction, often diverging from 'real' history (cf. Maguire, 1988). This argument should be borne in mind when interpreting these historical texts. The first text, involving shared historical memories, is similar to the romanticization of rural life that was displayed at other Games such as the Lillehammer Olympics. The meaning, however, is not generated by the individual texts; rather, these three texts must be combined and read together by the same dominant code in order to extract their specific meaning. Furthermore, the Nagano texts have a collective effect of presenting a specific Japaneseness, which also encompasses a specific order of Japanese culture and society.

Fujita Shozo (1966), known for his astute examination of imperialism, defined the foundation of the imperial-state as the fusion between the emperor's authority and Shintoism into a state norm. At the same time, imperialism retained a link with the communal principle of the traditional family. In his examination of the structure of the imperial state, Fujita also emphasized the concept of *bansei ikkei no tenno* (a hereditary emperor from an eternal line of descent). Considering a specific phrase, this concept has always been used to describe the Japanese emperor. Its invocation articulates a specific racial or ethnic claim, representing an exclusive social community based on the imagined bond of blood relations. Another important aspect of imperialism revolves around ancestor worship. According to Yoshino (1997), the symbolic discourse of 'Japanese blood' is invoked to draw a distinction between the Japanese and other Asian peoples such as Koreans and Chinese. This symbolic construction creates an 'us versus them' mentality and a sense of a 'Japanese' community based on a common ethnic and racial background. Thus, the three texts combine to focus on imperialism. After the rituals of purification and the invocation of divinity, the emperor made a divine appearance. Then, in front of the emperor's gaze at the centre of the order, the festival was sumptuously displayed. The producers created the representation of Japan around this point and, at the same time, presented specific principles of social integration.

In summarizing the first half of the ceremony, it is clear that the dominant representation of Japaneseness can be seen as a particularly emperor-centric Japanese order. This is articulated by intricate ties between imperial authority and Shintoism, the structure of the family state and the tenet of an ethnically homogenous nation. It is the underlying code that works along the paradigmatic axis of meaning which these three texts represent in relation to each other. This is what Roland Barthes (1973) has termed a 'myth' because of how it frames our thinking (cf. Hall, 1997). While it does, at first, appear to be a straightforward revival of past ways, it is much more of a reconstructed or newly re-invented 'tradition'. However, if we take into account the historical context of the late 1990s in the period after the Plaza Accord, this representation cannot be seen as a revival of traditional Japaneseness, nor does it force people to submit to this reactionary Japaneseness. After all, the second half of the ceremony emphasized Universalism as an Olympic ideal from a nationalistic perspective. How is it possible to explain the apparent paradox of the ceremony with its element of nationalism and these universal Olympic ideals?

In formulating an answer to this, two hundred students were asked to write a one page report on their impressions of the opening ceremony based on a video coverage. Most of them 'read' Nagano along the lines of the second theme, with its global orientation. I had suspected that this would be the case because of the predominant discourses about the Olympics that called for peace and co-operation among the peoples of the world. In creating a context for interpretation, this dominant theme inevitably shaped how people understood the Olympics. Moreover, newspaper articles that appeared after the ceremony strongly reinforced this interpretation. It should be noted, however, that the majority of students also described the representation of Japaneseness in their reports. Though it was not discussed in much detail, they recognized its presence nonetheless. Given these responses, it seems that the organizers of the opening ceremony were successful in broadcasting the intended world view.

The world view, represented in Nagano, did not only create a specific Japaneseness, but also framed the relationship between Japan and rest of the world. Mary Yoko Brannen's argument (1992) about a particular type of Japanese cultural imperialism at work at Tokyo Disneyland is an exemplary case of how such 'framing' operates. Brannen's analysis is focused on how Japanese society accepts a foreign concept like Disneyland in its entirety without making adjustments for Japanese distinctiveness. She observed that, from a Western point of view, this might appear to be an unquestioned acceptance of Western cultural imperialism, but she rejects this interpretation. Instead, she suggests that this phenomenon reflects a type of Japanese cultural imperialism that functions in a completely different way from the Western type. Because the Japanese keep their own culture fairly well defined, often in a very exclusive fashion, this enables them to accept other cultures as exotic and discrete. For this reason, then, they do not make adjustments according to Japanese society and culture. More accurately, what is retained as Japanese is not a pure culture, but an imagined Japaneseness and a belief in its community.

In much the same way the opening ceremony of Nagano, with its initial emphasis on Japan's individuality, does not necessarily contradict the theme of the second half of the event. Rather the two halves articulate a representation of a certain relationship between Japan and rest of the world. In this context, this is certainly an ethnocentric assertion, but not necessarily a reactionary one. Perhaps it would be more accurate to say that the representation of Japaneseness in Nagano can be characterized as the temporary product of a transitional period towards an era of globalization. It is the representation of the frame of a new world view through sport, 'a nation-state centred internationalism'. This is not traditional nationalism, rather the generation of a new one. Such an analysis is in accord with the argument of the political scientist Watanabe (1999, 2001). He postulated that as no agreement could be reached in the late 1990s, the upper social stratum was forced to progress under the joint interest of nationalism and internationalism.

If the boundaries of an 'imagined' country are determined culturally and conceptually then economic transformations cause inevitable changes in traditional boundaries. The Japanese economy was no longer determined by physical factors like geographical proximity, and this policy shift altered the very definition of Japaneseness. At the same time, this shift opened up serious conflicts between domestic-centred capitalism and Japanese global capitalism: most domestic Japanese companies found themselves struggling to survive under these new demands. Such economic conflicts are also projected on and find expression in sport. In reaction to this trend and towards globalization, conservative nationalism reappeared. It is this relationship that was represented at Nagano.

## The FIFA 2002 World Cup

Japanese people cheered the successful results of the Japanese national team during this tournament. This, on occasions, led to the false conclusion of some observers concerning a possible rebirth of reactionary nationalism. However, this view might be premature. We would be wrong to forget that the FIFA 2002

World Cup was a sporting event of a different genre from the Nagano Olympics and the passionate support of Japanese people for the Japanese national team was accompanied by an enthusiastic cheering for the Korean team as well. The World Cup existed on three social levels: level one was global; level two was regional politics, especially considering the peculiarities of past Japan-Korea relationships; and, level three concerned Japanese society and culture in relation to its domestic responses to the changes occurring on a global scale. In the social phenomenon that was the 2002 World Cup, these three levels intersected and are, in reality, closely interwoven.

The tone of the tournament was not set with nationalist overtones, but rather with regional politics at the forefront, especially concerning Japan and Korea. The question, therefore, is why was regionalism brought to the fore at this juncture? In order to gain a better understanding of the reasoning behind this, it is necessary to examine the Japanese capitalist strategy. High on their agenda was the restatement of boundaries in order to create a new order in East Asia, especially, the creation of a free trade area centred on Japan. However, this received increasing criticism from both political and academic observers, who labelled it the 'New Great East Asia Co-prosperity Sphere'. History was made as the 2002 World Cup became not only the first to be held in Asia, but also the first to be co-hosted. The real crux of the matter lies in the fact that this World Cup provided Japanese capitalists with their greatest opportunity to finally pacify strained relations between Korea and Japan.

The 2002 World Cup acted as an essential catalyst in this rebuilding process. It has to be remembered that the Japanese government has never offered an apology to any country that it invaded in the last seventy years. This displays the reluctance of the Japanese to reflect on their past conduct. It is this very attitude that has fuelled feelings of great indignation and distrust towards Japan from other Asian countries. This animosity has hindered the forward planning of Japanese capitalists. The 2002 World Cup thus provided them with the best opportunity to remove this hindrance. Immediately prior to the opening of the World Cup, the Japanese and the Korean governments reached an official agreement to implement an all-inclusive free trade plan between their respective countries.

In accordance with this decision, an image of a new kinship between Japan and Korea was expressed. This co-operative campaign used the mass media to convey this message to the public through special programmes on television, special articles in newspapers, together with symposiums held by the mass media and the local governments of the host cities. The food, tourist, music and film industries also capitalized on this movement. Consequently, the 'Korean Boom' occurred virtually overnight, particularly among the younger generation. Ironically, this movement was supported by those who had previously demanded an official government apology to the relevant Asian countries, despite the constant refusal by the government to address these concerns. However, with apparent disregard to this newly healed relationship,

President Koizumi worshipped at the Yasukuni Shrine, which is dedicated to Japanese World War II leaders.

The 2002 World Cup thus embodied the rejuvenated relationship between Japanese and Korean capitalism. However, we should not overlook that the structural outline represented in the World Cup was the universal idea of coexistence that disregards the specific history. It is obvious that this universalism attracted opposing groups. It is important to note, however, that the fundamental ideas behind the World Cup were of the same type as those on which the Nagano Olympics were based. These basic principles are in accordance with the world view that focused on a reinvented frame of reference for nationalism and internationalism. Watanabe indicated that this is linked with both globalization and a 'neo-great power ambition' (2001: 139). To trade in such broad areas as tourism and popular culture led to increased links between Japan and Korea. However, the reflection upon or the recognition of the historical relationship between the two countries, namely war responsibility, was dismissed. To a certain extent, therefore, Japanese capitalists can be seen to have detracted from the issue of World War II responsibility and, at the same time, have instilled in people their new framework for diplomatic relations via the 2002 World Cup.

We should also acknowledge other new trends that crossed the national borders. These trends took influences from both the local and global domains. As Maguire (1999) has argued, today's sport is constituted under the influence of the 'global sport figuration' and is embedded in it. In particular, he stresses the important point that today's sport exists as a sport-media complex and is linked with global commerce. Under these conditions, influential interactions have arisen, meaning that players, coaches, staff and capital are exchanged at ever increasing rates, and there is a greater and more widespread dissemination of sporting information and culture through the mass media. This is evident in the presence of a foreign coach and players in the Japanese national football team.

These trends result in two major changes. Firstly, today's sport depends much more on market strategies. This, in turn, urges sport to break away from its close ties with the nation state. In the recent FIFA World Cups for example, sponsoring companies and the media began to extend their influence to a greater degree. Therefore, host countries have begun to lose a significant part of their control over the game. This was indeed noticeable during the 2002 World Cup. Today's sporting events fail to be recognized as state events. As a result, the relationship between sport and the nation state, namely between sport and nationalism, has changed dramatically. The second change relates to the fact that the concept of national heroes has changed. Acting as a role model, they often secure the bonds between the nation state and its people. However, during the last decade, nationality has not necessarily affected public support. Some Japanese supporters who became familiar with European football leagues via satellite television, tended to identify with foreign players and teams more readily than with Japanese players and the national team.

In addition to such global influences, it is important to examine important aspects of sport on a more localized level. The FIFA 2002 World Cup was characteristic not only of globalization, but also of localization. The event was held across Japan at various local venues. It was especially significant that Tokyo, which represents the nation as its capital, was not a venue city. Consequently, each of the respective local cities and their citizens attached their own individual meaning to the World Cup, thus emphasizing localism more than nationalism. These local representations, to some extent, limited the opportunity to fully display nationalism. That is part of the reason why the new breed of Japanese football supporter grew rapidly after the establishment of the Japanese professional league (J-league) in 1991. These voluntary groups reflect the social conditions surrounding the World Cup and constitute what an Italian sociologist, Alberto Mellucci (1989), has called, a new social movement that represents local, regional and global influences. They have created not only vocal support for local teams, like cheering, but have also generated a wide range of activities, for example, a symposium on the local development of football and the provision of football for people with special needs (see Yamashita and Saka, 2002). Consequently, local interests became the focus of their agenda. Such an emergence of local representation has hardly been seen before in the field of sport in Japan.

On the other hand, it should be noted that these local supporters could play a vital role in the ambitions of the state by their support for the national team. This differs from the established links with nationalism. They ironically labelled themselves as 'nationalist for 90 minutes'. This intentionally limited description demonstrates an awareness of a distinction between themselves and traditional nationalists. They fly the *Hinomaru* (Japanese national flag) and sing the *Kimigayo* (Japanese national anthem) in a way more closely associated with the team than the country itself. Nevertheless, it is also true that they have the potential to articulate a new type of nationalism in a roundabout way.

Interviews conducted with such supporters reveal some possible explanations. It is true that many of them belong to the new generation that tends to have a more individual attitude towards sport than their nationalist predecessors. However, they share a world view in common with that of contemporary Japanese capitalists, namely neo-liberalism and the strange amalgam of nationalism and internationalism as previously discussed. Therefore, it seems that they now have an affinity with a new type of nationalism, together with neo-liberalism under globalization. Following this path, there is the possibility of linking neo-liberalism with a great power ambition. However, it is not possible any longer to confine sport to a single nation state. Rather the world sport system must be viewed as a global formation with free access to the world market. The relationship between sport and nationalism, for a long time to come, will fluctuate between two types of nationalisms, one based on internationalism and the other based on globalization.

## Conclusion

The above examples clearly demonstrate that the relationship between sport and nationalism is undergoing change in the current Japanese social context. They indicate the role of sport as part of the cultural apparatus which is currently in flux. These processes are not merely counter-actions to but a necessary ingredient of globalization itself. Therefore, as Brannen has argued (1992), the nation state is centred internationalism in the Japanese social context. I emphasize again that such processes are essentially parts of the globalizing processes. Consequently, the function and role of sport as part of the cultural apparatus has been altered. In addition, Slavoj Zizek (1998) argued that during the age of imperialism, cultural imperialism constituted the dominant ideology, but that has lately been replaced by the ideology of multiculturalism in the current period of global capitalism. This is, indeed, an adequate expression of the current ideological trends. By and large, from this ideology, different cultural trends have emerged and each demands open dealing with the world. It is important to note, however, that this ideology is an indispensable requirement for global capitalism because the world capitalist market has an intrinsic tendency to transcend any national borders. Conversely, the world capitalist market perceives nationalism as a means to its ends.

It should also be noted that this new world order still requires a certain hierarchy. Immanuel Wallerstein terms this the 'core–peripheral' hierarchy, and he explains that: 'ethnicization, or peoplehood, resolves one of the basic contradictions of historical capitalism – its simultaneous thirst for theoretical equality and practical inequality – and it does so by utilizing the mentalities of the world's working strata' (Balibar and Wallerstein, 1991: 84). To construct this order, the constitution of the nation is bound up not with the abstraction of the capitalist market, but with its concrete form, enabling the development of relations of unequal exchange and dominance (Balibar and Wallerstein, 1991: 89). As standards for the new hierarchy have not been set, the order is still based on the 'fictive ethnic and ideal nation', which is considered to be distinct and superior (96).

In this sense, nationalism, as a representation of Japaneseness through sport, is still in a transition and it is essentially a constructive illusion of nationalism. Tomlinson (1996) argued that this is situated in the paradox of globalization. Moreover, taking Japan into consideration, countries located at the centre (as per Wallerstein) will continuously re-make any ambiguous definition of 'Japaneseness'. Therefore, sport does not necessarily revive a traditional imagination, but has 'created new political forms, new myths and cults,' and is 'now to use old traditions and to adapt them to a new purpose' (Mosse, 1991: 1). However, it is important to stress that the emergence of a new trans-national trend, which, in Elias's terms, is 'a spread of a sense of responsibility among individuals for the fate of others far beyond the frontiers of their own country or continent' (1987: 168) has grown increasingly among people worldwide. Current sport, in fact, provides an opportunity for this new sensibility. This shows another possibility of globalization. Only time will tell whether this trend can achieve 'diminishing contrasts, increasing varieties' (Elias, 1987, 382–387) and create global friendship.

## Notes

1 Plaza Accord: An agreement on the exchange rate at the financial conference held at the Plaza Hotel in New York in September 1985 by members of the G5. In particular, by way of correcting trade imbalances, it was agreed to reduce the US dollar's value. Consequentially, to avoid a loss by an exchange appreciation of the Yen and keeping a strong competitive edge over exports, many Japanese companies were forced to move their factories and capital abroad, especially to South East Asia. In this respect, the Plaza Accord played an important role in transforming Japanese capitalism into a part of global capitalism and can thus be seen as a watershed.
2 Madame Butterfly was composed by Italian composer, Giacomo Puccini in 1904 and it is one of the examples of typical Orientalism, like Said's argument (Said, 1978).

## References

Anderson, B. (1991) *Imagined Communities: Reflections on the Origin and Spread of Nationalism* (revised edn), London: Verso.

Bakhtin, M. (1984, Russian original, 1965) *Rabelais and His World*, translated by H. Iswolsky, Bloomington and Indianapolis: Indiana University Press.

Balibar, E. and Wallerstein, I. (1991) *Race, Nation, Class: Ambiguous Identities*, London: Verso.

Barthes, R. (1973, French original, 1957) *Mythologies*, translated by A. Lavers, New York: Hill and Wang.

Brannen, Y. (1992) 'Bwana Mickey: constructing cultural consumption at Tokyo Disneyland', in Joseph Tobin (ed.) *Re-Made in Japan*, New Haven: Yale University Press.

Clarke, J. (1978) 'Football and working-class fans: Tradition and change' in R. Ingham (ed.), *Football Hooliganism: The Wider Context*, London: Inter-Action.

Defrance, J. and Pociello, C. (1993) 'Structure and functions of the field of sport in France (1960–1990)', *International Review for Sociology of Sport*, Vol. 28, part 1, 1–21.

Dicken, P. (2003) *Global Shift: Reshaping the Global Economic Map in the 21st Century* (4th edn), London: Sage Publications.

Elias, N. (1987) *The Society of Individuals*, Oxford: Blackwell Publishing.

Elias, N. (2000) *The Civilizing Process* (revised edn), Oxford: Blackwell Publishing.

Foucault, M. (1979) *Discipline and Punish*, Harmondsworth: Penguin.

Fujita, S. (1966) *Tennôsei kokka no shihai genri* (The Principles of Rule in the Emperor-state), Japan: Miraisha.

Gamble, A. (1988) *The Free Economy and The Strong State: The Politics of Thatcherism*, London: Macmillan Press.

Gray, John. (1998) *False Dawn: The Delusions of Global Capitalism*, London: Granta Books.

Grossberg, L. (1996) 'On postmodernism and articulation: an interview with Stuart Hall', in D. Morley (ed.) *Stuart Hall: Critical Dialogues in Cultural Studies*, London: Routledge.

Hall, S. (ed.) (1980) 'Encoding/Decoding' in S. Hall (*et al.*) *Culture, Media, Language*. London: Hutchinson.

Hall, S. (ed.) (1997) *Representation: Cultural Representations and Signifying Practices*, London: Sage Publications.

Hobsbawm, E. and Ranger, T. (eds) (1983) *The Invention of Tradition*, Cambridge: Cambridge University Press.

Iwai, T. (1987) *Tennôsei to Nihon Bunkaron* (The Emperor-state and Japanese Theories on Culture), Japan: Bunrikaku.

Iwai T. (1998) *Kindai tennôsei no ideorogi* (The Ideology of the Modern Emperor-state), Tokyo: Shin Nihon Press.

Maguire, J. (1988) 'Research note: doing figurational sociology: some preliminary observations on methodological issues and sensitizing concepts', *Leisure Studies*, Vol. 7, E & FN Spon Ltd.

Maguire, J. (1999) *Global Sport: Identities, Societies, Civilizations*, Oxford: Polity Press.

Melucci, A. (1989) *Nomads of The Present: Social Movements and Individual Needs in Contemporary Society*, edited by J. Keane and P. Mier, Philadelphia: Temple University Press.

Mosse, G. (1991) *The Nationalization of the Masses*, Ithaca: Cornell University Press.

Said, E. (1978) *Orientalism*, London: Routledge and Kegan Paul.

Taylor, I. (1982) 'On the sports violence question: hooliganism revisited' in A. Hargreaves (ed.) *Sport, Culture & Ideology*, London: Routledge and Kegan Paul.

Tomlinson, A. (1996) 'The Olympic spectacle: opening ceremonies and some paradoxes of globalization', in *Media, Culture & Society*, Vol. 18.

Watanabe, O. (1999) *Kigyô shakai Nippon wa doko e iku no ka* (The Future of Japanese Corporatized Society), Japan: Kyoiku Shiryô Press.

Watanabe, O. (2001) *Nihon no Taikokuka to Neo Nasionalism* (Japanese great-power ambition and a formation of neo-nationalism), Japan: Sakuraishoten.

Yamashita, T. (2001) 'The politics of representation: Nagano, re-Inventing Japaneseness in the global world order', KAHPERD (ed.), *Sport and Politics*, South Korea: KAHPERD.

Yamashita, T. (2002) 'Nagano Olympic: Re-inventing Japaneseness in global imagination', Institute of Humanities, Human and Social Sciences Ritsumeikan University (ed.), *Memoirs of Institute of Humanities, Human and Social Sciences*, No. 79.

Yamashita, T. (2003) 'Sports to nationalism: hennka no katei ni aru kankeisei' (Sport and nationalism: a changing relationship in Japanese current social context and globalization), Yuibutsuron Kenkyu Kai (ed.) *Yuibutsuron Kenkyu* (The Journal of Materialism), Tokyo: Aoki Shoten.

Yamashita, T. and Saka, N. (2002) 'Another kick off: the 2002 World Cup and soccer voluntary groups as a new social movement' in J. Horne and W. Manzenriter (eds.) *Korea, Japan and the FIFA World Cup 2002*, London: Routledge.

Yamashita, T. and Seino, M. (1995) 'Nihon no sport leisure kenkyu' (History of studies on sport and leisure in Japan), in D. Jary and M. Seino, J. Horne, T. Yamashita and J. Hashimoto, *Sport, Leisure Shyakaigaku: Alternative no Genzai* (Sociology of Sport and Leisure: Today's Alternatives), Tokyo: Dowa Syoin.

Yamashita, T. and Taneda, Y. (1997) 'A development of fitness business: a case study of People Co. Ltd', in The Society of Ritsumeikan Business Administration (ed.) *The Journal of Ritsumeikan Administration*, Vol. 35, 170–198.

Yoshino, K. (1997) *Bunka nashonarizumu no shakaigaku* (The Sociology of Cultural Nationalism), Nagoya: Nagoya Daigaku Shuppankai.

Zizek, S. (1998) 'Tabunka-shugi aruiwa takoku-seki shihon-shugi no bunka no ronri' (Multiculturalism, or the cultural logic of multinational capitalism), translated by T. Wada, in *Hihyô Kukan*, Vol. 18.

# Index

Abe, I. 42–3, 50
Aiba, J. 67
alumni associations 40
Amagasaki, A. 152
amateurism: and professional ideology
48–9; sponsorship 69–70
Anderson, B. 168
Asanuma, Y. 46–7
athletics, victory precedence 65–7

Barthes, R. 169
baseball 49–50; admission charges 42–3;
cult 23–4; expansion 28–9; fan clubs
*see* fan clubs; fraternity clubs 26; Japan
Baseball Club 46–7; Japan Sports
Association 43–4; professional
development 36–7, 43–6; Secondary
Schools' Baseball Championship 59
baseball spirit: and *bushido* 39–41, 46,
47–8, 50; frugality, decline 41–3;
historical types 36–8; and
professionalization 46–7; transitions
38–9
basketball, and team play 151 *Fig.*
Bates, A. 23
Beal, B. 100
Beckham, David 134
belief *see* ideology
Ben-Ari, E. 71
body: centripetal/centrifugal operations
146; extension 145–6; *see also* somatic
sensation
body-related differences 117–19
Brannen, M. Y. 169–70
Brannen, Y. 174
*budo* 9–11, 15, 16, 17
*bujutsu* 7–9, 17
Burnage, G. 133
bushi/bushido sports 32, 34

*bushido* spirit 37–8; and baseball ideology
39–41, 46, 47–8, 50
Butler, J. 121

Caillois, R. 117, 120
Clemens, S. C. 129
cognition 153–4; latent 152; team play
148–52
Collins, S. xi
commercialization 70–72
community sport, advocacy 67–9, 71–2
corporate welfare 61–5
creed *see* ideology
Crosset, T. 100
cultural products 99–100

dam lakes, use 84–6
Dan, T. 65
dance 152–3
Davis, N. xi
Defrance, J. 159–61
democratic values 58–61
Digel, H. 57
Donnelly, P. 99–100

E-boat movement 77–9; co-operative
association 87–8; dam lakes, use 84–6;
E-boat, definition/development 81,
86–7; framework 90 *Fig.*; organization
86; origins 79–81; as social experiment
79; flowchart 85 *Fig.*; methodology
82–4; in practice 84–8; *see also* green
sport
ecology *see* green sport
economic precedence, post-war 57–8,
72–3; as political policy 62–3, 67–8;
and traditional values 67–8; and values
61–7
Edo period 8–9, 119